13063

	DATE DUE		
03-19-99			

Enduring
Issues
in
Psychology

Other Books in the Enduring Issues Series:

Enduring
Issues
in
Psychology

Toni Blake

David L. Bender, *Publisher*
Bruno Leone, *Executive Editor*

Bonnie Szumski, *Series Editor*

Toni Blake, JD, MA, *Book Editor*

Greenhaven Press, Inc., San Diego, CA 92198-9009

Library of Congress Cataloging-in-Publication Data

Enduring issues in psychology : opposing viewpoints / Toni Blake, book editor.
      p.   cm.   — (Enduring issues series)
    Includes bibliographical references and index.
    ISBN 1-56510-253-3 (pbk.) — ISBN 1-56510-254-1 (lib. bdg.)
    1. Psychology. I. Blake, Toni. II. Series.
BF21.E53   1995
155—dc20   94-24936
                                                                CIP

Copyright © 1995 by Greenhaven Press, Inc.
PO Box 289009, San Diego, CA 92198-9009
Printed in the U.S.A.

Contents

Foreword

"When a thing ceases to be a subject of controversy, it ceases to be a subject of interest."

William Hazlitt

The Enduring Issues Series is based on the concept that certain fundamental disciplines remain interesting and vibrant because they remain controversial, debatable, and mutable. Indeed, it is through controversy that these disciplines were forged, and through debate that they continue to be defined.

Each book in the Enduring Issues Series aims to present the most seminal and thought-provoking issues in the most accessible way—by pitting the founders of each discipline against one another. This running debate style allows readers to compare and contrast major philosophical views, noting the major and minor areas of disagreement. In this way, the chronology of the formation of the discipline itself is traced. As American clergyman Lyman Beecher argued, "No great advance has ever been made in science, politics, or religion, without controversy."

In an effort to collect the most representative opinions of these disciplines, every editor of each book in the Enduring Issues Series has been chosen for his or her expertise in presenting these issues in the classroom. Each editor has chosen the materials for his or her book with these goals in mind: 1) To offer, both to the uninitiated and to the well read, classic questions answered by the leading historical and contemporary proponents. 2) To create and stimulate an interest and excitement in these academic disciplines by revealing that even in the most esoteric areas there are questions and views common to every person's search for life's meaning. 3) To reveal the development of ideas, and, in the process, plant the notion in the reader's mind that truth can only be unearthed in thoughtful examination and reexamination.

The editors of the Enduring Issues Series hope that readers will find in it a launching point to do their own investigation and form their own opinions about the issues raised by these academic disciplines. Because it is in the continued contemplation of these questions that these issues will remain alive.

Introduction

In 1964 a father crawls under his house to remove the dry, brittle remains of animals that have died there as his wife and four-year-old son watch. As he surfaces from under the house and sets a bucket of remains down, he notices his son's fascination with them.

> He had taken a great many of the bones from the bucket and was staring at them intently. From time to time, he would pick a few of them up, then let them fall with a brittle cracking sound that seemed to fascinate him. Over and over, he would pick up a fistful of bones, then let them drop back to the pile that remained on the bare ground. I went over to him, and as I bent down to gather up the bones and throw them away, Jeff released another small cluster of bones and let them clatter to the ground. He seemed oddly thrilled by the sound they made. "Like fiddlesticks," he said. Then he laughed and walked away. (From Lionel Dahmer's book *A Father's Story*)

Twenty-seven years later Jeffrey Dahmer was arrested and confessed to the brutal murders and dismemberment of seventeen men in the states of Wisconsin and Ohio.

What happens in the course of development to create a cold-blooded killer? Can a child's fascination with animal bones be a harbinger of future behavior? What are the components of an individual's personality that would allow him to commit such heinous acts? Can psychotherapy treat individuals at an early age so as to prevent these types of crimes? Psychology, defined as the scientific study of human behavior and mental processes, seeks to answer these questions.

The scientific investigation of human behavior originated in 1879 at a laboratory in Leipzig, Germany, under the direction of Wilhelm Wundt. Because Wundt trained a great many of the founders of psychology he is often referred to as the father of psychology. Wundt was a determinist; he believed that events have causes and he created a laboratory to systematically study those causes. Almost immediately after the laboratory opened, psychologists began to disagree as to the focus of psychology and began to proliferate into their own sub-disciplines. Titchener, a student of Wundt's, took the theories of his mentor to the United States where his revision of Wundt's psychology was referred to as structuralism. Titchener's structuralism differed from

Wundt's in that he studied the elements of the structure of consciousness instead of sensations and perceptions. At around the same time, American psychologist William James was trying to sell his theory of functionalism. He disagreed with Titchener's focus on the structure of consciousness and instead sought out to study the evolutionary functions of consciousness. From the original laboratory in Leipzig spawned Psychoanalytic and Behaviorist theories, followed by Humanist and Existentialist theories and others. These theoretical debates have continued since this time and it is these debates that make psychology an appropriate domain for this, the Enduring Issues Series.

Today, psychology has many different disciplines and applications. In its modern form, the field of psychology is broken up into two major divisions: clinical psychology and research oriented psychology. Clinical psychologists are interested in the therapeutic applications of psychology. They practice in private offices, mental health clinics, or school counseling centers, helping individuals obtain personal growth. Research psychologists, on the other hand, work in laboratories or universities, studying human behavior in a systematic fashion. These psychologists study, for example, why thirty-eight people in Queens, New York, stood by and watched the brutal and fatal attack of Kitty Genovese and no one called the police or attempted to intervene. They study how to make toys to help children learn, or how to pick a jury to receive a certain result, or how to make military troops combat ready.

This book looks at some of the enduring issues in psychology and how modern applications of these issues affect the world around us. The first three chapters of the book focus on the theoretical underpinnings that have created all or most of the debates in psychology. These chapters present the original views of the theorists that structured the field of psychology in its current form. The final two chapters focus on the debates generated by attempts to apply these theories in real world settings. Chapter four focuses on whether the psychological disorders of alcoholism, antisocial behavior, and depression are a product of socialization or biological factors. Chapter five looks at whether our psychological knowledge should influence public policy; specifically, whether psychology can lend data to debates surrounding repressed memories in the courtroom, involuntary commitment laws, or discussion regarding rational suicide.

Which Type of Psychotherapy Is Most Useful?

Chapter Preface

Throughout history, humans have questioned the source of their mental anguish and have sought guidance from clergy, physician, deity, and shaman to improve their psychological functioning. Treatment for severe mental illness has ranged from tonics, leeching, and religious healing to shock and drug therapies. Although many of these treatments could loosely be called psychotherapy, it wasn't until the late nineteenth century that psychotherapy developed into a method involving a client and a trained professional who, through talking, explored the client's mental state.

In the late 1880s in a laboratory in Vienna under the direction of Josef Breuer, a young physician named Sigmund Freud was developing the first of these talking cures in psychology. Breuer and Freud sought to tap into a client's unconscious mind through hypnosis, with the belief that the unconscious could give valuable clues to the origin of an individual's psychological disturbances. Freud later broke with Breuer and developed his theory of psychoanalysis.

Psychoanalysis immigrated to the United States just before the turn of the century but was, for all practical purposes, virtually unavailable until the 1920s. From the 1920s to the 1940s psychotherapy was available only to the very rich or very lucky through university counseling centers, psychoanalytic clinics, and child guidance centers.

In the late 1940s psychology began to gain popularity as a science. As World War II came to an end many soldiers returned home with inexplicable illnesses of both mind and body. In response, the government began expanding the Veterans Administration program to treat the psychological needs of veterans. In 1948 the National Institute of Mental Health was established to encourage research and training in psychology. In the private sector, health care insurance companies began to expand coverage to include mental health services and soon the growing demand for more psychotherapy providers inspired the development of training schools all over the country.

Although psychotherapy became more accessible and desirable in the 1940s, the American psychological community became frustrated with the traditional psychoanalytical theories as defined by Freud. Psychologists criticized psychoanalysis as being inefficient, impersonal, and ineffective. They began to develop shorter-term forms of therapy. Within the next 50 years more than 450 different styles of therapy would be practiced by counselors from many different disciplines. Although practicing psychologists today are more likely to use an eclectic approach that combines several theories, therapy styles are generally grouped into four distinct categories: psychodynamic, cognitive, behavioral, and humanist.

The psychoanalytic camp includes Sigmund Freud, Erik Erikson, Carl Jung, Karen Horney, and others. Psychoanalysts concentrate on the effects of past experiences and unconscious motives and how these motivate behavior. The psychoanalytic therapist seeks to minimize the effects of past experiences while helping the client to discover some of the unconscious roots of his or her behaviors. Psychoanalysts believe in remaining passive figures and allowing clients to reach the unconscious by their own accord.

Adherents of cognitive therapy believe that psychological disturbances originate from disabling thought processes rather than past experiences and biological drives. Cognitive therapists such as Albert Ellis, Aaron Beck, and Richard Lazarus concentrate on changing an individual's thought patterns rather than focusing on experiences that cannot be changed.

Humanist therapy is practiced by psychologists such as Carl Rogers, Abraham Maslow, and Gordon Allport. Humanist therapy rests on the idea that each individual possesses his or her own unique potential to achieve greatness. However, occasionally this potential becomes misaligned and it is the job of the humanist therapists to help clients realign themselves in order to achieve their goals.

Behavioral therapy has been furthered by theorists such as John Watson, E.L. Thorndike, Ivan Pavlov, and B.F. Skinner. Behaviorists differ from most other therapists in that they concentrate on changing an individual's maladaptive behaviors. The goal of behavioral therapy is to alter the reinforcement of behaviors so as to either increase or decrease the likelihood of the behavior occurring again.

In just over a century psychotherapy has been transformed from a technique practiced in a single man's private practice in

Vienna to a multibillion-dollar industry employing millions of practitioners. Psychotherapy in some form is practiced today by psychologists, psychiatrists, social workers, licensed family counselors, school counselors, and crisis hotline personnel. However, a recent study by Goldfried, Greenberg, and Marmar on the effectiveness of therapy estimated that only 66 percent of patients who engage in therapy with a trained psychologist experience any positive change from the experience. These studies and recent skepticism surrounding psychotherapists in general have caused some to question whether the psychotherapy industry is benefiting anyone or merely perpetuating itself. As the following viewpoints by Freud, Ellis, Rogers, and Skinner demonstrate, certain styles of psychotherapy are said to be more effective in dealing with certain psychological complaints than others.

VIEWPOINT

1

Psychotherapy Should Focus on Unconscious Traumas

SIGMUND FREUD

The following piece written by Sigmund Freud appeared as an encyclopedia article describing the requisite elements of his psychoanalytic therapy. In this article Freud discusses how his theory of psychoanalysis evolved from work done with Dr. Josef Breuer of Vienna. The work involved uncovering hidden mental traumas through hypnosis and "cathartic" therapy. When Freud broke away from Breuer and began to work on his theory of psychoanalysis he discovered that these hidden mental processes, which were known to produce psychological and physical traumas, could be accessed in ways other than hypnosis. He found that through the

Selected excerpts of about eight pages from *The Collected Papers*, vol. 5, by Sigmund Freud. Edited and translated by James Strachey. Published by Basic Books, Inc., by arrangement with The Hogarth Press, Ltd. and the Institute of Psycho-Analysis, London. Reprinted by permission of BasicBooks, a division of HarperCollins Publishers, Inc., and by permission of The Hogarth Press and the Institute of Psycho-Analysis.

process of free association, dream analysis and the analysis of chance actions and "Freudian Slips" a trained psychoanalyst could tap into the unconscious. It was here, according to Freud, that the root of a client's problems could be ascertained and then through transference (or redirection of emotions onto one's therapist) a change could be effected.

QUESTIONS

1. How does the process of free association aid in psychoanalysis? What are its rules?
2. What are transference and catharsis and what role do they play in Freud's psychoanalytic theory?
3. According to Freud, how do childhood milestones affect individuals in adult life?

Psycho-analysis is the name (1) of a procedure for the investigation of mental processes which are almost inaccessible in any other way, (2) of a method (based upon that investigation) for the treatment of neurotic disorders and (3) of a collection of psychological information obtained along those lines, which is gradually being accumulated into a new scientific discipline. . . .

Catharsis

The investigations which lay at the root of Breuer and [Freud speaks in the third person] Freud's studies led above all to two results, and these have not been shaken by subsequent experience: first, that hysterical symptoms have sense and meaning, being substitutes for normal mental acts; and secondly, that the uncovering of this unknown meaning is accompanied by the removal of the symptoms—so that in this case scientific research and therapeutic effort coincide. . . . From the very beginning the factor of *affect* was brought into the foreground; hysterical symptoms, the authors maintained, came into existence when a mental process with a heavy charge of affect was in any way prevented from equalizing that charge by passing along the normal paths leading to consciousness and movement (*i.e.*, from being '*abreacted*'), as a result of which the affect, which was in a sense *'strangulated'*, was diverted on to the wrong paths and found its discharge into the somatic innervation (a process named *'conversion'*). The occasions upon which 'pathogenic ideas' of this kind arose were described by Breuer and Freud as *'psychical traumas'*, and, since these often dated back to the very remote past, it was possible for the authors to say that hysterics suffered to a large extent from reminiscences (which had not been dealt with). Under the treatment, therefore, *'catharsis'* came about when the path to consciousness was opened and there was a normal discharge of affect. It will be seen that an essential part of this theory was the assumption of the existence of *unconscious* mental processes. . . .

Free Association

The effect of the hypnotic condition upon the patient had been so greatly to increase his ability to make associations that he was able to find straightaway the path—inaccessible to his conscious reflection—which led from the symptom to the thoughts and memories connected with it. The abandonment of hypnosis seemed to make the situation hopeless, until the writer recalled a remark of Hippolyte Bernheim's to the effect that things that had been experienced in a state of somnambulism were only *apparently* forgotten and that they could be brought into recollection at any time if the physician insisted forcibly enough that the patient knew them. The writer therefore endeavoured to press his *unhypnotized* patients into giving him their associations, so that from the material thus provided he might find the path leading to what had been forgotten or warded off. He noticed later that such pressure was unnecessary and that copious ideas almost always arose in the patient's mind, but that they were held back from being communicated and even from becoming conscious by certain objections put by the patient in his own way. . . .

The 'Fundamental Technical Rule'

The *'Fundamental Technical Rule'* of this procedure of 'free association' has from that time on been maintained in psycho-analytic work. The treatment is begun by the patient being required to put himself in the position of an attentive and dispassionate self-observer, merely to read off all the time the surface of his consciousness, and on the one hand to make a duty of the most complete candour while on the other not holding back any idea from communication, even if (1) he feels that it is too disagreeable or if (2) he judges that it is nonsensical or (3) too unimportant or (4) irrelevant to what is being looked for. It is uniformly found that precisely those ideas which provoke these last-mentioned reactions are of particular value in discovering the forgotten material.

Psycho-Analysis as an Interpretive Art

The new technique altered the picture of the treatment so greatly, brought the physician into such a new relation to the patient and produced so many surprising results that it seemed justifiable to distinguish the procedure from the cathartic method by giving it a new name. The present writer gave this method of treatment, which could now be extended to many other forms of neurotic disorder, the name of *psycho-analysis*. Now, in the first resort, this psycho-analysis was an art of *interpretation* and it set itself the task of carrying deeper the first of Breuer's great discoveries—namely, that neurotic symptoms are significant substitutes for other mental acts which have been omitted. It was now a matter of regarding the material produced by the patients' associations as though it hinted at a hidden meaning and of discovering that meaning from it. Experience soon showed that the attitude which the analytical physician could most advantageously adopt was to surrender himself to his own unconscious mental activity, in a state of *easy and impartial attention*, to avoid so far as possible reflection and the construction of conscious expectations, not to try to fix anything that he heard particularly in his memory, and by these means to catch the drift of the patient's unconscious with his own unconscious. It was then found that, except under conditions that were too unfavourable, the patient's associations emerged like allusions, as it were, to one particular theme and that it was only necessary for the physician to go a step further in order to guess the material which was concealed from the patient himself and to be able to communicate it to him. It is true that this work of interpretation was not to be brought under strict rules and left a great deal of play to the physician's tact and skill; but, with impartiality and practice, it was usually possible to obtain trustworthy results—that is to say, results which were confirmed by being repeated in similar cases. At a time when so little was as yet known of the unconscious, the structure of the neuroses and the pathological processes underlying them, it was a matter for satisfaction that a technique of this kind should be available, even if it had no better theoretical basis. Moreover it is still employed in analyses at the present day in the same manner, though with a sense of greater assurance and with a better understanding of its limitations.

The Interpretation of Parapraxes and Chance Actions

It was a triumph for the interpretative art of psycho-analysis when it succeeded in demonstrating that certain common mental acts of normal people, for which no one had hitherto attempted to put forward a psychological explanation, were to be regarded in the same light as the symptoms of neurotics: that is to say, they had a *meaning*, which was unknown to the subject but which could easily be discovered by analytic means. The phenomena in question were such events as the temporary forgetting of familiar words and names, forgetting to carry out prescribed tasks, everyday slips of the tongue and of the pen, misreadings, losses and mislayings of objects, certain mistakes, instances of apparently accidental self-injury, and finally habitual movements carried out seemingly without intention or in play, tunes hummed 'thoughtlessly', and so on. All of these were shorn of their physiological explanation, if any such had ever been attempted, and were shown to be strictly determined and were revealed as an expression of the subject's suppressed intentions or as a result of a clash between two intentions one of which was permanently or temporarily unconscious. The importance of this contribution to psychology was of many kinds. The range of mental determinism was extended by it in an unforeseen manner; the supposed gulf between normal and pathological mental events was narrowed;

in many cases a useful insight was afforded into the play of mental forces that must be suspected to lie behind the phenomena. Finally, a class of material was brought to light which is calculated better than any other to stimulate a belief in the existence of unconscious mental acts even in people to whom the hypothesis of something at once mental and unconscious seems strange and even absurd. The study of one's own parapraxes and chance actions, for which most people have ample opportunities, is even to-day the best preparation for an approach to psycho-analysis. In analytic treatment, the interpretation of parapraxes retains a place as a means of uncovering the unconscious, alongside the immeasurably more important interpretation of associations.

The Interpretation of Dreams

A new approach to the depths of mental life was opened when the technique of free association was applied to dreams, whether one's own or those of patients in analysis. In fact, the greater and better part of what we know of the processes in the unconscious levels of the mind is derived from the interpretation of dreams. Psycho-analysis has restored to dreams the importance which was generally ascribed to them in ancient times, but it treats them differently. It does not rely upon the cleverness of the dream-interpreter but for the most part hands the task over to the dreamer himself by asking him for his associations to the separate elements of the dream. By pursuing these associations further we obtain knowledge of thoughts which coincide entirely with the dream but which can be recognized—up to a certain point—as genuine and completely intelligible portions of waking mental activity. Thus the recollected dream emerges as the *manifest dream-content*, in contrast to the *latent dream-thoughts* discovered by interpretation. The process which has transformed the latter into the former, that is to say into 'the dream', and which is undone by the work of interpretation, may be called *'dream-work'*.

We also describe the latent dream-thoughts, on account of their connection with waking life, as *'residues of the [previous] day'*. By the operation of the dream-work (to which it would be quite incorrect to ascribe any 'creative' character) the latent dream-thoughts are *condensed* in a remarkable way, they are *distorted* by the *displacement* of psychical intensities, they are arranged with a view to being *represented in visual pictures*; and, besides all this, before the manifest dream is arrived at, they are submitted to a process of *secondary elaboration* which seeks to give the new product something in the nature of sense and coherence. But, strictly speaking, this last process does not form a part of dream-work. . . .

Symbolism

In the course of investigating the form of expression brought about by dream-work, the surprising fact emerged that certain objects, arrangements and relations are represented, in a sense indirectly, by 'symbols', which are used by the dreamer without his understanding them and to which as a rule he offers no associations. Their translation has to be provided by the analyst, who can himself only discover it empirically by experimentally fitting it into the context. It was later found that linguistic usage, mythology and folklore afford the most ample analogies to dream-symbols. Symbols, which raise the most interesting and hitherto unsolved problems, seem to be a fragment of extremely ancient inherited mental equipment. The use of a common symbolism extends far beyond the use of a common language.

The Aetiological Significance of Sexual Life—The second novelty which emerged after the hypnotic technique had been replaced by free associations was of a clinical nature. It was discovered in the course of the prolonged search for the traumatic experiences from which hysterical symptoms appeared to be derived. The more carefully the search was pursued the more extensive seemed to be the network of aetiologically significant impressions, but the further back, too, did they reach into the patient's puberty or childhood. At the same time they assumed a uniform character and eventually it became inevitable to bow before the evidence and recognize that at the root of the formation of every symptom there were to be found traumatic experiences from early sexual life. Thus a sexual trauma stepped into the place of an ordinary trauma and the latter was seen to owe its aetiological significance to an associative or symbolic connection with the former, which had preceded it. . . .

The Theory of Repression

These theoretical considerations, taken together with the immediate impressions derived from analytic work, lead to a view of the neuroses which may be described in the roughest outline as follows. The neuroses are the expression of conflicts between the ego and such of the sexual impulses as seem to the ego incompatible with its integrity or with its ethical standards. Since these impulses are not *ego-syntonic*, the ego has *repressed* them: that is to say, it has withdrawn its interest from them and has shut them off from becoming conscious as well as from obtaining satisfaction by motor discharge. If in the course of analytic work one attempts to make these repressed impulses conscious, one becomes aware of the repressive forces in the form of *resistance*. But the achievement of repression fails particularly easily in the case of the sexual instincts. Their dammed-up libido finds other ways out from the unconscious: for it *regresses* to earlier phases of development and earlier attitudes towards objects, and, at weak points in the libidinal development where there are infantile fixations, it breaks through into consciousness and obtains discharge. What results is a *symptom* and consequently in its essence a substitutive sexual satisfaction. Nevertheless the symptom cannot entirely escape from the repressive forces of the ego and must therefore submit to modifications and displacements—exactly as happens with dreams—by means of which its characteristic of being a sexual satisfaction becomes unrecognizable. Thus symptoms are in the nature of compromise-formations between the repressed sexual instincts and the repressive ego instincts; they represent a wish-fulfilment for both partners to the conflict simultaneously, but one which is incomplete for each of them. This is quite strictly true of the symptoms of hysteria, while in the symptoms of obsessional neurosis there is often a stronger emphasis upon the side of the repressive function owing to the erection of reaction-formations, which are assurances against sexual satisfaction.

Transference

If further proof were needed of the truth that the motive forces behind the formation of neurotic symptoms are of a sexual nature, it would be found in the fact that in the course of analytic treatment a special emotional relation is regularly formed between the patient and the physician. This goes far beyond rational limits. It varies between the most affectionate devotion and the most obstinate enmity and derives all of its characteristics from earlier emotional erotic attitudes of the patient's which have become unconscious. This *transference* alike in its positive and in its negative form is used as a weapon by the resistance; but in the hands of the physician it becomes the most powerful therapeutic instrument and it plays a part that can scarcely be overestimated in the dynamics of the process of cure. . . .

Criticisms and Misunderstandings of Psycho-Analysis

Most of what is brought up against psycho-analysis, even in scientific works, is based upon insufficient information which in its turn seems to be determined by emotional resistances. Thus it is a mistake to accuse psycho-analysis of 'pansexualism' and to allege that it derives all mental occurrences from sexuality and traces them all back to it. On the contrary, psycho-analysis has from the very first distinguished the sexual instincts from others which it has provisionally termed 'ego instincts'. It has never dreamt of trying to explain 'everything', and even the neuroses it has traced back not to sexuality alone but to the conflict between the sexual impulses and the ego. In psycho-analysis (unlike the works of C. G. Jung) the term *'libido'* does not mean psychical energy in general but the motive force of the sexual instincts. Some assertions, such as that every dream is the fulfilment of a sexual wish, have never been maintained by it at all. The charge of one-sidedness made against psycho-analysis, which, as *the science of the unconscious mind*, has its own definite and restricted field of work, is as inapplicable as it would be if it were made against chemistry. To believe that psycho-analysis seeks a cure for neurotic disorders by giving a free rein to sexuality is a serious misunderstanding which can only be justified by ignorance. The making conscious of repressed sexual desires in analysis makes it possible, on the contrary, to obtain a mastery over them which the previous repression had been unable to achieve. It can more truly be said that analysis sets the neurotic free from the chains of his sexuality. Moreover, it is quite unscientific to judge analysis by whether it is calculated to undermine religion, authority and morals; for, like all sciences, it is entirely non-tendentious and has only a single aim—namely to arrive at a consistent view of one portion of reality. Finally, one can only characterize as simple-minded the fear which is sometimes expressed that all the highest goods of humanity, as they are called—research, art, love, ethical and social sense—will lose their value or their dignity because psycho-analysis is in a position to demonstrate their origin in elementary and animal instinctual impulses.

Psychotherapy Should Focus on Irrational Thought Processes

ALBERT ELLIS

Rational Emotive Therapy (RET) was created by Albert Ellis in 1955 in an attempt to devise a more efficient form of therapy. Ellis began his career practicing psychoanalysis but soon grew frustrated with the amount of time and lack of progress that it produced. In response he created a short term therapy that would enable clients to alter their belief systems to mitigate their psychological disturbances. Utilizing a hybrid of cognitive and humanist theories, Ellis developed the ABC theory of Rational Emotive Therapy. The basis of Ellis' theory is that humans have two juxtaposing biological tendencies: 1) thinking irrationally and 2) acting in ways to change these irrational thought patterns. He says that it is this biological tendency to think irrationally that creates psychological disturbances in individuals and the biological tendency to try and change these thought patterns that enables individuals to move toward healthier thought patterns.

QUESTIONS

1. What is an irrational belief according to Ellis?
2. What are the ABCs of Rational Emotive Therapy according to Ellis?
3. What advantage does Ellis see to a therapy that works on current cognition rather than past experiences?
4. What are some of the techniques employed by Ellis to create a more efficient therapy? Do they meet that goal?

■　■　■

According to RET theory, humans are happiest when they establish important life goals and purposes and actively strive to attain these. It is argued that, in establishing and pursuing these goals and purposes, human beings had better mind the fact that they live in a social world and that a philosophy of self-interest, where a person places him or herself first, also implies putting others a close second. This is in contrast to a philosophy of selfishness where the desires of others are neither respected nor regarded. Given that humans will tend to be goal-directed, *rational* in RET theory means "that which helps people to achieve their basic goals and purposes, whereas 'irrational' means that which prevents them from achieving these goals and purposes." Thus, rationality is not defined in any absolute sense, but is relative in nature. . . .

The Interaction of Psychological Processes and the Place of Cognition

RET theory has from its inception stressed an interactive view of human psychological processes. Cognitions, emotions, and behaviors are not experienced in isolation and often, particularly in the realm of psychological disturbance, overlap to a significant degree. Recently RET has stressed the inferential nature of activating events and has shown how events (or, more correctly, how we perceive events) again interact with our cognitive evaluations, emotions, and behaviors. This point will be amplified in the section entitled "The ABC's of RET: An Expanded Framework."

Given this interactional view, it is true, however, that RET is most noted for the special place it has accorded cognition in human psychological processes, particularly the role that evaluative thought plays in psychological health and disturbance. One of RET's unique contributions to the field of cognitive-behavior therapy lies in its distinction between rational and irrational Beliefs. Rational Beliefs are evaluative cognitions of personal significance that are preferential (i.e., nonabsolute) in nature. They are expressed in the form of "desires," "preferences," "wishes," "likes," and "dislikes." Positive feelings of pleasure and satisfaction are experienced when humans get what they desire, whereas negative feelings of displeasure and dissatisfaction (e.g., sadness, concern, regret, annoyance) are experienced when they do not get what they desire. These negative feelings (the strength of which is closely related to the importance of the desire) are regarded as appropriate responses to negative events and do not significantly interfere with the pursuit of established or new goals and purposes. These Beliefs, then, are "rational" in two respects. First, they are relative, and second, they do not impede the attainment of basic goals and purposes.

Irrational Beliefs, on the other hand, differ in two respects from rational beliefs. First, they are absolute (or dogmatic) in nature and are expressed in the form of "musts," "shoulds," "oughts," "have-to's," etc. Second, as such they lead to negative emotions that largely interfere with goal pursuit and attainment (e.g., depression, anxiety, guilt, anger). Rational Beliefs strongly tend to underlie functional behaviors, whereas irrational Beliefs underpin dysfunctional behaviors such as withdrawal, procrastination, alcoholism, and substance abuse. . . .

The ABC's of RET: An Expanded Framework

When RET was originally established I (AE) employed a simple ABC assessment framework to conceptualize clients' psychological problems. In this schema, "A" stood for the Activating event, "B" represented a person's Belief about that event, and "C" denoted the person's emotional and behavioral responses or Consequences to holding the particular Beliefs at "B." The major advantage of the ABC framework lay in its simplicity. However, its simplicity was also a disadvantage in that important distinctions between different types of cognitive activity were glossed over. It is important to note that different RET therapists use different expanded versions of the original ABC framework. There is thus no absolutely correct way of conceptualizing clients' problems according to such an expanded schema. What is presented below is one version of the expanded ABC framework.

Activating Events or Activators (A's) of Cognitive, Emotional, and Behavioral Consequences (C's)

The RET theory of personality and personality disturbances begins with people trying to fulfill their Goals (G's) in some kind of environment and encountering a set of Activating events or Activators (A's) that tend to help them achieve or block these Goals. The A's they encounter usually are present or current events or their own thoughts, feelings, or behaviors about these events, but they may be imbedded in memories or thoughts (conscious or unconscious) about past experiences. People are prone to seek out and respond to these A's because of (1) their biological or genetic predispositions; (2) their constitutional history; (3) their prior interpersonal and social learning; and (4) their innately predisposed and acquired habit patterns.

A's (Activating events) virtually never exist in a pure or monolithic state; they almost always interact with and partly include B's and C's. People bring themselves (their goals, thoughts, desires, and physiological propensities) to A's.

Beliefs (B's) About Activating Events (A's)

According to RET theory, people have almost innumerable Beliefs (B's)—cognitions, thoughts, or ideas—about their Activating events (A's); and these B's importantly and directly tend to exert strong influences on their cognitive, emotional, and behavioral Consequences (C's). Although A's often seem to directly "cause" or contribute to C's, this is rarely true, because B's normally serve as important mediators between A's and C's and therefore more directly "cause" or "create" C's. People largely bring their Beliefs to A; and they prejudicially view or experience A's in the light of these biased Beliefs (expectations, evaluations) and also in the light of their emotional Consequences (C's). Therefore, humans virtually never experience A without B and C; but they also rarely experience B and C without A.

B's take many different forms because people have many kinds of cognitions. In RET, however, we are mainly interested in their rational Beliefs (rB's), which we hypothesize lead to their self-helping behaviors, and in their irrational Beliefs (iB's), which we theorize lead to their self-defeating (and societal-defeating) behaviors. We can list some of the main (but not the only) kinds of B's as follows: . . .

Consequences (C's) of Activating Events (A's) and Beliefs (B's about A's)

C's (cognitive, affective, and behavioral Consequences) follow from the interaction of A's and B's. We can say, mathematically, that A X B = C, but this formula may actually be too simple and we may require a more complex one to express the relationship adequately. C is almost always significantly affected or influenced but not exactly "caused" by A, because humans naturally to some degree react to stimuli in their environments. Moreover, when A is powerful (e.g., a set of starvation conditions or an earthquake) it tends to affect C profoundly.

When C consists of emotional disturbance (e.g., severe feelings of anxiety, depression, hostility, self-deprecation, and self-pity), B usually (but not always) mainly or more directly creates or "causes" C. Emotional disturbance, however, may at times stem from powerful A's—for example, from enviornmental disasters such as floods or wars. Emotional disturbance may also follow from factors in the organism—for example, hormonal or disease factors—that are somewhat independent of yet may actually "cause" Consequences (C's).

When strong or unusual A's significantly contribute to or "cause" C's, or when physiological factors "create" C's, they are usually accompanied by contributory B's too. Thus, if people are caught in an earthquake or if they experience powerful hormonal changes and they "therefore" become depressed, their A's and their physiological processes probably are strongly influencing them to create irrational Beliefs (iB's), such as, "This earthquake shouldn't have occurred! Isn't it awful! I can't stand it!" These iB's, in turn, add to or help create their feelings of depression at C.

C's usually consist of feelings and behaviors but may also consist of thoughts (e.g., obsessions). C's (Consequences) that follow from A's and B's are virtually never pure or monolithic but also partially include and inevitably interact with A and B. Thus if A is an obnoxious event (e.g., a job refusal) and B is, first, a rational Belief (e.g.,"I hope I don't get rejected for this job!") as well as, second, an irrational Belief (e.g.,"I must have this job! I'm no good if I don't get it!"), C tends to be, first, healthy feelings of frustration and disappointment and, second, unhealthy feelings of severe anxiety, inadequacy, and depression.

So A X B = C. But people also *bring* feelings (as well as hopes, goals, and purposes) to A. They would not keep a job unless they desired or favorably evaluated it or unless they enjoyed some aspect of it. Their A therefore partially includes their B and C. The three, from the beginning, are related rather than completely disparate.

At the same time, people's Beliefs (B's) also partly or intrinsically relate to and include their A's and their C's. Thus, if they tell themselves, at B, "I want to get a good job," they partly create the Activating event at A (going for a job interview), and they partly create their emotional and behavioral Consequences at C (feeling disappointed when they encounter a job rejection). Without their evaluating a job as good they would not try for it nor have any particular feeling about being rejected.

A, B, and C, then, are all closely related and none of them tends to exist without the other.

The Nature of Psychological Disturbance and Health

Psychological Disturbance

Rational-emotive theory, then, posits that at the heart of psychological disturbance lies the tendency of humans to make devout, absolutistic evaluations of the perceived events in their lives. As has been shown, these evaluations are couched in the form of dogmatic "musts," "shoulds," "have-to's," "got-to's," and "oughts." We hypothesize that these absolutistic cognitions are at the core of a philosophy of religiosity that is the central feature of human emotional and behavioral disturbance. These Beliefs are deemed to be irrational in RET theory in that they usually (but not invariably) impede and obstruct people in the pursuit of their basic goals and purposes. Absolute musts do not invariably lead to psychological disturbance because it is possible for a person to devoutly believe "I must succeed at all important projects," have confidence that he or she will be successful in these respects, and actually succeed in them and thereby not experience psychological disturbance. However, the person remains vulnerable in this respect because there is always the possibility that he or she may fail in the future. So while on probabilistic grounds RET theory argues that an absolutistic philosophy will frequently lead to such disturbance, it does not claim that this is absolutely so. Thus, even with respect to its view of the nature of human disturbance RET adopts an antiabsolutistic position.

RET theory goes on to posit that if humans adhere to a philosophy of "musturbation" they will strongly tend to make a number of core irrational conclusions that are deemed to be derivatives of these "musts." These major derivatives are viewed as irrational because they too tend to sabotage a person's basic goals and purposes.

The first major derivative is known as *"awfulizing."* This occurs when a perceived event is rated as being more than 100% bad—a truly exaggerated and magical conclusion that stems from the Belief: "This must not be as bad as it is."

The second major derivative is known as *"I-can't-stand-it-itis."* This means believing that one cannot experience virtually any happiness at all, under any conditions, if an event that "must" not happen actually occurs or threatens to occur.

The third major derivative, known as *"damnation,"* represents a tendency for humans to rate themselves and other people as "subhuman" or "undeserving" if self or other does something that they "must" not do or fail to do something that they "must" do. "Damnation" can also be applied to world or life conditions that are rated as being "rotten" for failing to give the person what he or she must have.

While RET holds that "awfulizing," "I-can't-stand-it-itis," and "damnation" are secondary irrational processes in that they stem from the philosophy of "musts," these processes can sometimes be primary. Indeed, Richard L. Wessler has argued that they are more likely to be primary and that "musts" are derived from them. However, the philosophy of "musts," on the one hand, and those of "awfulizing," "I-can't-stand-it-itis," and "damnation," on the other, are, in all probability, interdependent processes and often seem to be different sides of the same "cognitive" coin.

RET notes that humans also make numerous kinds of illogicalities when they are disturbed. In this respect RET agrees with cognitive therapists that such cognitive distortions are a feature of psychological disturbance. However, RET theory holds that such distortions almost always stem from the "musts.". . .

Psychological Health

If the philosophy of musturbation is at the core of much psychological disturbance, then what philosophy is characteristic of psychological health? RET theory argues that a philosophy of relativism or "desiring" is a central feature of psychologically healthy humans. This philosophy acknowledges that humans have a large variety of desires, wishes, wants, preferences, etc., but if they refuse to escalate these nonabsolute values into grandiose dogmas and demands they will not become psychologically disturbed. They will, however, experience appropriate negative emotions (e.g., sadness, regret, disappointment, annoyance) whenever their desires are not fulfilled. These emotions are considered to have constructive motivational properties in that they both help people to remove obstacles to goal attainment and help them to make constructive adjustments when their desires cannot be met.

Three major derivatives of the philosophy of desiring are postulated by rational-emotive theory. They are deemed to be rational in that they tend to help people reach their goals or formulate new goals if their old ones cannot be realized.

The first major derivative, known as *rating or evaluating badness*, is the rational alternative to "awfulizing." Here, if a person does not get what she wants she acknowledges that this is bad. However, because she does not believe "I have to get what I want," she contains her evaluation along a 0-100% continuum of badness and does not therefore rate this situation as "awful"—a magical rating that is placed on a nonsensical 101%-infinity continuum. In general, when the person adheres to the desiring philosophy, the stronger her desire the greater her rating of badness will be when she does not get what she wants.

The second major derivative is known as *"tolerance"* and is the rational alternative to "I-can't-stand-it-itis." Here the person (1) acknowledges that an undesirable event has happened (or may happen); (2) believes that the event should empirically occur if it does; (3) rates the event along the badness continuum; (4) attempts to change the undesired event or accepts the "grim" reality if it cannot be modified, and (5) actively pursues other goals even though the situation cannot be altered.

The third major derivative, known as *"acceptance,"* is the rational alternative to "damnation." Here the person accepts herself and others as fallible human beings who do not have to act other than they do and as too complex and fluid to be given any legitimate or global rating. In addition, life conditions are accepted as they exist. People who have the philosophy of acceptance fully acknowledge that the world is highly complex and exists according to laws that are often outside their personal control. It is important to emphasize here that acceptance does not imply resignation. A rational philosophy of acceptance means that the person acknowledges that whatever exists empirically should exist but does not absolutely have to exist forever. This prompts the person to make active attempts to change reality. The person who is resigned to a situation usually does not attempt to modify it. . . .

The Theory of Therapeutic Change

We have argued that the rational-emotive view of the person is basically an optimistic one, since although it posits that humans have a distinct biological tendency to think irrationally, it also holds that they have the capacity to *choose* to work toward changing this irrational thinking and its self-defeating effects.

There are various levels of change. Rational-emotive theory holds that the most elegant and long-lasting changes that humans can effect are ones that involve philosophic restructuring of irrational Beliefs. Change at this level can be specific or general. Specific philosophic change means that individuals change their irrational absolutistic demands ("musts," "shoulds") and *given* situations to rational relative preferences. General philosophic change involves people adopting a nondevout attitude toward life events in general.

To effect a philosophic change at either the specific or general level, people are advised to:

1. First, realize that they create, to a large degree, their own psychological disturbances and that while environmental conditions can contribute to their problems they are in general of secondary consideration in the change process.
2. Fully recognize that they do have the ability to significantly change these disturbances.
3. Understand that emotional and behavioral disturbances stem largely from irrational, absolutistic dogmatic Beliefs.
4. Detect their irrational Beliefs and discriminate them from their rational alternatives.
5. Dispute these irrational Beliefs using the logico-empirical methods of science.
6. Work toward the internalization of their new rational Beliefs by employing cognitive, emotive, and behavioral methods of change.
7. Continue this process of challenging irrational Beliefs and using multimodal methods of change for the rest of their lives.

When people effect a philosophic change at B in the ABC model they often are able to spontaneously correct their distorted inferences of reality (overgeneralizations, faulty attributions, etc.). However, they can often benefit from challenging these distorted inferences more directly, as RET has always emphasized and as Aaron Beck has also stressed.

While rational-emotive theory argues that irrational Beliefs are the breeding ground for the development and maintenance of inferential distortions, it is possible for people to effect inferentially based changes without making a profound philosophic change. Thus, they may regard their inferences as hunches about reality rather than facts, may generate alternative hypotheses, and may seek evidence and/or carry out experiments that test out each hypothesis. They may then accept the hypothesis that represents the "best bet" of those available.

Consider a man who thinks that his co-workers view him as a fool. To test this hypothesis he might first specify their negative reactions to him. These constitute the data from which he quickly draws the conclusion, "They think I'm a fool." He might then realize that what he has interpreted to be negative responses to him might not be negative. If they seem to be negative, he might then carry out an experiment to test out the meaning he attributes to their responses. Thus, he might enlist the help of a colleague whom he trusts to carry out a "secret ballot" of others' opinions of him. Or he could test his hunch more explicitly by directly asking them for their view of him. As a result of these strategies this person may conclude that his co-workers find some of his actions foolish rather than considering him to be a complete fool. His mood may lift because his inference of the situation has changed, but he may still believe, "If others think I'm a fool, they're right, I am a fool and that would be awful." Thus, he has made an inferential change but not a philosophic one. If this person were to attempt to make a philosophic change he would *first* assume that his inference was true, *then* address himself to his evaluations about this inference and hence challenge these if they were discovered to be irrational (i.e., musturbatory evaluations). Thus he might conclude, "Even if I act foolishly that makes me a *person with* foolish behavior, not a *foolish person.* And even if they deem me a total idiot, that is simply *their* view, with which I can choose to disagree." Rational-emotive therapists hypothesize that people are more likely to make a profound philosophic change if they first assume that their inferences are true and then challenge their irrational Beliefs, rather than if they first correct their inferential distortions and then challenge their underlying irrational Beliefs. However, this hypothesis awaits full empirical enquiry.

People can also make direct changes of the situation at A. Thus, in the example quoted above the man could leave his job or distract himself from the reactions of his colleagues by taking on extra work and devoting himself to this. Or he might carry out relaxation exercises whenever he comes in contact with his co-workers and thus distract himself once again from their perceived reactions. Additionally, the man might have a word with his supervisor, who might then instruct the other workers to change their behavior toward the man.

When we use this model to consider behavioral change, it is apparent that a person can change his or her behavior to effect inferential and/or philosophic change. Thus, again using the above example, a man whose co-workers view him as a fool might change his own behavior toward them and thus elicit a different set of responses from them that would lead him to reinterpret his previous inference (behavior change to effect inferential change). However, if it could be determined that they did indeed consider him to be a fool, then the man could actively seek them out and show himself that he could stand the situation and that just because they think him a fool does not make him one, that is, he learns to accept himself in the face of their views while exposing himself to their negative reactions (behavior change to effect philosophic change).

While rational-emotive therapists prefer to help their clients make profound philosophic changes at B, they do not dogmatically insist that their clients make such changes. If it becomes apparent that clients are not able at any given time to change their irrational Beliefs, then RET therapists would endeavor to help them either to change A directly (by avoiding the troublesome situation or by behaving differently) or to change their distorted inferences about the situation.

VIEWPOINT

3

Psychotherapy Should Focus on an Individual's Potential

CARL ROGERS

Humanist psychologist Carl Rogers was raised under highly
structured religious ideals which eventually produced a life-
long struggle between religion and psychology. After gradu-
ating with a psychology major Rogers joined the seminary.
While at the seminary he continued to question the religious
dogma being espoused. Finally the incompatibility of psychology and the religious teaching of the seminary drove
Rogers to pursue a Ph.D in clinical psychology. In his new
discipline he would go on to create the leading Humanist
Theory of psychotherapy and to elevate the encounter-
group (a form of group therapy) to its current form. The following article is an attempt to convey the essential components of Rogerian Person Centered Therapy. Building on his
theory that all organisms have an innate tendency to move
toward self-actualization, he sets forth a framework from
which to conduct a successful therapeutic relationship.
Rogers here discusses the six elements that must be present
in any relationship to effect personality change.

Excerpted from "The Necessary and Sufficient Conditions of Therapeutic Personality Change" by Carl Rogers, *Journal of Consulting Psychology* 21 (1957): 95-103.

QUESTIONS

1. What does Rogers mean when he says that a client must be in a state of incongruity?
2. How does Rogers suggest that a therapist achieve genuineness?
3. How does Rogers' concept of empathy differ from standard definitions of sympathy?
4. What is the role of the therapist in person-centered therapy?

■ ■ ■

For many years I have been engaged in psychotherapy with individuals in distress. In recent years I have found myself increasingly concerned with the process of abstracting from that experience the general principles which appear to be involved in it. I have endeavored to discover any orderliness, any unity which seems to inhere in the subtle, complex tissue of interpersonal relationship in which I have so constantly been immersed in therapeutic work. One of the current products of this concern is an attempt to state, in formal terms, a theory of psychotherapy, of personality, and of interpersonal relationships which will encompass and contain the phenomena of my experience. What I wish to do in this paper is to take one very small segment of that theory, spell it out more completely, and explore its meaning and usefulness. . . .

The Conditions

As I have considered my own clinical experience and that of my colleagues, together with the pertinent research which is available, I have drawn out several conditions which seem to me to be *necessary* to initiate constructive personality change, and which, taken together, appear to be *sufficient* to inaugurate that process. As I have worked on this problem I have found myself surprised at the simplicity of what has emerged. The statement which follows is not offered with any assurance as to its correctness, but with the expectation that it will have the value of any theory, namely that it states or implies a series of hypotheses which are open to proof or disproof, thereby clarifying and extending our knowledge of the field.

Since I am not, in this paper, trying to achieve suspense, I will state at once, in severely rigorous and summarized terms, the six conditions which I have come to feel are basic to the process of personality change. The meaning of a number of the terms is not immediately evident, but will be clarified in the explanatory sections which follow. It is hoped that this brief statement will have much more significance to the reader when he has completed the paper. Without further introduction let me state the basic theoretical position.

For constructive personality change to occur, it is necessary that these conditions exist and continue over a period of time.

1. Two persons are in psychological contact.
2. The first, whom we shall term the client, is in a state of incongruence, being vulnerable or anxious.
3. The second person, whom we shall term the therapist, is congruent or integrated in the relationship.
4. The therapist experiences unconditional positive regard for the client.
5. The therapist experiences an empathic understanding of the client's internal frame of reference and endeavors to communicate this experience to the client.
6. The communication to the client of the therapist's empathic understanding and unconditional positive regard is to a minimal degree achieved.

No other conditions are necessary. If these six conditions exist, and continue over a period of time, this is sufficient. The process of constructive personality change will follow.

A Relationship

The first condition specifies that a minimal relationship, a psychological contact, must exist. I am hypothesizing that significant positive personality change does not occur except in a relationship. This is of course in hypothesis, and it may be disproved.

Conditions 2 through 6 define the characteristics of the relationship which are regarded as essential by defining the necessary characteristics of each person in the relationship. All that is intended by this first condition is to specify that the two people are to some degree in contact, that each makes some perceived difference in the experiential field of the other. Probably it is sufficient if each makes some "subceived" difference, even though the individual may not be consciously aware of this impact. . . .

This first condition of therapeutic change is such a simple one that perhaps it should be labeled an assumption or a precondition in order to set it apart from those that follow. Without it, however, the remaining items would have no meaning, and that is the reason for including it.

The State of the Client

It was specified that it is necessary that the client be "in a state of incongruence, being vulnerable or anxious." What is the meaning of these terms?

Incongruence is a basic construct in the theory we have been developing. It refers to a discrepancy between the actual experience of the organism and the self picture of the individual insofar as it represents that experience. Thus a student may experience, at a total or organismic level, a fear of the university and of examinations which are given on the third floor of a certain building, since these may demonstrate a fundamental inadequacy in him. Since such a fear of his inadequacy is decidedly at odds with his concept of himself, this experience is represented (distortedly) in his awareness as an unreasonable fear of climbing stairs in this building, or any building, and soon an unreasonable fear of crossing the open campus. Thus there is a fundamental discrepancy between the experienced meaning of the situation as it registers in his organism and the symbolic representation of that experience in awareness in such a way that it does not conflict with the picture he has of himself. In this case to admit a fear of inadequacy would contradict the picture he holds of himself: to admit incomprehensible fears does not contradict his self concept.

Another instance would be the mother who develops vague illnesses whenever her only son makes plans to leave home. The actual desire is to hold on to her only source of satisfaction. To perceive this in awareness would be inconsistent with the picture she holds of herself as a good mother. Illness, however, is consistent with her self concept, and the experience is symbolized in this distorted fashion. Thus again there is a basic incongruence between the self as perceived (in this case as an ill mother needing attention) and the actual experience (in this case the desire to hold on to her son).

When the individual has no awareness of such incongruence in himself, then he is merely vulnerable to the possibility of anxiety and disorganization. Some experience might occur so suddenly or so obviously that the incongruence could not be denied. Therefore, the person is vulnerable to such a possibility.

If the individual dimly perceives such an incongruence in himself, then a tension state occurs which is known as anxiety. The incongruence need not be sharply perceived. It is enough that it is subceived—that is, discriminated as threatening to the self without any awareness of the content of that threat. Such anxiety is often seen in therapy as the individual approaches awareness of some element of his experience which is in sharp contradiction to his self concept. . . .

The Therapist's Genuineness in the Relationship

The third condition is that the therapist should be, within the confines of this relationship, a *congruent, genuine, integrated person*. It means that within the relationship he is freely and deeply himself, with his actual experience accurately represented by his awareness of himself. It is the opposite of presenting a facade, either knowingly or unknowingly.

It is not necessary (nor is it possible) that the therapist be a paragon who exhibits this degree of integration, of wholeness, in every aspect of his life. It is sufficient that he is accurately himself in this hour of this relationship, that in this basic sense he is what he actually is, in this moment of time.

It should be clear that this includes being himself even in ways which are not regarded as ideal for psychotherapy. His experience may be "I am afraid of this client" or "My attention is so focused on my own problems that I can scarcely listen to him." If the therapist is not denying these feelings to awareness, but is able freely to be them (as well as being his other feelings), then the condition we have stated is met.

It would take us too far afield to consider the puzzling matter as to the degree to which the therapist overtly communicates this reality in himself to the client. Certainly the aim is not for the therapist to express or talk out his own feelings, but primarily that he should not be deceiving the client as to himself. At times he may need to talk out some of his own feelings (either to the client, or to a colleague or supervisor) if they are standing in the way of the two following conditions. . . .

Unconditional Positive Regard

To the extent that the therapist finds himself experiencing a warm acceptance of each aspect of the client's experience as being a part of that client, he is experiencing unconditional positive regard. This concept has been developed by Stanley Standal. It means that there are no *conditions* of acceptance, no feeling of "I like you only *if* you are thus and so." It means a "prizing" of the person, as Dewey has used that term. It is at the opposite pole from a selective evaluating attitude—"You are bad in these ways, good in those." It involves as much feeling of acceptance for the client's expression of negative, "bad," painful, fearful, defensive, abnormal feelings as for his expression of "good," positive, mature, confident, social feelings, as much acceptance of ways in which he is inconsistent as of ways in which he is consistent. It means a caring for the client, but not in a possessive way or in such a way as simply to satisfy the therapist's own needs. It means a caring for the client as a *separate* person, with permission to have his own feelings, his own experiences. One client describes the therapist as "fostering my possession of my own experience . . . that [this] is *my* experience and that I am actually having it: thinking what I think, feeling what I feel, wanting what I want, fearing what I fear: no 'ifs,' 'buts,' or 'not reallys.'" This is the type of acceptance which is hypothesized as being necessary if personality change is to occur. . . .

Empathy

The fifth condition is that the therapist is experiencing an accurate, empathic understanding of the client's awareness of his own experience. To sense the client's private world as if it were your own, but without ever losing the "as if" quality—this is empathy, and this seems essential to therapy. To sense the client's anger, fear, or confusion as if it were your own, yet without your own anger, fear, or confusion getting bound up in it, is the condition we are endeavoring to describe. When the client's world is this clear to the therapist, and he moves about in it freely, then he can both communicate his understanding of what is clearly known to the client and can also voice meanings in the client's experience of which the client is scarcely aware. As one client described this second aspect: "Every now and again, with me in a tangle of thought and feeling, screwed up in a web of mutually divergent lines of movement, with impulses from different parts of me, and me feeling the feeling of its being all too much and suchlike—then whomp, just like a sunbeam thrusting its way through cloudbanks and tangles of foliage to spread a circle of light on a tangle of forest paths, came some comment from you. [It was] clarity, even disentanglement, an additional twist to the picture, a putting in place. Then the consequence—the sense of moving on, the relaxation. These were sunbeams.". . .

The Client's Perception of the Therapist

The final condition as stated is that the client perceives, to a minimal degree, the acceptance and empathy which the therapist experiences for him. Unless some communication of these attitudes has been achieved, then such attitudes do not exist in the relationship as far as the client is concerned, and the therapeutic process could not, by our hypothesis, be initiated.

Since attitudes cannot be directly perceived, it might be somewhat more accurate to state that therapist behaviors and words are perceived by the client as meaning that to some degree the therapist accepts and understands him. . . .

The Resulting Hypotheses

The major value of stating any theory in unequivocal terms is that specific hypotheses may be drawn from it which are capable of proof or disproof. Thus, even if the conditions which have been postulated as necessary and sufficient conditions are more incorrect than correct (which I hope they are not), they could still advance science in this field by providing a base of operations from which fact could be winnowed out from error.

The hypotheses which would follow from the theory given would be of this order:

If these six conditions (as operationally defined) exist, then constructive personality change (as defined) will occur in the client.

If one or more of these conditions is not present, constructive personality change will not occur.

These hypotheses hold in any situation whether it is or is not labeled "psychotherapy."

Only Condition 1 is dichotomous (it either is present or is not), and the remaining five occur in varying degree, each on its continuum. Since this is true, another hypothesis follows, and it is likely that this would be the simplest to test:

If all six conditions are present, then the greater the degree to which Conditions 2 to 6 exist, the more marked will be the constructive personality change in the client.

At the present time the above hypothesis can only be stated in this general form—which implies that all of the conditions have equal weight. Empirical studies will no doubt make possible much more refinement of this hypothesis. It may be, for example, that if anxiety is high in the client, then the other conditions are less important. Or if unconditional positive regard is high (as in a mother's love for her child), then perhaps a modest degree of empathy is sufficient. But at the moment we can only speculate on such possibilities.

Some Implications

Significant Omissions

If there is any startling feature in the formulation which has been given as to the necessary conditions for therapy, it probably lies in the elements which are omitted. In present-day clinical practice, therapists operate as though there were many other conditions in addition to those described, which are essential for psychotherapy. To point this up it may be well to mention a few of the conditions which, after thoughtful consideration of our research and our experience, are not included.

For example, it is *not* stated that these conditions apply to one type of client, and that other conditions are necessary to bring about psychotherapeutic change with other types of client. Probably no idea is so prevalent in clinical work today as that one works with neurotics in one way, with psychotics in another; that certain therapeutic conditions must be provided for compulsives, others for homosexuals, etc. Because of this heavy weight of clinical opinion to the contrary, it is with some "fear and trembling" that I advance the concept that the essential conditions of psychotherapy exist in a single configuration, even though the client or patient may use them very differently.

It is *not* stated that these six conditions are the essential conditions for client-centered therapy, and that other conditions are essential for other types of psychotherapy. I certainly am heavily influenced by my own experience, and that experience has led me to a viewpoint which is termed "client centered." Nevertheless my aim in stating this theory is to state the conditions which apply to *any* situation in which constructive personality change occurs, whether we are thinking of classical psychoanalysis, or any of its modern offshoots, or Adlerian psychotherapy, or any other. It will be obvious then that in my judgment much of what is considered to be essential would not be found, empirically, to be essential. Testing of some of the stated hypotheses would throw light on this perplexing issue. We may of course find that various therapies produce various types of personality change, and that for each psychotherapy a separate set of conditions is necessary. Until and unless this is demonstrated, I am hypothesizing that effective psychotherapy of any sort produces similar changes in personality and behavior, and that a single set of preconditions is necessary.

It is *not* stated that psychotherapy is a special kind of relationship, different in kind from all others which occur in everyday life. It will be evident instead that for brief moments, at least, many good friendships fulfill the six conditions. Usually this is only momentarily, however, and then empathy falters, the positive regard becomes conditional, or the congruence of the "therapist" friend becomes overlaid by some degree of facade or defensiveness. Thus the therapeutic relationship is seen as a heightening of the constructive qualities which often exist in part in other relationships, and an extension through time of qualities which in other relationships tend at best to be momentary.

It is *not* stated that special intellectual professional knowledge—psychological, psychiatric, medical, or religious—is required of the therapist. Conditions 3, 4, and 5, which apply especially to the therapist, are qualities of experience, not intellectual information. If they are to be acquired, they must, in my opinion, be acquired through an experiential training—which may be, but usually is not, a part of professional training. It troubles me to hold such a radical point of view, but I can draw no other conclusion from my experience. Intellectual training and the acquiring of information has, I believe, many valuable results—but becoming a therapist is not one of those results.

It is *not* stated that it is necessary for psychotherapy that the therapist have an accurate psychological diagnosis of the client. Here too it troubles me to hold a viewpoint so at variance with my clinical colleagues. When one thinks of the vast proportion of time spent in any psychological, psychiatric, or mental hygiene center on the exhaustive psychological evaluation of the client or patient, it seems as though this *must* serve a useful purpose insofar as psychotherapy is concerned. Yet the more I have observed therapists, and the more closely I have studied research such as that done by Fiedler and others, the more I am forced to the conclusion that such diagnostic knowledge is not essential to psychotherapy. It may even be that its defense as a necessary prelude to psychotherapy is simply a protective alternative to the admission that it is, for the most part, a colossal waste of time. There is only one useful purpose I have been able to observe which relates to psychotherapy. Some therapists cannot feel secure in the relationship with the client unless they possess such diagnostic knowledge. Without it they feel fearful of him, unable to be empathic, unable to experience unconditional regard, finding it necessary to put up a pretense in the relationship. If they

46

know in *advance* of suicidal impulses they can somehow be more acceptant of them. Thus, for some therapists, the security they perceive in diagnostic information may be a basis for permitting themselves to be integrated in the relationship, and to experience empathy and full acceptance. In these instances a psychological diagnosis would certainly be justified as adding to the comfort and hence the effectiveness of the therapist. But even here it does not appear to be a basic precondition for psychotherapy.

Perhaps I have given enough illustrations to indicate that the conditions I have hypothesized as necessary and sufficient for psychotherapy are striking and unusual primarily by virtue of what they omit. If we were to determine, by a survey of the behaviors of therapists, those hypotheses which they appear to regard as necessary to psychotherapy, the list would be a great deal longer and more complex.

Is This Theoretical Formulation Useful?

Aside from the personal satisfaction it gives as a venture in abstraction and generalization, what is the value of a theoretical statement such as has been offered in this paper? I should like to spell out more fully the usefulness which I believe it may have.

In the field of research it may give both direction and impetus to investigation. Since it sees the conditions of constructive personality change as general, it greatly broadens the opportunities for study. Psychotherapy is not the only situation aimed at constructive personality change. Programs of training for leadership in industry and programs of training for military leadership often aim at such change. Educational institutions or programs frequently aim at development of character and personality as well as at intellectual skills. Community agencies aim at personality and behavioral change in delinquents and criminals. Such programs would provide an opportunity for the broad testing of the hypotheses offered. If it is found that constructive personality change occurs in such programs when the hypothesized conditions are not fulfilled, then the theory would have to be revised. If however the hypotheses are upheld, then the results, both for the planning of such programs and for our knowledge of human dynamics, would be significant. In the field of psychotherapy itself, the application of consistent hypotheses to the

work of various schools of therapists may prove highly profitable. Again the disproof of the hypotheses offered would be as
important as their confirmation, either result adding significantly to our knowledge.

For the practice of psychotherapy the theory also offers
significant problems for consideration. One of its implications
is that the techniques of the various therapies are relatively
unimportant except to the extent that they serve as channels
for fulfilling one of the conditions. In client-centered therapy,
for example, the technique of "reflecting feelings" has been
described and commented on. In terms of the theory here
being presented, this technique is by no means an essential
condition of therapy. To the extent, however, that it provides a
channel by which the therapist communicates a sensitive empathy and an unconditional positive regard, then it may serve
as a technical channel by which the essential conditions of
therapy are fulfilled. In the same way, the theory I have presented would see no essential value to therapy of such techniques as interpretation of personality dynamics, free association, analysis of dreams, analysis of the transference,
hypnosis, interpretation of life style, suggestion, and the like.
Each of these techniques may, however, become a channel for
communicating the essential conditions which have been formulated. An interpretation may be given in a way which communicates the unconditional positive regard of the therapist.
A stream of free association may be listened to in a way which
communicates an empathy which the therapist is experiencing. In the handling of the transference an effective therapist
often communicates his own wholeness and congruence in
the relationship. Similarly for the other techniques. But just as
these techniques *may* communicate the elements which are essential for therapy, so any one of them may communicate attitudes and experiences sharply contradictory to the hypothesized conditions of therapy. Feeling may be "reflected" in a
way which communicates the therapist's lack of empathy. Interpretations may be rendered in a way which indicates the
highly conditional regard of the therapist. Any of the techniques may communicate the fact that the therapist is ex-
pressing one attitude at a surface level, and another contradictory attitude which is denied to his own awareness. Thus
one value of such a theoretical formulation as we have offered

is that it may assist therapists to think more critically about those elements of their experience, attitudes, and behaviors which are essential to psychotherapy, and those which are nonessential or even deleterious to psychotherapy.

Finally, in those programs—educational, correctional, military, or industrial—which aim toward constructive changes in the personality structure and behavior of the individual, this formulation may serve as a very tentative criterion against which to measure the program. Until it is much further tested by research, it cannot be thought of as a valid criterion, but, as in the field of psychotherapy, it may help to stimulate critical analysis and the formulation of alternative conditions and alternative hypotheses.

Summary

Drawing from a larger theoretical context, six conditions are postulated as necessary and sufficient conditions for the initiation of a process of constructive personality change. A brief explanation is given of each condition, and suggestions are made as to how each may be operationally defined for research purposes. The implications of this theory for research, for psychotherapy, and for educational and training programs aimed at constructive personality change, are indicated. It is pointed out that many of the conditions which are commonly regarded as necessary to psychotherapy are, in terms of this theory, nonessential.

Psychotherapy Should Focus on Changing Behaviors

B.F. SKINNER

Burrhus Frederick Skinner was an avid inventor and a college
rebel. As a psychologist Skinner criticized the tendency of scientists to study only internal mental processes. He suggested
instead that the only measurable clues to mental functioning
lie in an organism's behavior. With an affinity toward mechan-
ics he built the famous "Skinner Box," (an aparatus to deliver
reinforcements and record data on laboratory animals). His
mechanical inclinations later led him to create a "Teaching
Machine" for use in an automated classroom and the Skinner-
Air-Crib, a soundproof environmentally controlled crib in
which he raised his youngest daughter for more than two
years. Based on his theories of reinforcement, Skinnerian
Therapy seeks to shape behavior through positive and negative reinforcement.

QUESTIONS

1. What role do "feelings" play in Skinner's theory?

From "The Operant Side of Behavior Therapy" by B.F. Skinner, *Journal of Be-
havior Therapy and Experimental Psychiatry*, vol. 19, no. 12 (1988), pp. 171-76.
Reprinted by permission of Elsevier Science, Ltd., Pergamon Imprint, Oxford,
England.

2. What is the difference between operant and respondent behavior therapy, according to Skinner?
3. How do positive and negative reinforcers differ according to Skinner?
4. What effect do differing schedules of reinforcement have on behavior modification, according to the author?

■ ■ ■

In 1913 John B. Watson issued his famous manifesto: The subject matter of psychology was behavior. It is easy to forget how radical that must have seemed. Psychology had always been the science of mental life, and that life was to be studied through introspection, a process of self-examination borrowed from the philosophers, who had used it for more than twenty-four hundred years. People were seen to behave in given ways because of what they were feeling or thinking about, and feelings and thoughts were therefore the things to study. If animals sometimes behaved rather like people, they probably had feelings and some kind of mental life, although they might not know they had.

Seventy-five years have seen a great change. Introspection has been returned to the philosophers. There are no longer any "trained observers" in the Wundtian tradition, and cognitive psychologists no longer observe the mental processes they talk about. The processes are hypotheses, to be confirmed either by inferences from the behavior they are said to explain or by a different kind of observation—namely, of the nervous system.

Meanwhile, two flourishing sciences of behavior have appeared. Ethology is one of them. The behavior of animals in a natural environment is no longer explained by imagining what the animals are feeling or thinking about but by the contributions the behavior may have made to the future of their genes. In the other science, the experimental analysis of behavior, animals are observed in the laboratory, where many of the conditions of which their behavior is a function can be controlled. Most of the behavior is traced to operant reinforcement, a different kind of selective consequence acting during the lifetime of the individual.

As more and more of the variables of which behavior is a function are identified and their role analysed, less remains to be explained in mentalistic ways. There are proportionate gains in the application of the analysis. It has always been difficult to do very much with feelings and states of mind because of their inaccessibility. The environmental variables are often within reach. Contact between the basic analysis and its applications is therefore important. Although new facts often turn up in the course of applying a science, the science itself usually moves more rapidly into new territory. In what follows I review some well known practices in behavior therapy from the point of view of behavior analysis and discuss a few current theoretical issues. I do so, not to correct or instruct practitioners, but to reassure them. The experimental analysis of behavior is developing rapidly, and at every step the principles of behavior therapy gain authority. Troublesome behavior is due to troublesome contingencies of reinforcement, not to troublesome feelings or states of mind, and to correct the trouble we should correct the contingencies.

Respondent Behavior Therapy

Psychotherapy has often been concerned with feelings—with anxiety, fear, anger and the like. An early step toward behavior therapy was the realization that what was felt was not a "feeling" but a state of the body. The point was made before the advent of behaviorism by William James and Carl Lange. Lange looked for possibly relevant states, but James put the argument in its best known form: we do not cry because we are sad, we are sad because we cry.

A further step was needed, however. We do not cry *because* we are sad or feel sad *because* we cry, we cry *and* feel sad because something has happened. Perhaps a friend has died. We must know something about the earlier event if we are to explain either the crying or the state felt. That is the behavioristic position: turn to environmental antecedents to explain what one does and, at the same time, what one feels while doing it. For every state felt and given the name of a feeling there is presumably a prior environmental event of which it is the product. Behavior therapy addresses the prior event rather than the feeling.

What are felt as emotions are largely the responses of glands and smooth muscle. Efforts were once made to define a given emotion as a particular pattern of such responses. The variables of which the behavior is a function are a more promising alternative. Some aggressive behavior, for example, is genetic; it has evolved because of its contribution to the survival of the species. Variables of that sort are largely out of reach in dealing with the behavior of an individual, although aggressive behavior can often be allowed to adapt out. Much more can be done when emotional responses result from respondent (Pavlovian) conditioning. Troublesome behavior can then often be extinguished or other behavior can be conditioned to replace it. Both adaptation and extinction have fewer unwanted side effects when stimuli are presented with gradually increasing intensities. The process is called, of course, desensitization.

Operant Behavior Therapy

Therapists have been as much concerned with what people do as with what they feel. Behavior therapists trace what is done to two kinds of selective consequences, innate behavior to natural selection and learned behavior to operant reinforcement. A given instance is usually a joint product of both. There is an operant side to emotion, for example. Fear is not only a response of glands and smooth muscle, it is a reduced probability of moving toward a feared object and a heightened probability of moving away from it. The operant side of anger is a greater probability of hurting someone and a lesser probability of acting to please. Where the bodily state resulting from respondent conditioning is usually called a feeling, the state resulting from operant conditioning, observed through introspection, is called a state of mind.

Important distinctions are obscured, however, when behavior is attributed to a state of mind. An operant is strengthened, for example, when a response has reinforcing consequences, but subsequent responses occur because of what has happened, not what is going to happen. When we say that we do something "with the intention of having a given effect," for example, we attribute our behavior to something that lies in the future, but both the behavior and the state introspectively observed at the time are due to what has happened in the past.

"Expectation" misrepresents the facts in the same way. To take an operant example, when a reinforcing consequence has followed something we have done, we are said to expect that it will follow when we do it again. What is introspectively observed is the bodily state resulting from the past occurrence. When one stimulus has often followed another, regardless of anything we may have done, we are said to expect the second whenever the first occurs. That expectation is a bodily state resulting from respondent conditioning.

Terms for states of mind have never been very consistently used. The nervous systems which bring our behavior into contact with various parts of our own body are not very efficient because they evolved for other reasons, and we cannot observe the bodily states of other people at all, at least while they are alive. In any case explanations of that sort must themselves be explained. We make no progress by explaining one state of mind as the effect of another; we must get back to something that can be directly observed and, if possible, put to use. That means, of course, the genetic and personal histories responsible both for the behavior and, in passing, the states of the body introspectively observed.

Some Examples

The operant side of behavior therapy can be illustrated by considering a few characteristic problems, in each of which behavior is traced to a contingency of natural selection or operant reinforcement rather than to a state of mind. Positively reinforced behavior is often accompanied by a state which we report by saying that we are doing "what we want to do", "like to do", or "love to do". There is a special reason why such behavior is often troublesome. The reinforcing effect of a particular consequence may have evolved under conditions which no longer prevail. For example, most of us are strongly reinforced by salty or sweet foods, not because large quantities are good for us now, but because salty and sweet foods were in short supply in the early history of the species. Those who, thanks to genetic variations, found them especially reinforcing were more likely to eat them and survive. The increased susceptibility to reinforcement then led to the discovery and processing of vast quantities of salty and sweet foods, and we now eat too much of them and may turn to therapy for help.

An increased susceptibility to reinforcement by sexual contact would also have had great survival value in a world subject to famine, pestilence, and predation, and it now raises problems, not only for individuals but for an already overpopulated world. A strong susceptibility to reinforcement by signs that one has hurt another person could also have evolved because such signs shape and maintain skillful combat. (The boxer who shows that he has been hurt has taught his opponent how to hurt.) Hence, the strong reinforcement of aggressive behavior which, like that of sexual behavior, raises problems both for the individual and the world.

Problems also arise from reinforcers which have never had any evolutionary advantage. *Homo sapiens* is not the only species to have discovered them. The reinforcing effects of alcohol, heroin, cocaine, and other drugs are presumably accidental. They are particularly troublesome when their use leads to the powerful negative reinforcers we call withdrawal symptoms. The craving from which an addict is said to suffer is a bodily state which accompanies behavior due to an anomalous reinforcer.

A different problem arises when a repertoire of behavior conditioned in one environment undergoes extinction in another. The relevant bodily state may be called discouragement, a sense of failure, helplessness, a loss of confidence, or depression. A different kind of depression follows when, having acquired a large and effective repertoire in one place, one moves to another in which it cannot be executed. The behavior is not extinguished; there are things one still wants to do, but appropriate occasions are lacking. The student who has acquired an effective repertoire in college may find no place for it in the world to which he moves upon graduation. The person who moves to a new city may suffer the same kind of depression when a repertoire appropriate to the old city does not work well in the new.

The addiction due to anomalous reinforcers is quite different from the addiction due to certain schedules of reinforcement. The so-called variable-ratio schedule is especially likely to cause trouble. It is a useful schedule because it maintains behavior against extinction when reinforcers occur only infrequently. The behavior of the dedicated artist, writer, business-man, or scientist is sustained by an occasional, unpredictable re-inforcement. We play games because our behavior is reinforced on a variable ratio schedule, and for the same reason we gamble. In the long run gamblers lose because those who maintain the contingencies must win. As with the behavior due to anomalous reinforcers, gambling is an addiction in the sense that there is no ultimate gain, at least for most of those who gamble.

Many problems calling for therapy arise from a fault in op-erant conditioning itself. The process presumably evolved be-cause behavior was strengthened when it produced important consequences for both individual and species. The process could not, however, take into account the *manner* in which the consequences were produced. It was enough that conse-quences usually followed because they were produced by what was done. Conditioning nevertheless occurs when rein-forcing consequences follow for any reason whatsoever. Acci-dental consequences yield the behavior we call superstition. We fall ill, take a pill or perform a ritual, and get well; we then are more likely to take a pill or perform the ritual when we fall ill again, regardless of whether there was any actual effect. The superstition may stand in the way of a better measure. Therapy is often a matter of destroying the reinforcing effects of adven-titious consequences.

Aversive consequences are responsible for many kinds of problems. As negative reinforcers they can have the faults we have just seen in positive reinforcers. As punishment their side effects may be severe. We learned to crawl, walk, run and ride a bicycle because getting around the world reinforced our cor-rectly doing so but also because we were hurt when we made mistakes. That sort of punishment is immediately contingent on behavior and may reduce its probability of occurrence, but it can also suppress behavior in a different way through respondent conditioning. The situation in which the behavior occurs or some aspect of the behavior itself becomes aversive, and it can then negatively reinforce alternative forms of behavior. The punished person remains as strongly inclined to behave in the punished way as ever but escapes from the threat of punishment by doing something else instead. When punishment is imposed by other people, as it often is, it is seldom immediately contin-gent on what is done and works via respondent conditioning.

The bodily state resulting from the threat of deferred punishment is named according to its sources. When punished by one's peers it is called shame, when by a government guilt and when by a religious agency a sense of sin. One way to escape is to confess and take the punishment, but when the behavior upon which a deferred punishment was contingent is not clear, escape can be difficult. Merely accidental aversive contingencies generate unexplained feelings of shame, guilt or sin, and a person may then turn to a therapist for help in escaping.

Here, then, are a few examples of troublesome contingencies of operant reinforcement, together with a few "states of mind" to which the behavior is often attributed. Other examples could be given (the list seems endless), but these are perhaps enough to show the precision and potential of the operant analysis. It does not follow, however, that behavior therapists should never ask their clients what they are feeling or thinking about. From their answers something may be inferred about genetic or personal histories. Asking such questions is, in fact, often the only way in which therapists can learn about a personal history. They lack facilities for direct investigations, and to investigate without permission is regarded as unethical. But asking about feelings and thoughts is only a convenience—the very convenience, in fact, which explains why people have asked about them for so many centuries—and we must turn to more accessible variables if we are to have a scientific analysis or use it to do something about personal problems.

The argument for operant behavior therapy is essentially this: What is felt as feelings or introspectively observed as states of mind are states of the body, and they are the products of certain contingencies of reinforcement. The contingencies can be much more easily identified and analysed than the feelings or states of mind, and by turning to them as the thing to be changed, behavior therapy gains a special advantage. An important question remains to be answered, however. How are contingencies to be changed?

Changing the Contingencies

The conditions of which behavior is a function are under control in homes, for example, and in schools, workplaces, hospitals and prisons. Therapists may change them for their own purposes if they are part of a family or if they teach, employ workers, or administer hospitals or prisons. Professionally, they advise those who do so. They help parents with their children or spouses with their spouses; they advise teachers; they suggest new practices in hospitals and prisons. They can do so because some of the conditions under which people live can be controlled.

The word control raises a familiar issue. What right has a therapist to manipulate the conditions of which a person's behavior is a function? The question is more often asked about the use of punitive consequences by governments or positive reinforcers by business and industry. If it is not so often asked of psychotherapists, perhaps it is because they have not demonstrated any threatening power or because, like Carl Rogers, they insist that they are not exercising control at all. The question is more likely to be asked of behavior therapists because their practices are more often effective. Token economies in hospitals or prisons, for example, have been challenged precisely because they work. Food, even institutional food, is a reinforcer and can often be made contingent on behavior. That can be done to the advantage of those who are reinforced, but it is perhaps more often done to solve problems of management. The ethical question would seem to be *cui bono*, who profits? Control is ethical if it is exerted for the sake of the controlled.

That principle could play a greater part in current demands for legislative action to prohibit the use of aversive measures by therapists. It is easy to argue for banning the use of aversives because they are unpleasant things. By definition they are things we turn away from, and as punishment they interfere with things we want to do. But who eventually profits? The dentist's drill is aversive, but we accept it to escape from a toothache. We accept the punitive practices of governments and religions in return for some measure of order, security, and peace of mind. When aversive stimuli are used to stop the bizarre behavior of autistic people long enough to bring them under the control of nonaversive practices, they would seem to be justified. But only if no other measure can be used. Too ready an acceptance of aversive measures blocks progress along other lines. It is only recently that strong sanctions have been imposed upon child abuse and the battering of spouses, and corporal punishment is only now being strongly challenged in schools. We are not yet ready to replace a police force or close the Pentagon. Applied behavior analysis has contributed to alternative measures, however, and we may hope that the problems of the autistic will soon be solved in better ways.

The Clinic

Homes, schools, workplaces, hospitals and prisons are environments in which people spend a great deal of their time. Face-to-face therapy in the clinic is different. Only a small part of the client's life is spent in the presence of a therapist. Only a few reinforcers can be used, and most of the time only to reinforce social, especially verbal, behavior. There is a great deal of mutual shaping of behavior in face-to-face confrontations; some of it possibly harmful.

What the client does in the clinic is not of immediate concern, however. What happens there is preparation for a world which is not under the control of the therapist. Instead of arranging current contingencies of reinforcement, as in a home, school, workplace or hospital, therapists give advice. Modelling behavior to be copied is a kind of advice, but verbal advice has a broader scope. It may take the form of an order ("Do this, stop doing that") or it may describe contingencies of reinforcement ("Doing this will probably have a reinforcing effect." "If you do that the consequences may be punishing.").

Traditionally, advice has been thought of as communication. Something called knowledge of the world is said to pass from speaker to listener. But a useful distinction has been made between knowing by acquaintance and knowing by description. Knowing because something you have done has had reinforcing consequences is very different from knowing because you have been told what to do. It is the difference between contingency-shaped and rule-governed behavior.

But why is advice taken? Children often do as they are told because they have been punished when they have not done so, and something of the sort is suggested in therapy when it is said that the therapist should become an authority figure, perhaps that of a father or mother. But children also do as they are told because positive reinforcers have followed. Parents who contrive consequences having that effect are said to "reward" their children for doing as they are told. Teachers contrive similar reinforcing consequences, such as commendation or good grades, to induce their students to study. There is no natural connection between the behavior and its consequence, but the practice is justified on the grounds that genuine consequences will take over in the world at large. Very little of that sort of thing is suitable in therapy. The only reinforcing consequences which induce clients to continue to take advice are largely to be found outside the clinic.

Therapists who resemble people whose advice has often proved to be worth taking have an advantage. Those who do not must work in other ways. In traditional terms, they must build "confidence" or "trust". That can sometimes be done by giving bits of advice which are not only easily followed but will almost certainly have reinforcing consequences.

Face-to-face advice may also take the form of rules for effective action. The proverbs and maxims of cultures are rules of that sort. Rules are especially useful because therapists may not be available to help in solving future problems. Not every problem can be solved by applying a rule, however, and therapists may need to take a further step and teach their clients how to construct their own rules. That means teaching them something about the analysis of behavior. It is usually easier than teaching them how to change their feelings or states of mind.

CHAPTER

2

What Is Personality and How Is It Measured?

Chapter Preface

The origins of modern medical theories of personality date back to 450 B.C. when Hippocrates theorized that mental illness, like physical illness, could be traced to genetic predispositions and physical causes such as imbalances in bodily fluids. These bodily fluids or "humors" produced psychological disturbances. An excess of blood, for example, produced sanguinity; black bile produced melancholy; yellow bile produced cholera; and phlegm resulted in apathy. Hippocrates argued that it was the physician's objective to return these fluids to natural homeostatic proportions. Though some of Hippocrates' theories seem far-fetched today, the fact that he linked hormones to temperament was extremely advanced for his time. Hippocrates' theories influenced modern personality theories considerably. In fact, like Hippocrates, Sigmund Freud attributed hysteria in women to a wandering uterus.

Later theories on personality attempted to explain personality by studying an individual's cranial bumps (Gall's phrenology), body structures (Sheldon's physique classification), or outward appearances (Aristotle's physiognomy). These theories, however, held a transient influence in psychology until the late 1800s when Freud combined an amalgam of past personality theories to create his own—one that continues to influence psychology.

Ironically, current studies of personality mirror that of ancient Greece, the same debates arise today as were contemplated by Hippocrates and others. Debates in personality theory cover three main areas: 1) What are the basic components of personality? 2) How is personality determined (motivated)? and 3) How is personality measured?

The first issue, on the components of personality, centers on the motivation for behavior—whether it is driven by the unconscious, or by needs and feelings. The second question of personality asks how personalities are formed. The third issue that arises is how to measure personality. Personality theorists argue whether personality should be analyzed in the form of stable characteristics or traits or in terms of the whole personality.

Unconscious Instincts Motivate Personality

SIGMUND FREUD

Sigmund Freud's psychoanalytic theory spawned a theory of personality. Much has been written about Freud's overemphasis on sexuality, however, it is important to remember that Freud was the first to recognize sexuality's constant influence throughout the life span. Freud's characterization of the unconscious mind has changed both psychologists' and lay people's understanding of personality. Because no chapter on personality is complete without a discussion of Freud's influence on these theories, a short piece by Freud is provided for a description of some of the better known elements of his theory.

QUESTIONS

1. According to Freud, what are the characteristics of the id, ego, and superego and how are they acquired?
2. What role do instincts play in Freud's theory?
3. Does Freud believe all instincts exert equal power? Why or why not?
4. How does Freud define the libido and the role it plays?

The Mind and Its Workings

The Psychical Apparatus

Psycho-analysis makes a basic assumption, the discussion of which is reserved to philosophical thought but the justification for which lies in its results. We know two kinds of things about what we call our psyche (or mental life): firstly, its bodily organ and scene of action, the brain (or nervous system) and, on the other hand, our acts of consciousness, which are immediate data and cannot be further explained by any sort of description. Everything that lies between is unknown to us, and the data do not include any direct relation between these two terminal points of our knowledge. If it existed, it would at the most afford an exact localization of the processes of consciousness and would give us no help towards understanding them.

Our two hypotheses start out from these ends or beginnings of our knowledge. The first is concerned with localization. We assume that mental life is the function of an apparatus to which we ascribe the characteristics of being extended in space and of being made up of several portions—which we imagine, that is, as resembling a telescope or microscope or something of the kind. Notwithstanding some earlier attempts in the same direction, the consistent working-out of a conception such as this is a scientific novelty.

We have arrived at our knowledge of this psychical apparatus by studying the individual development of human beings. To the oldest of these psychical provinces or agencies we give the name of *id*. It contains everything that is inherited, that is present at birth, that is laid down in the constitution—above all, therefore, the instincts, which originate from the somatic organization and which find a first psychical expression here [in the id] in forms unknown to us.

Under the influence of the real external world around us, one portion of the id has undergone a special development. From what was originally a cortical layer, equipped with the organs for receiving stimuli and with arrangements for acting as a protective shield against stimuli, a special organization has arisen which henceforward acts as an intermediary between the id and the external world. To this region of our mind we have given the name of *ego*.

Here are the principal characteristics of the ego. In consequence of the pre-established connection between sense perception and muscular action, the ego has voluntary movement at its command. It has the task of self-preservation. As regards *external* events, it performs that task by becoming aware of stimuli, by storing up experiences about them (in the memory), by avoiding excessively strong stimuli (through flight), by dealing with moderate stimuli (through adaptation) and finally by learning to bring about expedient changes in the external world to its own advantage (through activity). As regards *internal* events, in relation to the id, it performs that task by gaining control over the demands of the instincts, by deciding whether they are to be allowed satisfaction, by postponing that satisfaction to times and circumstances favorable in the external world or by suppressing their excitations entirely. It is guided in its activity by consideration of the tensions produced by stimuli, whether these tensions are present in it or introduced into it. The raising of these tensions is in general felt as *unpleasure* and their lowering as *pleasure*. It is probable, however, that what is felt as pleasure or unpleasure is not the *absolute* height of this tension but something in the rhythm of the changes in them. The ego strives after pleasure and seeks to avoid unpleasure. An increase in unpleasure that is expected and foreseen is met by a *signal of anxiety*; the occasion of such an increase, whether it threatens from without or within, is known as a danger. From time to time the ego gives up its connection with the external world and withdraws into the state of sleep, in which it makes far-reaching changes in its organization. It is to be inferred from the state of sleep that this organization consists in a particular distribution of mental energy.

The long period of childhood, during which the growing human being lives in dependence on his parents, leaves behind it as a precipitate the formation in his ego of a special agency in which this parental influence is prolonged. It has received the name of *super-ego*. In so far as this super-ego is differentiated from the ego or is opposed to it, it constitutes a third power which the ego must take into account.

An action by the ego is as it should be if it satisfies simultaneously the demands of the id, of the super-ego and of reality—that is to say, if it is able to reconcile their demands with one another. The details of the relation between the ego and the super-ego become completely intelligible when they are traced back to the child's attitude to its parents. This parental influence of course includes in its operation not only the personalities of the actual parents but also the family, racial and national traditions handed on through them, as well as the demands of the immediate social *milieu* which they represent. In the same way, the super-ego, in the course of an individual's development, receives contributions from later successors and substitutes of his parents, such as teachers and models in public life of admired social ideals. It will be observed that, for all their fundamental difference, the id and the super-ego have one thing in common: they both represent the influences of the past—the id the influence of heredity, the super-ego the influence, essentially, of what is taken over from other people—whereas the ego is principally determined by the individual's own experience, that is by accidental and contemporary events.

This general schematic picture of a psychical apparatus may be supposed to apply as well to the higher animals which resemble man mentally. A super-ego must be presumed to be present wherever, as is the case with man, there is a long period of dependence in childhood. A distinction between ego and id is an unavoidable assumption. Animal psychology has not yet taken in hand the interesting problem which is here presented.

The Theory of the Instincts

The power of the id expresses the true purpose of the individual organism's life. This consists in the satisfaction of its innate needs. No such purpose as that of keeping itself alive or of protecting itself from dangers by means of anxiety can be attributed to the id. That is the task of the ego, whose business it also is to discover the most favourable and least perilous method of obtaining satisfaction, taking the external world into account. The super-ego may bring fresh needs to the fore, but its main function remains the limitation of satisfactions.

The forces which we assume to exist behind the tensions caused by the needs of the id are called *instincts*. They represent the somatic demands upon the mind. Though they are the ultimate cause of all activity, they are of a conservative nature; the state, whatever it may be, which an organism has reached gives rise to a tendency to re-establish that state so soon as it has been abandoned. It is thus possible to distinguish an indeterminate number of instincts, and in common practice this is in fact done. For us, however, the important question arises whether it may not be possible to trace all these numerous instincts back to a few basic ones. We have found that instincts can change their aim (by displacement) and also that they can replace one another—the energy of one instinct passing over to another. This latter process is still insufficiently understood. After long hesitancies and vacillations we have decided to assume the existence of only two basic instincts, *Eros* and *the destructive instinct*. (The contrast between the instincts of self-preservation and the preservation of the species, as well as the contrast between ego-love and object-love, fall within Eros.) The aim of the first of these basic instincts is to establish ever greater unities and to preserve them thus—in short, to bind together; the aim of the second is, on the contrary, to undo connections and so to destroy things. In the case of the destructive instinct we may suppose that its final aim is to lead what is living into an inorganic state. For this reason we also call it the *death instinct*. If we assume that living things came later than inanimate ones and arose from them, then the death instinct fits in with the formula we have proposed to the effect that instincts tend towards a return to an earlier state. In the case of Eros (or the love instinct) we cannot apply this formula. To do so would presuppose that living substance was once a unity which had later been torn apart and was now striving towards re-union.

In biological functions the two basic instincts operate against each other or combine with each other. Thus, the act of eating is a destruction of the object with the final aim of incorporating it, and the sexual act is an act of aggression with the purpose of the most intimate union. This concurrent and mutually opposing action of the two basic instincts gives rise to the whole variegation of the phenomena of life. The analogy of our two basic instincts extends from the sphere of living things to the pair of opposing forces—attraction and repulsion—which rule in the inorganic world.

Modifications in the proportions of the fusion between the instincts have the most tangible results. A surplus of sexual aggressiveness will turn a lover into a sex-murderer, while a sharp diminution in the aggressive factor will make him bashful or impotent.

There can be no question of restricting one or the other of the basic instincts to one of the provinces of the mind. They must necessarily be met with everywhere. We may picture an initial state as one in which the total available energy of Eros, which henceforward we shall speak of as 'libido', is present in the still undifferentiated ego-id and serves to neutralize the destructive tendencies which are simultaneously present. (We are without a term analogous to 'libido' for describing the energy of the destructive instinct.) At a later stage it becomes relatively easy for us to follow the vicissitudes of the libido, but this is more difficult with the destructive instinct.

So long as that instinct operates internally, as a death instinct, it remains silent; it only comes to our notice when it is diverted outwards as an instinct of destruction. It seems to be essential for the preservation of the individual that this diversion should occur; the muscular apparatus serves this purpose. When the super-ego is established, considerable amounts of the aggressive instinct are fixated in the interior of the ego and operate there self-destructively. This is one of the dangers to health by which human beings are faced on their path to cultural development. Holding back aggressiveness is in general unhealthy and leads to illness (to mortification). A person in a fit of rage will often demonstrate how the transition from aggressiveness that has been prevented to self-destructiveness is brought about by diverting the aggressiveness against himself: he tears his hair or beats his face with his fists, though he would evidently have preferred to apply this treatment to someone else. Some portion of self-destructiveness remains within, whatever the circumstances; till at last it succeeds in killing the individual, not, perhaps, until his libido has been used up or fixated in a disadvantageous way. Thus it may in general be suspected that the *individual* dies of his internal conflicts but that the *species* dies of its unsuccessful struggle against the external world if the latter changes in a fashion which cannot be adequately dealt with by the adaptations which the species has acquired.

It is hard to say anything of the behaviour of the libido in the id and in the super-ego. All that we know about it relates to the ego, in which at first the whole available quota of libido is stored up. We call this state absolute, primary *narcissism*. It lasts till the ego begins to cathect the ideas of objects with libido, to transform narcissistic libido into object-libido. Throughout the whole of life the ego remains the great reservoir from which libidinal cathexes are sent out to objects and into which they are also once more withdrawn, just as an amoeba behaves with its pseudopodia. It is only when a person is completely in love that the main quota of libido is transferred on to the object and the object to some extent takes the place of the ego. A characteristic of the libido which is important in life is its *mobility*, the facility with which it passes from one object to another. This must be contrasted with the *fixation* of the libido to particular objects, which often persists throughout life.

There can be no question but that the libido has somatic sources, that it streams to the ego from various organs and parts of the body. This is most clearly seen in the case of that portion of the libido which, from its instinctual aim, is described as sexual excitation. The most prominent of the parts of the body from which this libido arises are known by the name of 'erotogenic zones', though in fact the whole body is an erotogenic zone of this kind. The greater part of what we know about Eros—that is to say, about its exponent, the libido—has been gained from a study of the sexual function, which, indeed, on the prevailing view, even if not according to our theory, coincides with Eros. We have been able to form a picture of the way in which the sexual urge, which is destined to exercise a decisive influence on our life, gradually develops out of successive contributions from a number of component instincts, which represent particular erotogenic zones.

Social Feeling Motivates Personality

ALFRED ADLER

Alfred Adler was educated in the Freudian psychoanalytic school but later broke with Freud to develop "individual psychology." Adler's childhood was riddled with constant illness and hospitalization and some theorize that this constant vulnerability served as the impetus for his inferiority theory. Adler's theory is premised on the belief that individuals exist within a social context. He believed that this social context provides a feeling of group unity or membership (Gemeinschaftsgefühl) that causes individuals to assess themselves relative to others. The source of maladjusted personality, according to Adler, is improper development of this social interest, not improper psychosexual development. Adler saw society as the source for every individual's journey—we must first assess and then compensate for our inferiority. The following is a small sample of Adler's theory of individual psychology.

From Alfred Adler, "Individual Psychology and Experimental Psychology," *Character and Personality*, June 1993, pp. 265-67. Copyright Duke University Press, 1993. Reprinted with permission.

QUESTIONS

1. What role does illness play in Adler's theory of personality?
2. According to Adler, what can be done about a lack of social feeling?
3. How does Adler's social feeling differ from conventional notions of altruism?
4. How does Adler's theory diverge from that of Freud? What aspects of Freud's teachings does Adler retain?

■　■　■

Individual psychology is compelled to adopt a friendly attitude as soon as it begins to consider the various sciences and scientific tendencies. It takes up what may be described as a central position among the various schools of psychological thought and it admits the claims of every school provided that it is seen to pursue what must be the aim of every science, namely, the promotion of human development. It is one of the fundamental claims of individual psychology that this development requires a fostering of the social feeling. For this, and various other scientific reasons, individual psychology is committed to an uncompromising position on psychoanalysis—to give but one example of a science which follows laboriously in the rear of individual psychology which, in its turn, has its sphere of activity at the very centre of human evolution.

The claims of individual psychology to describe personality and character, not by means of the inevitable ambiguity of words and concepts but by means of detailed descriptions, stand and fall with the fundamental assumption that mankind in general, as well as individuals, behaves "correctly," "normally," "reasonably," "intellectually soundly," if it possesses these qualities at any given moment *sub specie aeterna* and if it be seen from the point of view of an ideal community. In that case every aberration would have to be ascribed as an erroneous attitude; and the fact that this ideal may never be attained and that mankind is compelled never to do more than laboriously approach it, does nothing to invalidate the certainty of this view. And it may well be that every scientist is aware of this fact without necessarily understanding it.

71

Accordingly whenever we pass judgment on an individual—and every individual is unique; whence the justification of the term "individual psychology"—four main questions must be answered; these questions must be supplemented by other and more detailed questions if the investigation is to be at all exact.

1. In what direction does the evolutionary urge of the individual under examination tend? The significance of this question in my science has been clearly set out in the discussion of aims in the life of the soul and of the urge towards perfection (taken as an individual perfection). This view, I imagine, has today been adopted by all serious psychologists and psychiatrists, under such names as purposivism, teleology, ideal-ego, etc., although no adequate description of this urge has been given outside the range of individual psychology.

2. This perfection which must be the aim of the individual has only one standard of measurement, viz., the ideal of a community. Accordingly what we have to measure is a relation. In our view of the inviolable unity of the individual this relation is one between his various traits (all of which are to be taken solely from the social point of view) and all the other forms in which his psyche finds expression. In this question individual psychology expresses a judgment of values and in doing so it is doing the same as every other science which attempts to substitute the better for the worse. In this science, more perhaps than in others, any error of the object of investigation due to his creative force takes up the foreground of our study.

3. We have to reject typology as being inadequate to emphasize the uniqueness of a personality. Again all the formulae, numbers, and classification, by whatever means they are reached, can only be treated as statistical probabilities and should be used only in order to throw light upon the sphere within which the personality for which we are looking may be found. It is the exact agreement between the part and the whole which is decisive for the final result of the investigation. A result once discovered may be considered as confirmed only if all the partial movements, thoughts, feelings, volitions, and attitudes (as referred to the main questions of life in the social sense) which we think we have "understood" agree with the totality of the individual within the meaning of 1 and 2. Adequate investigations of this kind have hitherto been made only by individual psychologists, and they have been available for some considerable time. The degree of social coöperation is most clearly expressed in connection with vital questions which imply a serious problem for the individual on account of his style of life. Artificial questions can touch the sore spot of a style of life never or only by accident. Accordingly the decisive problem for us is to discover the sore spot, in other words the error in the style of life.

4. Life, with some few fortunate exceptions, tries each individual and tests his preparation for the evolutionary meaning of life. I have investigated these questions and trials in every conceivable situation and have discovered that they invariably imply the necessity of coöperation. If there is failure of any kind it invariably arises in connection with the question whether the individual is fit for the community, when it is seen that this is not the case. Question 4 now arises: "Why is it that so many men do not possess an adequate social feeling?" I was able to discover that the full measure of social feeling is reached in the very earliest years and that it can be augmented only if the individual recognizes the inadequacies in the structure of his style of life. The capacity for developing a social feeling is absent only in the feeble-minded. With other persons the obstacles which stand in the way of a fairly adequate development of social feeling appear clearly in the course of this investigation and, once they have been discovered, provide us with the possibility of understanding how it is that they have acted as a barrier preventing further development of social feeling. Among these barriers both of a fundamental and of an accidental nature, an important part is played by the spoiling of children; when a child is spoiled his interest is drawn away from real life.

Thus for individual psychology the past life of the individual and any interruptions it may have suffered become the central point of the investigation. Extraneous causes here appear as definite as regular tests. On the other hand experiments do not assume a more scientific appearance and in fact look only like a shadow of reality. Nevertheless it follows from our previous remarks that they can provide good results for students trained in individual psychology, and that, not only with regard to the characterological level of a group; they also allow them to understand the individual, since the results which have been reached can be further tested. It is possible to demonstrate that they agree with other forms of expression and with the individual personality, as well as to determine the unvarying distance from the ideal social feeling.

A Hierarchy of Needs Motivates Personality

ABRAHAM H. MASLOW

The following viewpoint from Abraham H. Maslow is taken
from his book *Motivation and Personality*, published in 1954.
Maslow studied exceptional students and psychologists because he believed that the study of healthy, motivated individuals produced valuable information about the progression of
personality. Maslow believed that individuals are motivated
by their own need to achieve their highest potential. This motivation toward greatness causes them to climb a "hierarchy of
needs." Each level of this hierarchy represents a more sophisticated desire and as each level of needs is satisfied, it is 4
succeeded by the next, more sophisticated level of needs.

QUESTIONS

1. How does the deprivation of lower level needs differ from
   the deprivation of higher level needs in Maslow's theory?
2. How does Maslow's study of exceptional individuals influence his theory?

3. How does Maslow define self-actualization?
4. What is homeostasis and what role does it play in Maslow's theory?

■ ■ ■

The Basic Needs

The Physiological Needs

The needs that are usually taken as the starting point for motivation theory are the so-called physiological drives. Two recent lines of research make it necessary to revise our customary notions about these needs: first, the development of the concept of homeostasis, and second, the finding that appetites (preferential choices among foods) are a fairly efficient indication of actual needs or lacks in the body.

Homeostasis refers to the body's automatic efforts to maintain a constant, normal state of the blood stream. . . .

It seems impossible as well as useless to make any list of fundamental physiological needs, for they can come to almost any number one might wish, depending on the degree of specificity of description. We cannot identify all physiological needs as homeostatic. That sexual desire, sleepiness, sheer activity and exercise, and maternal behavior in animals are homeostatic has not yet been demonstrated. Furthermore, this list would not include the various sensory pleasures (tastes, smells, tickling, stroking), which are probably physiological and which may become the goals of motivated behavior. Nor do we know what to make of the fact that the organism has simultaneously a tendency to inertia, laziness and least effort and also a need for activity, stimulation, and excitement. . . .

Physiological drives or needs are to be considered unusual rather than typical because they are isolable, and because they are localizable somatically. That is to say, they are relatively independent of each other, of other motivations, and of the organism as a whole, and second, in many cases, it is possible to demonstrate a localized, underlying somatic base for the drive. This is true less generally than has been thought (exceptions are fatigue, sleepiness, maternal responses) but it is still true in the classic instances of hunger, sex, and thirst.

It should be pointed out again that any of the physiological needs and the consummatory behavior involved with them serve as channels for all sorts of other needs as well. That is to say, the person who thinks he is hungry may actually be seeking more for comfort, or dependence, than for vitamins or proteins. Conversely, it is possible to satisfy the hunger need in part by other activities such as drinking water or smoking cigarettes. In other words, relatively isolable as these physiological needs are, they are not completely so.

Undoubtedly these physiological needs are the most prepotent of all needs. What this means specifically is that in the human being who is missing everything in life in an extreme fashion, it is most likely that the major motivation would be the physiological needs rather than any others. A person who is lacking food, safety, love, and esteem would most probably hunger for food more strongly than for anything else.

If all the needs are unsatisfied, and the organism is then dominated by the physiological needs, all other needs may become simply nonexistent or be pushed into the background. It is then fair to characterize the whole organism by saying simply that it is hungry, for consciousness is almost completely preëmpted by hunger. All capacities are put into the service of hunger-satisfaction, and the organization of these capacities is almost entirely determined by the one purpose of satisfying hunger. The receptors and effectors, the intelligence, memory, habits, all may now be defined simply as hunger-gratifying tools. Capacities that are not useful for this purpose lie dormant, or are pushed into the background. The urge to write poetry, the desire to acquire an automobile, the interest in American history, the desire for a new pair of shoes are, in the extreme case, forgotten or become of secondary importance. For the man who is extremely and dangerously hungry, no other interests exist but food. He dreams food, he remembers food, he thinks about food, he emotes only about food, he perceives only food, and he wants only food. The more subtle determinants that ordinarily fuse with the physiological drives in organizing even feeding, drinking, or sexual behavior, may now be so completely overwhelmed as to allow us to speak at this time (but *only* at this time) of pure hunger drive and behavior, with the one unqualified aim of relief.

Another peculiar characteristic of the human organism when it is dominated by a certain need is that the whole philosophy of the future tends also to change. For our chronically and extremely hungry man, Utopia can be defined simply as a place where there is plenty of food. He tends to think that, if only he is guaranteed food for the rest of his life, he will be perfectly happy and will never want anything more. Life itself tends to be defined in terms of eating. Anything else will be defined as unimportant. Freedom, love, community feeling, respect, philosophy, may all be waved aside as fripperies that are useless, since they fail to fill the stomach. Such a man may fairly be said to live by bread alone.

It cannot possibly be denied that such things are true, but their *generality* can be denied. Emergency conditions are, almost by definition, rare in the normally functioning peaceful society. That this truism can be forgotten is attributable mainly to two reasons. First, rats have few motivations other than physiological ones, and since so much of the research upon motivation has been made with these animals, it is easy to carry the rat picture over to the human being. Second, it is too often not realized that culture itself is an adaptive tool, one of whose main functions is to make the physiological emergencies come less and less often. In most of the known societies, chronic extreme hunger of the emergency type is rare, rather than common. In any case, this is still true in the United States. The average American citizen is experiencing appetite rather than hunger when he says, "I am hungry." He is apt to experience sheer life-and-death hunger only by accident and then only a few times through his entire life.

Obviously a good way to obscure the higher motivations, and to get a lopsided view of human capacities and human nature, is to make the organism extremely and chronically hungry or thirsty. Anyone who attempts to make an emergency picture into a typical one, and who will measure all of man's goals and desires by his behavior during extreme physiological deprivation is certainly being blind to many things. It is quite true that man lives by bread alone—when there is no bread. But what happens to man's desires when there *is* plenty of bread and when his belly is chronically filled?

At once other (and higher) needs emerge and these, rather than physiological hungers, dominate the organism. And when these in turn are satisfied, again new (and still higher) needs emerge, and so on. This is what we mean by saying that the basic human needs are organized into a hierarchy of relative prepotency.

One main implication of this phrasing is that gratification becomes as important a concept as deprivation in motivation theory, for it releases the organism from the domination of a relatively more physiological need, permitting thereby the emergence of other more social goals. The physiological needs, along with their partial goals, when chronically gratified cease to exist as active determinants or organizers of behavior. They now exist only in a potential fashion in the sense that they may emerge again to dominate the organism if they are thwarted. But a want that is satisfied is no longer a want. The organism is dominated and its behavior organized only by unsatisfied needs. If hunger is satisfied, it becomes unimportant in the current dynamics of the individual.

This statement is somewhat qualified by a hypothesis to be discussed more fully later, namely, that it is precisely those individuals in whom a certain need has always been satisfied who are best equipped to tolerate deprivation of that need in the future, and that furthermore, those who have been deprived in the past will react differently to current satisfactions than the one who has never been deprived.

The Safety Needs

If the physiological needs are relatively well gratified, there then emerges a new set of needs, which we may categorize roughly as the safety needs (security; stability; dependency; protection; freedom from fear, from anxiety and chaos; need for structure, order, law, limits; strength in the protector; and so on). All that has been said to the physiological needs is equally true, although in less degree, of these desires. The organism may equally well be wholly dominated by them. They may serve as the almost exclusive organizers of behavior, recruiting all the capacities of the organism in their service, and we may then fairly describe the whole organism as a safety-seeking mechanism. Again we may say of the receptors, the effectors, of the intellect, and of the other capacities that they are primarily safety-seeking tools. Again, as in the hungry man, we find that the dominating goal is a strong determinant not only of his current world outlook and philosophy but also of his philosophy of the future and of values. Practically everything looks less important than safety and protection (even sometimes the physiological needs, which, being satisfied, are now underestimated). A man in this state, if it is extreme enough and chronic enough, may be characterized as living almost for safety alone.

Although we are interested primarily in the needs of the adult, we can approach an understanding of his safety needs perhaps more efficiently by observation of infants and children, in whom these needs are much more simple and obvious. One reason for the clearer appearance of the threat or danger reaction in infants is that they do not inhibit this reaction at all, whereas adults in our society have been taught to inhibit it at all costs. Thus even when adults do feel their safety to be threatened, we may not be able to see this on the surface. Infants will react in a total fashion and as if they were endangered, if they are disturbed or dropped suddenly, startled by loud noises, flashing light, or other unusual sensory stimulation, by rough handling, by general loss of support in the mother's arms, or by inadequate support.

In infants we can also see a much more direct reaction to bodily illnesses of various kinds. Sometimes these illnesses seem to be immediately and *per se* threatening, and seem to make the child feel unsafe. For instance, vomiting, colic, or other sharp pains seem to make the child look at the whole world in a different way. At such a moment of pain, it may be postulated that, for the child, the whole world suddenly changes from sunniness to darkness, so to speak, and become a place in which anything at all might happen, in which previously stable things have suddenly become unstable. Thus a child who because of some bad food is taken ill may for a day or two develop fear, nightmares, and a need for protection and reassurance never seen in him before his illness. The recent work on the psychological effects of surgery on children demonstrates this richly.

Another indication of the child's need for safety is his preference for some kind of undisrupted routine or rhythm. He seems to want a predictable, lawful, orderly world. For instance, injustice, unfairness, or inconsistency in the parents seems to make a child feel anxious and unsafe. This attitude may be not so much because of the injustice *per se* or any particular pains involved, but rather because this treatment threatens to make the world look unreliable, or unsafe, or unpredictable. Young children seem to thrive better under a system that has at least a skeletal outline of rigidity, in which there is a schedule of a kind, some sort of routine, something that can be counted upon, not only for the present but also far into the future. Child psychologists, teachers, and psychotherapists have found that permissiveness within limits, rather than unrestricted permissiveness is preferred as well as *needed* by children. Perhaps one could express this more accurately by saying that the child needs an organized and structured world rather than an unorganized or unstructured one.

The central role of the parents and the normal family setup are indisputable. Quarreling, physical assault, separation, divorce, or death within the family may be particularly terrifying. Also parental outbursts of rage or threats of punishment directed to the child, calling him names, speaking to him harshly, handling him roughly, or actual physical punishment sometimes elicit such total panic and terror that we must assume more is involved than the physical pain alone. While it is true that in some children this terror may represent also a fear of loss of parental love, it can also occur in completely rejected children, who seem to cling to the hating parents more for sheer safety and protection than because of hope of love.

Confronting the average child with new, unfamiliar, strange, unmanageable stimuli or situations will too frequently elicit the danger or terror reaction, as for example, getting lost or even being separated from the parents for a short time, being confronted with new faces, new situations, or new tasks, the sight of strange, unfamiliar, or uncontrollable objects, illness, or death. Particularly at such times, the child's frantic clinging to his parents is eloquent testimony to their role as protectors (quite apart from their roles as food givers and love givers).

From these and similar observations, we may generalize and say that the average child and, less obviously, the average adult in our society generally prefers a safe, orderly, predictable, lawful, organized world, which he can count on and in which unexpected, unmanageable, chaotic, or other dangerous things do not happen, and in which, in any case, he has powerful parents or protectors who shield him from harm.

That these reactions may so easily be observed in children is in a way proof that children in our society feel too unsafe (or, in a word, are badly brought up). Children who are reared in an unthreatening, loving family do *not* ordinarily react as we have described. In such children the danger reactions are apt to come mostly to objects or situations that adults too would consider dangerous.

The healthy and fortunate adult in our culture is largely satisfied in his safety needs. The peaceful, smoothly running, stable, good society ordinarily makes its members feel safe enough from wild animals, extremes of temperature, criminal assault, murder, chaos, tyranny, and so on. Therefore, in a very real sense, he no longer has any safety needs as active motivators. Just as a sated man no longer feels hungry, a safe man no longer feels endangered. If we wish to see these needs directly and clearly we must turn to neurotic or near-neurotic individuals, and to the economic and social underdogs, or else to social chaos, revolution, or breakdown of authority. In between these extremes, we can perceive the expressions of safety needs only in such phenomena as, for instance, the common preference for a job with tenure and protection, the desire for a savings account, and for insurance of various kinds (medical, dental, unemployment, disability, old age).

Other broader aspects of the attempt to seek safety and stability in the world are seen in the very common preference for familiar rather than unfamiliar things, or for the known rather than the unknown. The tendency to have some religion or world philosophy that organizes the universe and the men in it into some sort of satisfactorily coherent, meaningful whole is also in part motivated by safety seeking. Here too we may list science and philosophy in general as partially motivated by the safety needs.

Otherwise the need for safety is seen as an active and dominant mobilizer of the organism's resources only in real emergencies, e.g., war, disease, natural catastrophes, crime waves, societal disorganization, neurosis, brain injury, breakdown of authority, chronically bad situations.

Some neurotic adults in our society are, in many ways, like the unsafe child in their desire for safety, although in the former it takes on a somewhat special appearance. Their reaction is often to unknown, psychological dangers in a world that is perceived to be hostile, overwhelming, and threatening. Such a person behaves as if a great catastrophe were almost always impending, i.e., he is usually responding as if to an emergency. His safety needs often find specific expression in a search for a protector, or a stronger person on whom he may depend, perhaps a Fuehrer.

The neurotic individual may be described with great usefulness as a grown-up person who retains his childhood attitudes toward the world. That is to say, a neurotic adult may be said to behave as if he were actually afraid of a spanking, or of his mother's disapproval, or of being abandoned by his parents, or having his food taken away from him. It is as if his childish attitudes of fear and threat reaction to a dangerous world had gone underground, and untouched by the growing up and learning processes, were now ready to be called out by any stimulus that would make a child feel endangered and threatened. Horney especially has written well about "basic anxiety."

The neurosis in which the search for safety takes its clearest form is in the compulsive-obsessive neurosis. Compulsive-obsessives try frantically to order and stabilize the world so that no unmanageable, unexpected, or unfamiliar dangers will ever appear. They hedge themselves about with all sorts of ceremonials, rules, and formulas so that every possible contingency may be provided for and so that no new contingencies may appear. They are much like the brain-injured cases, described by Kurt Goldstein, who manage to maintain their equilibrium by avoiding everything unfamiliar and strange and by ordering their restricted world in such a neat, disciplined, orderly fashion that everything in the world can be counted on. They try to arrange the world so that anything unexpected (dangers) cannot possibly occur. If, through no fault of their own, something unexpected does occur, they go into a panic reaction as if this unexpected occurrence constituted a grave danger. What we can see only as a none-too-strong preference in the healthy person, e.g., preference for the familiar, becomes a life-and-death necessity in abnormal cases. The healthy taste for the novel and unknown is missing or at a minimum in the average neurotic.

The safety needs can become very urgent on the social scene whenever there are real threats to law, to order, to the authority of society. The threat of chaos or of nihilism can be expected in most human beings to produce a regression from any higher needs to the more prepotent safety needs. A common, almost an expectable reaction, is the easier acceptance of dictatorship or of military rule. This tends to be true for all human beings, including healthy ones, since they too will tend to respond to danger with realistic regression to the safety need level, and will prepare to defend themselves. But it seems to be most true of people who are living near the safety line. They are particularly disturbed by threats to authority, to legality, and to the representatives of the law.

The Belongingness and Love Needs

If both the physiological and the safety needs are fairly well gratified, there will emerge the love and affection and belongingness needs, and the whole cycle already described will repeat itself with this new center. Now the person will feel keenly, as never before, the absence of friends, or a sweetheart, or a wife, or children. He will hunger for affectionate relations with people in general, namely, for a place in his group or family, and he will strive with great intensity to achieve this goal. He will want to attain such a place more than anything else in the world and may even forget that once, when he was hungry, he sneered at love as unreal or unnecessary or unimportant. Now he will feel sharply the pangs of loneliness, of ostracism, of rejection, of friendlessness, of rootlessness.

We have very little scientific information about the belongingness need, although this is a common theme in novels, autobiographies, poems, and plays and also in the newer sociological literature. From these we know in a general way the destructive effects on children of moving too often; of disorientation; of the general over-mobility that is forced by industrialization; of being without roots, or of despising one's roots, one's origins, one's group; of being torn from one's home and family, and friends and neighbors; of being a transient or a newcomer rather than a native. We still underplay the deep importance of the neighborhood, of one's territory, of one's clan, of one's own "kind," one's class, one's gang, one's familiar working colleagues. I will content myself with recommending a single book that says all this with great poignancy and conviction and that helps us understand our deeply animal tendency to herd, to flock, to join, to belong. Perhaps also, Ardrey's *Territorial Imperative* will help to make all of this conscious. Its very rashness was good for me because it stressed as crucial what I had been only casual about and forced me to think seriously about the matter. Perhaps it will do the same for the reader.

I believe that the tremendous and rapid increase in T-groups and other personal growth groups and intentional communities may in part be motivated by this unsatisfied hunger for contact, for intimacy, for belongingness and by the need to overcome the widespread feelings of alienation, aloneness, strangeness, and loneliness, which have been worsened by our mobility, by the breakdown of traditional groupings, the scattering of families, the generation gap, the steady urbanization and disappearance of village face-to-faceness, and the resulting shallowness of American friendship. My strong impression is also that *some* proportion of youth rebellion groups—I don't know how many or how much—is motivated by the profound hunger for groupiness, for contact, for real togetherness in the face of a common enemy, *any* enemy that can serve to form an amity group simply by posing an external threat. The same kind of thing was observed in groups of soldiers who were pushed into an unwonted brotherliness and intimacy by their common external danger, and who may stick together throughout a lifetime as a consequence. Any good society must satisfy this need, one way or another, if it is to survive and be healthy.

In our society the thwarting of these needs is the most commonly found core in cases of maladjustment and more severe pathology. Love and affection, as well as their possible expression in sexuality, are generally looked upon with ambivalence and are customarily hedged about with many restrictions and inhibitions. Practically all theorists of psychopathology have stressed thwarting of the love needs as basic in the picture of maladjustment. Many clinical studies have therefore been made of this need, and we know more about it perhaps than any of the other needs except the physiological ones. Janene Suttie has written an excellent analysis of our "taboo on tenderness."

One thing that must be stressed at this point is that love is not synonymous with sex. Sex may be studied as a purely physiological need. Ordinarily sexual behavior is multidetermined, that is to say, determined not only by sexual but also by other needs, chief among which are the love and affection needs. Also not to be overlooked is the fact that the love needs involve both giving *and* receiving love.

The Esteem Needs

All people in our society (with a few pathological exceptions) have a need or desire for a stable, firmly based, usually high evaluation of themselves, for self-respect, or self-esteem, and for the esteem of others. These needs may therefore be classified into two subsidiary sets. These are, first, the desire for strength, for achievement, for adequacy, for mastery and competence, for confidence in the face of the world, and for independence and freedom. Second, we have what we may call the desire for reputation or prestige (defining it as respect or esteem from other people), status, fame and glory, dominance, recognition, attention, importance, dignity, or appreciation. These needs have been relatively stressed by Alfred Adler and his followers, and have been relatively neglected by Freud. More and more today, however, there is appearing widespread appreciation of their central importance, among psychoanalysts as well as among clinical psychologists.

Satisfaction of the self-esteem need leads to feelings of self-confidence, worth, strength, capability, and adequacy, of being useful and necessary in the world. But thwarting of these needs produces feelings of inferiority, of weakness, and of helplessness. These feelings in turn give rise to either basic discouragement or else compensatory or neurotic trends. An appreciation of the necessity of basic self-confidence and an understanding of how helpless people are without it can be easily gained from a study of severe traumatic neurosis.

From the theologians' discussion of pride and *hubris*, from the Frommian theories about the self-perception of untruth to one's own nature, from the Rogerian work with self, from essayists like Ayn Rand and from other sources as well, we have been learning more and more of the dangers of basing self-esteem on the opinions of others rather than on real capacity, competence, and adequacy to the task. The most stable and therefore most healthy self-esteem is based on *deserved* respect from others rather than on external fame or celebrity and unwarranted adulation. Even here it is helpful to distinguish the actual competence and achievement that is based on sheer will power, determination and responsibility, from that which comes naturally and easily out of one's own true inner nature, one's constitution, one's biological fate or destiny, or as Horney puts it, out of one's Real Self rather than out of the idealized pseudo-self.

The Need for Self-Actualization

Even if all these needs are satisfied, we may still often (if not always) expect that a new discontent and restlessness will soon develop, unless the individual is doing what *he*, individually, is fitted for. A musician must make music, an artist must paint, a poet must write, if he is to be ultimately at peace with himself. What a man *can* be, he *must* be. He must be true to his own nature. This need we may call self-actualization.

This term, first coined by Kurt Goldstein, is being used in this viewpoint in a much more specific and limited fashion. It refers to man's desire for self-fulfillment, namely, to the tendency for him to become actualized in what he is potentially. This tendency might be phrased as the desire to become more and more what one idiosyncratically is, to become everything that one is capable of becoming.

The specific form that these needs will take will of course vary greatly from person to person. In one individual it may take the form of the desire to be an ideal mother, in another it may be expressed athletically, and in still another it may be expressed in painting pictures or in inventions. At this level, individual differences are greatest.

The clear emergence of these needs usually rests upon some prior satisfaction of the physiological, safety, love, and esteem needs.

The Preconditions for the
Basic Need Satisfactions

There are certain conditions that are immediate prerequisites for the basic need satisfactions. Danger to these is reacted to as if it were direct danger to the basic needs themselves. Such conditions as freedom to speak, freedom to do what one wishes so long as no harm is done to others, freedom to express oneself, freedom to investigate and seek for information, freedom to defend oneself, justice, fairness, honesty, orderliness in the group are examples of such preconditions for basic need satisfactions. Thwarting in these freedoms will be reacted to with a threat or emergency response. These conditions are not ends in themselves but they are *almost* so since they are so closely related to the basic needs, which are apparently the only ends in themselves. These conditions are defended because without them the basic satisfactions are quite impossible, or at least, severely endangered.

If we remember that the cognitive capacities (perceptual, intellectual, learning) are a set of adjustive tools, which have, among other functions, that of satisfaction of our basic needs, then it is clear that any danger to them, any deprivation or blocking of their free use, must also be indirectly threatening to the basic needs themselves. Such a statement is a partial solution of the general problems of curiosity, the search for knowledge, truth, and wisdom, and the ever-persistent urge to solve the cosmic mysteries. Secrecy, censorship, dishonesty, blocking of communication threaten *all* the basic needs.

Personality Is a Combination of Thousands of Traits

GORDON W. ALLPORT

Gordon Allport can probably best be characterized as the father of American personality theories as well as modern trait theories of personality. As a professor and mentor at Harvard he taught the first course on personality offered at an American university. He was adored by his students and admired by his colleagues. Allport emphasized the merits of cross discipline research and tried to conduct his own in an effort to improve society as a whole. In 1936 in the effort to reduce personality to its smallest measureable units Allport and his colleagues set out to list all of the words in the dictionary that could viably be classified as "Personality Traits." He came up with over 4000 traits. His traits were eventually reduced to sixteen by Raymond Catell and finally to "The Big Five" theory which you will read later in this chapter.

QUESTIONS

1. What is a trait, according to Allport?
2. How are traits determined, according to Allport?
3. According to the author, how do traits influence personality?
4. How do traits differ from habits, according to Allport?

■ ■ ■

At the heart of all investigation of personality lies the puzzling problem of the nature of the unit or element that is the carrier of the distinctive behavior of a man. *Reflexes* and *habits* are too specific in reference and connote constancy rather than consistency in behavior. *Attitudes* are ill-defined and, as employed by various writers, refer to determining tendencies that range in inclusiveness from the *Aufgabe* to the *Weltanschauung*. *Dispositions* and *tendencies* are even less definitive. But *traits*, although appropriated by all manner of writers for all manner of purposes, may still be salvaged, I think, and may be limited in their reference to a certain definite conception of a generalized response-unit in which resides the distinctive quality of behavior that reflects personality. Foes as well as friends of the doctrine of traits will gain from a more consistent use of the term.

The doctrine itself has never been explicitly stated. It is my purpose, with the aid of eight criteria, to define *trait* and to state the logic and some of the evidence for the admission of this concept to good standing in psychology.

1. *A trait has more than nominal existence.* A trait may be said to have the same kind of existence that a habit of a complex order has. Habits of a complex, or higher, order have long been accepted as household facts in psychology. There is no reason to believe that the mechanism that produces such a habit (integration, *Gestaltung* or whatever it may be) stops short of producing the more generalized habits which are here called traits of personality.

2. *A trait is more generalized than a habit.* Within a personality there are, of course, many independent habits; but there is also so much integration, organization and coherence among habits that we have no choice but to recognize great

90

systems of interdependent habits. If the habit of brushing one's teeth can be shown, statistically or genetically, to be unrelated to the habit of dominating a tradesman, there can be no question of a common trait involving both these habits; but, if the habit of dominating a tradesman can be shown, statistically or genetically, to be related to the habit of bluffing one's way past guards, there is the presumption that a common trait of personality exists that includes these two habits. Traits may conceivably embrace anywhere from two habits to a legion of habits. In this way, there may be said to be both major, widely extensified traits and minor, less generalized traits in the same personality.

3. *A trait is dynamic, or at least determinative.* The stimulus is not the crucial determinant in behavior that expresses personality; the trait itself is decisive. Once formed, a trait seems to have the capacity of directing responses to stimuli into characteristic channels. This emphasis upon the dynamic nature of traits, ascribing to them a capacity for guiding the specific response, is variously recognized by many writers. The principle is nothing more than that which has been subscribed to in various connections by Woodworth, Prince, Sherrington, Coghill, Kurt Lewin, Troland, Lloyd Morgan, Thurstone, Bentley, Stern and others.

From this general point of view, traits might be called "derived drives" or "derived motives." Whatever they are called, they may be regarded as playing a motivating role in each act, thus endowing the separate adjustments of the individual to specific stimuli with that *adverbial* quality that is the very essence of personality.

Some psychologists may balk at the doctrine of the absorption of driving power into the integrated mechanism of traits. If so, it is equally possible, without violence to the other criteria of this essay, to accept the view that a trait is a generalized neural set, which is activated ecphorically or redintegratively. But it seems to me that this second doctrine is only slightly less dynamic than the first. The difference is simply one between trait considered as a drive aroused through the operation of a specific stimulus, and trait conceived as powerfully directive when an effective stimulus arouses the organism to action.

4. *The existence of a trait may be established empirically or statistically.* In order to know that a person has a habit, it is necessary to have evidence of repeated reactions of a constant type. Similarly, in order to know that an individual has a trait, it is necessary to have evidence of repeated reactions that, though not necessarily constant in type, seem none the less to be consistently a function of the same underlying determinant. If this evidence is gathered casually by mere observation of the subject or through the reading of a case-history or biography, it may be called empirical evidence.

More exactly, of course, the existence of a trait may be established with the aid of statistical techniques that determine the degree of coherence among the separate responses. Although this employment of statistical aid is highly desirable, it is not necessary to wait for such evidence before speaking of traits, any more than it would be necessary to refrain from speaking of the habit of biting fingernails until the exact frequency of the occurrence is known. Statistical methods are at present better suited to intellective than to conative functions, and it is with the latter that we are chiefly concerned in our studies of personality.

5. *Traits are only relatively independent of each other.* The investigator desires, of course, to discover what the fundamental traits of personality are—that is to say, what broad trends in behavior do exist independently of one another. Actually, with the test methods and correlational procedures in use, completely independent variation is seldom found. In one study, expansion correlated with extroversion to the extent of +.39; ascendance with conservatism, +.22; humor with insight, +.83; and so on. This overlap may be due to several factors, the most obvious being the tendency of the organism to react in an integrated fashion: when concrete acts are observed or tested, they reflect not only the trait under examination but also, and simultaneously, other traits. Several traits may thus converge into a final common path. It seems safe, therefore, to predict that traits can never be completely isolated for study, since they never show more than a relative independence of one another.

In the instance just cited, it is doubtful whether humor and insight (provided their close relationship is verified in subsequent studies) represent distinct traits. In the future, it may be possible to agree upon a certain magnitude of correlation, below which it will be acceptable to speak of separate traits, and above which only one trait will be recognized. If only one trait is indicated, it will presumably represent a broadly generalized disposition. For example, if humor and insight cannot be established as independent traits, it will be necessary to recognize a more inclusive trait and name it, perhaps, "sense of proportion."

6. *A trait of personality, psychologically considered, is not the same as moral quality.* A trait of personality may or may not coincide with some well-defined, conventional social concept. Extroversion, ascendance, social participation and insight are free from preconceived moral significance, largely because each is a word newly coined or adapted to fit a psychological discovery. It would be ideal if we could, in this way, find our traits first and then name them. But honesty, loyalty, neatness and tact, though encrusted with social significance, *may* likewise represent true traits of personality. The danger is that, in devising scales for their measurement, we may be bound by the conventional meanings and thus be led away from the precise integration as it exists in a given individual. Where possible, it would be well for us to find our traits first and then seek devaluated terms with which to characterize our discoveries.

7. *Acts, and even habits, that are inconsistent with a trait are not proof of the nonexistence of the trait.* The objection most often considered fatal to the doctrine of traits has been illustrated as follows: "An individual may be habitually neat with respect to his person and characteristically slovenly in his handwriting or the care of his desk."

In the first place, this observation fails to state that there are cases frequently met where a constant level of neatness is maintained in all of a person's acts, giving unmistakable empirical evidence that the trait of neatness is, in some people at least, thoroughly and permanently integrated. Not everyone will show the same degree of integration in respect to a given trait. What is a major trait in one personality may be a minor trait, or even nonexistent, in another personality.

In the second place, there may be opposed integrations—that is, contradictory traits—in a single personality. The same individual may have traits *both* of neatness *and* of carelessness, of ascendance *and* of submission, although these will frequently be of unequal strength.

In the third place, there are in every personality instances of acts that are unrelated to existent traits, the product of the stimulus and the attitude of the moment. Even the characteristically neat person may become careless when he is hurrying to catch a train. But to say that not all of a person's acts reflect some higher integration is not to say that no such higher integrations exist.

8. *A trait may be viewed either in the light of the personality that contains it or in the light of its distribution in the population at large.* Each trait has both its unique and its universal aspect. In its unique aspect, the trait takes its significance entirely from the role it plays in the personality as a whole. In its universal aspect, the trait is arbitrarily isolated for study, and a comparison is made between individuals in respect to it. From this second point of view, traits merely extend the familiar field of the psychology of individual differences.

Personality Is a Combination of Five Major Factors

ROBERT McCRAE AND OLIVER JOHN

Unlike some of the other theories of personality, the five-factor model of personality is endorsed by many researchers today. Though proponents of the five-factor model sometimes disagree on how to label each of the respective factors, there has been general agreement that there are indeed five main personality factors that can be used to understand personality and personality measurement. The five-factor model currently enjoys considerable popularity among personality theories because of its vast empirical support. The following piece is just one of many articles written on the five-factor model. Robert McCrae and Oliver John provide an excellent summary of the five-factor model and its components.

QUESTIONS

1. How do Allport's traits differ from factors under the five-factor model discussed by McCrae and John?

Excerpted from "An Introduction to the Five-Factor Model and Its Applications" by Robert R. McCrae and Oliver P. John, *Journal Of Personality*, vol. 60, no. 2 (June 1992), pp. 175-215.

2. How do McCrae and John define the five factors and what they represent?
3. What is the utility of the five factor model, according to the authors?

■ ■ ■

What are the basic dimensions of personality, the most important ways in which individuals differ in their enduring emotional, interpersonal, experiential, attitudinal, and motivational styles? Personality theorists have offered hundreds of candidates, and for decades factor analysts attempted to bring order to the resulting confusion by factoring personality scales. Instead of resolving the issue, however, these studies only contributed another layer of controversy, most familiar in the competing systems of Guilford, Raymond Catell, and H. J. Eysenck. So when Tupes and Christal found five recurrent factors in analyses of personality ratings in eight different samples, they were understandably surprised:

> In many ways it seems remarkable that such stability should be found in an area which to date has granted anything but consistent results. Undoubtedly the consistency has always been there, but it has been hidden by inconsistency of factorial techniques and philosophies, the lack of replication using identical variables, and disagreement among analysts as to factor titles.

Despite their work—and the more widely read replication of Norman—the importance of these five factors remained hidden from most personality psychologists throughout the 1960s and 1970s. In the 1980s, however, researchers from many different traditions were led to conclude that these factors were fundamental dimensions of personality, found in self-reports and ratings, in natural languages and theoretically based questionnaires, in children, college students, and older adults, in men and women, and in English, Dutch, German, and Japanese samples. All five factors were shown to have convergent and discriminant validity across instruments and observers, and to endure across decades in adults. As a brief introduction to their nature, Table 1 lists definers of the positive pole of each of these factors. . . .

If this hypotheses is correct—if we have truly discovered the basic dimensions of personality—it marks a turning point for personality psychology. Instead of the interminable disputes among competing systems that so long paralyzed the field, we could see cooperative research and cumulative findings. Instead of the redundancy that results from measuring the same construct under a dozen different names, we could see an efficient integration of the literature across many instruments. And instead of the lost insights that a haphazard selection of personality variables is likely to produce, we could see a complete and systematic pursuit of personality correlates. The FFM [five factor model] could provide a common language for psychologists from different traditions, a basic phenomenon for personality theorists to explain, a natural framework for organizing research, and a guide to the comprehensive assessment of individuals that should be of value to educational, industrial/organizational, and clinical psychologists.

Even its most ardent defenders do not claim that the FFM is the last word in the description of personality. There are disputes among five-factorists about the best interpretation of the factors; there are certainly important distinctions to be made at the level of the more molecular traits that define the factors; and it is possible that there are other basic dimensions of personality. But some version of these five dimensions is at least *necessary* for an adequate description of individual differences, and if all personality researchers compare their preferred system to this framework, it should soon become clear whether and in what ways the model is deficient.

The consensus that five-factorists see among themselves may be puzzling to outsiders because the "disagreement among analysts as to factor titles" that Tupes and Christal noted still plagues the field. Factor names reflect historical accidents, conceptual positions, and the entrenchment that comes from a published body of literature and from published instruments. There are two prominent systems for naming the factors, one derived from the lexical tradition and one from the questionnaire tradition.

Many writers take Norman's annunciation of an "adequate taxonomy of personality attributes" derived from Catell's reduction of natural language trait terms as the formal beginning

TABLE 1 Examples of Adjectives, Q-Sort Items, and Questionnaire Scales Defining the Five Factors

Factor			Factor definers	
Name	Number	Adjectives[a]	Q-sort items[b]	Scales[c]
Extraversion (E)	I	Active	Talkative	Warmth
		Assertive	Skilled in play, humor	Gregariousness
		Energetic	Rapid personal tempo	Assertiveness
		Enthusiastic	Facially, gesturally expressive	Activity
		Outgoing	Behaves assertively	Excitement Seeking
		Talkative	Gregarious	Positive Emotions
Agreeableness (A)	II	Appreciative	Not critical, skeptical	Trust
		Forgiving	Behaves in giving way	Straightforwardness
		Generous	Sympathetic, considerate	Altruism
		Kind	Arouses liking	Compliance
		Sympathetic	Warm, compassionate	Modesty
		Trusting	Basically trustful	Tender-Mindedness
Conscientiousness (C)	III	Efficient	Dependable, responsible	Competence
		Organized	Productive	Order
		Planful	Able to delay gratification	Dutifulness
		Reliable	Not self-indulgent	Achievement Striving
		Responsible	Behaves ethically	Self-Discipline
		Thorough	Has high aspiration level	Deliberation
Neuroticism (N)	IV	Anxious	Thin-skinned	Anxiety
		Self-pitying	Brittle ego defenses	Hostility
		Tense	Self-defeating	Depression
		Touchy	Basically anxious	Self-Consciousness
		Unstable	Concerned with adequacy	Impulsiveness
		Worrying	Fluctuating moods	Vulnerability
Openness (O)	V	Artistic	Wide range of interests	Fantasy
		Curious	Introspective	Aesthetics
		Imaginative	Unusual thought processes	Feelings
		Insightful	Values intellectual matters	Actions
		Original	Judges in unconventional terms	Ideas
		Wide interests	Aesthetically reactive	Values

a. Adjective Check List items defining the factor in a study of 280 men and women rated by 10 psychologists serving as observers during an assessment weekend at the Institute of Personality Assessment and Research (John, 1989a).
b. California Q-Set items from self-sorts by 403 men and women in the Baltimore Longitudinal Study of Aging (McCrae, Costa, & Busch, 1986).
c. Revised NEO Personality Inventory facet scales from self-reports by 1,539 adult men and women (Costa, McCrae, & Dye, 1991).

of the FFM, and the factor numbers and names Norman chose—I: Extraversion or Surgency; II: Agreeableness; III: Conscientiousness; IV: Emotional Stability; and V: Culture—are often used. Peabody and Goldberg have noted that the order in which these factors emerged roughly parallels their representation among English language trait terms in the dictionary: Many more words can be found to describe aspects of Factors I through III than of Factors IV and V. The factor numbers, I to V, are thus meaningful designations. Roman numerals also have the advantage of being theoretically neutral; they seem to stand above the fray of disputed factor interpretations.

The second tradition that led to the modern FFM comes from the analysis of questionnaires, and particularly from the work of H. J. Eysenck, who identified Extraversion (E) and Neuroticism (N) as major components of psychological tests. (It was Wiggins, 1968, who dubbed these the "Big Two," setting the stage for Goldberg's 1981 designation of the FFM as the "Big Five.") Costa and McCrae added a dimension they called Openness to Experience (O), and later created scales to measure Agreeableness (A) and Conscientiousness (C). A number of publications have adopted this nomenclature. Note that N corresponds to low Emotional Stability, –IV, and O is a variant of Norman's Factor V.

If the advantage of the Norman numbers is their theoretical neutrality, the disadvantage is their low mnemonic value. Initials, originally popularized by H. J. Eysenck, are easier to interpret, and they may be less theoretically laden than full names. To those for whom Neuroticism connotes psychiatric disorder, negative affectivity or simply nervousness may seem more apt; all can be characterized by N. Likewise, E can also stand for energy or enthusiasm; O for originality; A for affiliation or affection; and C for constraint, or control.

The claim of five-factor theorists is that these factors, singly or in combination, can be found in virtually all personality instruments, and a number of authors have compiled tables showing the putative assignment of standard personality scales or factors to the five. The table can be extremely useful not only as a demonstration of the nature and pervasiveness of the five factors, but also as a guide to researchers and meta-analysts who need to identify alternative measures of the same fundamental construct. Similarly, researchers sometimes interpret their own factor analyses in terms of these five. Here, too, the communicative power of the model is exploited.

The danger is that such identifications may be wrong. Hogan classified Costa and McCrae's Openness scale as a measure of Conscientiousness; Noller et al. interpreted a factor combining liberal thinking, assertiveness, rebelliousness, and imagination as (low) A; Costa and McCrae interpreted a similar factor as O. The integrative value of the model is clearly compromised by such discrepancies.

Two approaches have been used to resolve such problems of classification. John formalized a rational strategy: A group of 10 judges familiar with the classic literature on the FFM assigned the 300 items of Gough and Heilbrun's Adjective Check List (ACL) to one of the factors. Coefficient alpha reliabilities of the mean judgments exceeded .90 for all five dimensions. This study demonstrated that substantial interrater agreement on the content of the factors is possible, and produced lists of items that correspond to common conceptions of the five factors. McCrae, Piedmont, and Costa had raters judge the extent to which items of the California Psychological Inventory were indicative or contraindicative of each of the five factors and analyzed CPI scales in terms of this item content. Item-by-item analysis by multiple raters increases the objectivity of rational scale interpretation.

A complementary approach is empirical: Scales or new factors can be correlated with standard measures of the five factors. Briggs describes and evaluates available measures of the factors. Ideally, researchers would include at least two standard markers of each factor to examine the replicability of results. . . .

The problem of what to call the factors is not merely a matter of convention. The labels reflect conceptualizations, and five-factor advocates differ in the details of their views on the factors, and thus in their preferred names. At one level, about which a good deal has been written, these differences are descriptive: Precisely which traits define each factor, and which are central, which peripheral? At another level, the differences are theoretical: Why are there universal dimensions of personality, and why these dimensions and not others? Considerably less has been said about this topic, and we hope in the present article to outline some of the possible explanations. Obviously, the two levels of conceptualization are related, because theory must be tailored to the phenomenon to be explained.

There is probably the least controversy about the definition of N. N represents individual differences in the tendency to experience distress, and in the cognitive and behavioral styles that follow from this tendency. High N scorers experience chronic negative affects and are prone to the development of a variety of psychiatric disorders. The recurrent nervous tension, depression, frustration, guilt, and self-consciousness that such individuals feel is often associated with irrational thinking, low self-esteem, poor control of impulses and cravings, somatic complaints, and ineffective coping. Individuals low in N are not necessarily high in positive mental health, however that may be defined—they are simply calm, relaxed, even-tempered, unflappable.

Despite the long and common use of the term Extraversion, there is less consensus about E. Most of the differences can be traced to the fact that E and A together define the Interpersonal Circumplex, around which interpersonal terms are spaced almost evenly. The traditional axes of the circumplex are Dominance (or Status) and Affiliation (or Love), and the major dispute about E (Norman's Factor I) concerns its alignment with these axes. Goldberg, guided by his analyses of English language trait terms, and Wiggins (in press), guided by the interpersonal tradition, identify this factor with Dominance. McCrae and Costa argue that E is best seen as located midway between Dominance and Warmth (although perhaps a bit closer to Dominance). This position, which Peabody and Goldberg designate as I', is close to the location of such traditional questionnaire measures of E as H. J. Eysenck and S. B. G. Eysenck's E scale and the EI scale of the MBTI [Myers-Briggs Type Indicator].

The advantage of the I' position is that it aligns the factor more closely with its noninterpersonal aspects, particularly positive emotionality. As Watson and Clark describe, the tendencies to experience positive and negative emotions are not opposites, but orthogonal dimensions that define an affective plane. People who are cheerful, enthusiastic, optimistic, and energetic are not necessarily low in anxiety or depression—that depends on their level of N. But cheerful people consistently tend to be dominant, talkative, sociable, and warm, and Watson and Clark (in press) argue that positive emotionality should be seen as the core of E. This somewhat unorthodox view is probably a useful corrective to the narrowly interpersonal interpretation of E as sociability.

E is distinguished by its breadth of content. In their review, Watson and Clark identified [six] components of E: Venturesomeness, affiliation, positive affectivity, energy, ascendance, and ambition. As Table I shows, Costa and McCrae's view of E is similarly broad, although they would divide affiliation into warmth and gregariousness and assign ambition to C. The fact that such a wide variety of interpersonal, affective, and temperamental variables covary probably accounts for the fact that this factor is so well represented in English language adjectives and so often described by personality theorists.

The lexical literature suggests that individuals low in E can be described as quiet, reserved, retiring, shy, silent, and withdrawn, and Q-sort correlates point to emotional blandness and overcontrol of impulses as additional attributes. Nowhere in this description is introspectiveness seen: Low E must be distinguished from Guilford's Thinking Introversion (which is more closely related to O and C). The confusion between social and thinking introversions is perpetuated in the MBTI, where both kinds of traits are attributed to individuals classified as Introverts. In fact, the MBTI EI scale is a relatively pure measure of low E.

The label Agreeableness has been almost universally used for Norman's Factor II, but as Digman (1990) noted, "Agreeableness . . . seems tepid for a dimension that appears to involve the more humane aspects of humanity—characteristics such as altruism, nurturance, caring, and emotional support at the one end of the dimension, and hostility, indifference to others, self-centeredness, spitefulness, and jealousy at the other." Digman and Takemoto-Chock offered "Friendly Compliance versus Hostile Noncompliance" as an alternative descriptor for the factor, and Graziano and Eisenberg (in press) adopted the contrast "Agreeableness versus Antagonism."

Because A must be orthogonal to E, the location-and thus the interpretation-of A depends to some extent on one's view of E. Again, Goldberg and Wiggins see this factor as Love or Warmth; Costa et al. note a cluster of attributes that blend Warmth and Submission, including trust, modesty, and compliance.

Like A, C is a highly evaluated dimension; indeed, A and C are the classic dimensions of character, describing "good" versus "evil" and "strong-willed" versus "weak-willed" individuals. Perhaps it was these moral overtones that often led scientific psychologists to ignore these factors, but in fact, both represent objectively observable dimensions of individual differences. Some people are thorough, neat, well-organized, diligent, and achievement-oriented, whereas others are not, and self-reports of these characteristics can be validated by peer or spouse ratings.

A number of different conceptions of C have been offered. Tellegen's Constraint and Hogan's Prudence reflect an inhibitive view of C as a dimension that holds impulsive behavior in check. Digman and Takemoto-Chock's Will to Achieve represents a proactive view of C as a dimension that organizes and directs behavior. The term Conscientiousness combines both aspects, because it can mean either governed by conscience or diligent and thorough. Empirically, both kinds of traits seem to covary.

The greatest controversy concerns O, and the root of the controversy is the disparity between natural language and questionnaire studies. Studies of trait adjectives in English and German typically show a factor defined by such items as intelligent, imaginative, and perceptive, and researchers from Fiske to Hogan and Digman have identified this factor as some form of Intellect. However, many traits related to O are not represented among English trait adjectives—there is, for example, no single English word that means "sensitive to art and beauty." Researchers using questionnaires have typically found a much broader factor that includes, in addition to creativity and intellectual interests, differentiated emotions, aesthetic sensitivity, need for variety, and unconventional values. This broader concept can be traced to Rogers, Rokeach, and Coan; McCrae and Costa have argued that O is seen structurally in the depth, scope, and permeability of consciousness, and motivationally in the need for variety and experience. Ideas, of course, form an important aspect of consciousness, but fantasies, feelings, sensations, and values are also experiences to which individuals can be more or less open.

How Does Psychological Development Occur?

Chapter Preface

Historically, seminal debates in developmental psychology have arisen in three main areas: 1) nature versus nurture, 2) continuity versus discontinuity, and 3) focus. Though recently some have focused on child rearing as a major factor in development, the framework for most if not all questions about development is set in terms of the first three controversies.

The first area of debate, nature vs. nurture, questions the source of psychological phenomena. Discovering the origin of behaviors such as resilience, addiction, mental abilities, and coping styles is the single most researched area in developmental psychology. Determining whether personality characteristics, intelligence, and psychological disorders are caused by prewired biological forces (nature) or environmental factors (nurture) is at the heart of the nature versus nurture debate. Proponents of nature over nurture argue that certain psychological disorders as well as the fairly predictable pattern of child development are both inherited. Those who espouse these biological arguments cite studies showing that patterns of alcoholism, depression, and learning disabilities often occur across generations. Those who endorse the nurture argument, however, argue that environmental factors may explain the exact same behaviors. They argue that nonbiological children who are raised by alcoholic parents often manifest signs of alcoholism, which supports the argument that environmental exposure produced the patterns.

The second debate, continuity versus discontinuity, centers on whether children develop in a continuous fashion throughout life or develop in distinct stages arising at particular ages. Those that advocate stages generally focus on the rigidity and consistency of child development and cite age norms of development as support for their position. Proponents of a more fluid view of human development stress the gradual, yet constant acquisition of knowledge.

The third area of disagreement in developmental psychology arises in the context of focus. This debate makes distinctions between social, intellectual, and physical development. This is the easier of the three debates to settle because the debate does not assume a single focal point for human development: Social and intellectual development may progress differently without interfering with each other.

These three debates have endured through much discussion and it is unlikely that they will be settled during our lifetime. It is important, however, for students of psychology to explore and identify the strengths and weaknesses in each theory.

Development Occurs in a Series of Psychosexual Stages

SIGMUND FREUD

Sigmund Freud's contributions to the field of psychology permeate every one of its disciplines so it is only right that we should present a small sample of his theory of psychosexual development. Freud believed that a majority of a child's development occurs before the age of five and so emphasized early childhood as paramount to healthy development. Freud theorized that children developed through five psychosexual stages beginning from birth and ending at puberty. He believed that children who encountered major obstacles at any of these stages would become "fixated" at that stage and would return to problems of a similar nature throughout their lives.

QUESTIONS

1. According to Freud, what motivates personality?
2. What are the erogenous zones according to Freud and what is their function?

3. What does Freud say are the major obstacles of childhood?

■   ■   ■

The Development of the Sexual Function

According to the prevailing view human sexual life consists essentially in an endeavor to bring one's own genitals into contact with those of someone of the opposite sex. With this are associated, as accessory phenomena and introductory acts, kissing this extraneous body, looking at it and touching it. This endeavor is supposed to make its appearance at puberty—that is, at the age of sexual maturity—and to serve the purposes of reproduction. Nevertheless, certain facts have always been known which do not fit into the narrow framework of this view. (1) It is a remarkable fact that there are people who are only attracted by individuals of their own sex and by their genitals. (2) It is equally remarkable that there are people whose desires behave exactly like sexual ones but who at the same time entirely disregard the sexual organs or their normal use; people of this kind are known as 'perverts'. (3) And lastly it is a striking thing that some children (who are on that account regarded as degenerate) take a very early interest in their genitals and show signs of excitation in them.

It may well be believed that psycho-analysis provoked astonishment and denials when, partly on the basis of these three neglected facts, it contradicted all the popular opinions on sexuality. Its principal findings are as follows:

(a) Sexual life does not begin only at puberty, but starts with plain manifestations soon after birth.

(b) It is necessary to distinguish sharply between the concepts of 'sexual' and 'genital'. The former is the wider concept and includes many activities that have nothing to do with the genitals.

(c) Sexual life includes the function of obtaining pleasure from zones of the body—a function which is subsequently brought into the service of reproduction. The two functions often fail to coincide completely.

The chief interest is naturally focused on the first of these assertions, the most unexpected of all. It has been found that in early childhood there are signs of bodily activity to which only an ancient prejudice could deny the name of sexual and which are linked to psychical phenomena that we come across later in adult erotic life—such as fixation to particular objects, jealousy, and so on. It is further found, however, that these phenomena which emerge in early childhood form part of an ordered course of development, that they pass through a regular process of increase, reaching a climax towards the end of the fifth year, after which there follows a lull. During this lull progress is at a standstill and much is unlearnt and there is much recession. After the end of this period of latency, as it is called, sexual life advances once more with puberty; we might say that is has a second efflorescence. And here we come upon the fact that the onset of sexual life is diphasic, that it occurs in two waves—something that is unknown except in man and evidently has an important bearing on hominization. It is not a matter of indifference that the events of this early period, except for a few residues, fall a victim to infantile amnesia. Our views on the aetiology of the neuroses and our technique of analytic therapy are derived from these conceptions; and our tracing of the developmental processes in this early period has also provided evidence for yet other conclusions.

The first organ to emerge as an erotogenic zone and to make libidinal demands on the mind is, from the time of birth onwards, the mouth. To begin with, all psychical activity is concentrated on providing satisfaction for the needs of that zone. Primarily, of course, this satisfaction serves the purpose of self-preservation by means of nourishment; but physiology should not be confused with psychology. The baby's obstinate persistence in sucking gives evidence at an early stage of a need for satisfaction which, though it originates from and is instigated by the taking of nourishment, nevertheless strives to obtain pleasure independently of nourishment and for that reason may and should be termed sexual.

During this *oral phase* sadistic impulses already occur sporadically along with the appearance of the teeth. Their extent is far greater in the second phase, which we describe as the *sadistic-anal one*, because satisfaction is then sought in aggression and in the excretory function. Our justification for including aggressive urges under the libido is based on the view that sadism is an instinctual fusion of purely libidinal and purely destructive urges, a fusion which thenceforward persists uninterruptedly.

The third phase is that known as the *phallic* one, which is, as it were, a forerunner of the final form taken by sexual life and already much resembles it. It is to be noted that it is not the genitals of both sexes that play a part at this stage, but only the male ones (the phallus). The female genitals long remain unknown: in children's attempts to understand the sexual processes they pay homage to the venerable cloacal theory—a theory which has a genetic justification.

With the phallic phase and in the course of it the sexuality of early childhood reaches its height and approaches its dissolution. Thereafter boys and girls have different histories. Both have begun to put their intellectual activity at the service of sexual researches; both start off from the premiss of the universal presence of the penis. But now the paths of the sexes diverge. The boy enters the *Oedipus phase*; he begins to manipulate his penis and simultaneously has phantasies of carrying out some sort of activity with it in relation to his mother, till, owing to the combined effect of a threat of castration and the sight of the absence of a penis in females, he experiences the greatest trauma of his life and this introduces the period of latency with all its consequences. The girl, after vainly attempting to do the same as the boy, comes to recognize her lack of a penis or rather the inferiority of her clitoris, with permanent effects on the development of her character; as a result of this first disappointment in rivalry, she often begins by turning away altogether from sexual life.

It would be a mistake to suppose that these three phases succeed one another in a clear-cut fashion. One may appear in addition to another; they may overlap one another, may be present alongside of one another. In the early phases the different component instincts set about their pursuit of pleasure independently of one another; in the phallic phase there are the beginnings of an organization which subordinates the other urges to the primacy of the genitals and signifies the start of a coordination of the general urge towards pleasure into the sexual function. The complete organization is only achieved at puberty, in a fourth, *genital phase.* A state of things is then established in which (1) some earlier libidinal cathexes are retained, (2) others are taken into the sexual function as preparatory, auxiliary acts, the satisfaction of which produces what is known as fore-pleasure, and (3) other urges are excluded from the organization, and are either suppressed altogether (repressed) or are employed in the ego in another way, forming character-traits or undergoing sublimation with a displacement of their aims.

This process is not always performed faultlessly. Inhibitions in its development manifest themselves as the many sorts of disturbance in sexual life. When this is so, we find fixations of the libido to conditions in earlier phases, whose urge, which is independent of the normal sexual aim, is described as perversion. One such developmental inhibition, for instance, is homosexuality when it is manifest. Analysis shows that in every case a homosexual object-tie was present and in most cases persisted in a *latent* condition. The situation is complicated by the fact that as a rule the processes necessary for bringing about a normal outcome are not completely present or absent, but partially present, so that the final result remains dependent on these quantitative relations. In these circumstances the genital organization is, it is true, attained, but it lacks those portions of the libido which have not advanced with the rest and have remained fixated to pregenital objects and aims. This weakening shows itself in a tendency, if there is an absence of genital satisfaction or if there are difficulties in the real external world, for the libido to hark back to its earlier pregenital cathexes (regression).

During the study of the sexual functions we have been able to gain a first, preliminary conviction, or rather a suspicion, of two discoveries which will later be found to be important over the whole of our field. Firstly, the normal and abnormal manifestations observed by us (that is, the phenomenology of the subject) need to be described from the point of view of their dynamics and economics (in our case, from the point of view of the quantitative distribution of the libido). And secondly, the aetiology of the disorders which we study is to be looked for in the individual's developmental history—that is to say, in his early life.

VIEWPOINT

2

Development Occurs in a Series of Psychosocial Stages

ERIK ERIKSON

Erik Erikson was raised in Germany by Danish parents. In 1927 as a starving artist he traveled to Vienna where he was later trained in psychoanalysis under Freud. Then, after a break with Freud he immigrated to America in 1933 where he taught and researched child development. In contrast to that of his mentor Freud, Erikson's theory of ego psychology deemphasized the power of the id and the libido and concentrated more on a child's interaction with society. Erikson believed that personality develops in a somewhat continuous fashion throughout the life cycle. However, like Freud, Erikson believed that obstacles arise at each of the stages of life and that development of a healthy personality depends on how these obstacles are met. The following viewpoint first appeared in the *International Encyclopedia of the Social Sciences* in 1968 and was later modified in *A Way of Looking at Things: A Collection of Erikson's Works*. It illustrates the dilemmas encountered in the various stages of Erikson's ego psychology.

1. What does Erikson mean by "Psychosocial Stages of Development"?
2. How does Erikson's theory differ from Freud's? How are they similar?
3. What is the cause of poor development, according to Erikson?
4. What does Erikson say are the major obstacles of childhood?

■ ■ ■

The Eight Stages of Life

Man's protracted childhood must be provided with the psychosocial protection and stimulation which, like a second womb, permits the child to develop in distinct steps as he unifies his separate capacities. In each stage, we assume a new drive-and-need constellation, an expanded radius of potential social interaction, and social institutions created to receive the growing individual within traditional patterns. To provide an evolutionary rationale for this (for prolonged childhood and social institutions must have evolved together), two basic differences between animal and man must be considered.

We are, in Ernst Mayr's terms, the "generalist" animal, prepared to adapt to and to develop cultures in the most varied environments. A long childhood must prepare the newborn of the species to become specialized as a member of a pseudo species, i.e., in tribes, cultures, castes, etc., each of which behaves as if it were the only genuine realization of man as the heavens planned and created him. Furthermore, man's drives are characterized by instinctual energies, which are, in contrast to other animals, much less bound to instinctive patterns (or inborn release mechanisms). A maximum of free instinctual energy thus remains ready to be invested in basic psychosocial encounters which tend to fix developing energies into cultural patterns of mutuality, reliability, and competence. Freud has shown the extent to which maladaptive anxiety and rage accompany man's instinctuality, while postulating the strength of the ego in its defensive and in its adaptive aspects. We can attempt to show a systematic relationship between man's maladjustments and those basic strengths which must emerge in each life cycle and reemerge from generation to generation. . . .

Infancy (Basic Trust Versus Mistrust—Hope)

The resolution of the first psychosocial crisis is performed primarily by maternal care. The newborn infant's more or less coordinated readiness to incorporate by mouth and through the senses meets the mother's and the society's more or less coordinated readiness to feed him and to stimulate his awareness. The mother must represent to the child an almost somatic conviction that she (his first "world") is trustworthy enough to satisfy and to regulate his needs. But the infant's demeanor also inspires hope in adults and makes them wish to give hope; it awakens in them a strength which they, in turn, are ready and needful to have confirmed in the experience of care. This is the onto-genetic basis of hope, that first and basic strength which gives man a semblance of instinctive certainty in his social ecology.

Unavoidable pain and delay of satisfaction, however, and inexorable weaning make this stage also prototypical for a sense of abandonment and helpless rage. This is the first of the human estrangements against which hope must maintain itself throughout life.

In psychopathology, a defect in basic trust can be evident in early malignant disturbances or can become apparent later in severe addiction or in habitual or sudden withdrawal into psychotic states.

Biological motherhood needs at least three links with social experience—the mother's past experience of being mothered, a method of care in trustworthy surroundings, and some convincing image of providence. The infant's hope, in turn, is one cornerstone of the adult's faith, which throughout history has sought an institutional safeguard in organized religion. However, where religious institutions fail to give ritual actuality to their formulas they may become irrelevant to psychosocial strength.

Hope, then, is the first psychosocial strength. It is the enduring belief in the attainability of primal wishes in spite of the anarchic urges and rages of dependency.

Early Childhood (Autonomy Versus Shame, Doubt—Will Power)

Early childhood sets the stage for psychological autonomy by rapid gains in muscular maturation, locomotion, verbalization, and discrimination. All of these, however, create limits in the form of spatial restrictions and of categorical divisions between "yes and no," "good and bad," "right and wrong," and "yours and mine." Muscular maturation sets the stage for an ambivalent set of social modalities—holding on and letting go. To hold on can become a destructive retaining or restraining, or a pattern of care—to have and to hold. To let go, too, can turn into an inimical letting loose, or a relaxed "letting pass" and "letting be." Freud calls this the anal stage of libido development because of the pleasure experienced in and the conflict evoked over excretory retention and elimination.

This stage, therefore, becomes decisive for the ration of good will and willfulness. A sense of self-control without loss of self-esteem is the ontogenetic source of confidence in free will; a sense of over-control and loss of self-control can give rise to a lasting propensity for doubt and shame. The matter is complicated by the different needs and capacities of siblings of different ages—and by their rivalry.

Shame is the estrangement of being exposed and conscious of being looked at disapprovingly, of wishing to "bury one's face" or "sink into the ground." This potentiality is exploited in the "shaming" used throughout life by some cultures and causing, on occasion, suicide. While shame is related to the consciousness of being upright and exposed, doubt has much to do with the consciousness of having a front and a back (and of the vulnerability of being seen and influenced from behind). It is the estrangement of being unsure of one's will and of those who would dominate it.

From this stage emerges the propensity for compulsive overcompliance or impulsive defiance. If denied a gradual increase in autonomy of choice the individual may become obsessed by repetitiveness and develop an overly cruel conscience. Early self-doubt and doubt of others may later find their most malignant expression in compulsion neuroses or in paranoiac apprehension of hidden critics and secret persecutors threatening from behind.

We have related basic trust to the institutions of religion. The enduring need of the individual to have an area of free choice reaffirmed and delineated by formulated privileges and limitations, obligations and rights has an institutional safeguard in the principles of law and order and of justice. Where this is impaired, however, the law itself is in danger of becoming arbitrary or formalistic, i.e., "impulsive" or "compulsive" itself.

Will power is the unbroken determination to exercise free choice as well as self-restraint in spite of the unavoidable experience of shame, doubt, and a certain rage over being controlled by others. Good will is rooted in the judiciousness of parents guided by their respect for the spirit of the law.

Play Age (Initiative Versus Guilt—Purpose)

Able to move independently and vigorously, the child, now in his third or fourth year, begins to comprehend his expected role in the adult world and to play out roles worth imitating. He develops a sense of initiative. He associates with age-mates and older children as he watches and enters into games in the barnyard, on the street corner, or in the nursery. His learning now is intrusive; it leads him into ever-new facts and activities, and he becomes acutely aware of differences between the sexes. But if it seems that the child spends on his play a purposefulness out of proportion to "real" purposes, we must recognize the human necessity to simultaneously bind together infantile wish and limited skill, symbol and fact, inner and outer world, a selectively remembered past and a vaguely anticipated future—all before adult "reality" takes over in sanctioned roles and adjusted purposes.

The fate of infantile genitality remains determined by the sex roles cultivated and integrated in the family. In the boy, the sexual orientation is dominated by phallic-intrusive initiative; in the girl, by inclusive modes of attractiveness and "motherliness."

Conscience, however, forever divides the child within himself by establishing an inner voice of self-observation, self-guidance, and self-punishment. The estrangement of this stage, therefore, is a sense of guilt over goals contemplated and acts done, initiated, or merely fantasied. For initiative includes competition with those of superior equipment. In a final contest for favored position with the mother, "oedipal" feelings are aroused in the boy, and there appears to be an intensified fear of finding the genitals harmed as punishment for the fantasies attached to their excitability.

Infantile guilt leads to the conflict between unbounded initiative and repression or inhibition. In adult pathology this residual conflict is expressed in hysterical denial, general inhibition, and sexual impotence, or in overcompensatory exhibitionism and psychopathic acting-out.

The word "initiative" has for many a specifically American, or "entrepreneur," connotation. Yet man needs this sense of initiative for whatever he learns and does, from fruit gathering to commercial enterprise—or the study of books.

The play age relies on the existence of some form of basic family, which also teaches the child by patient example where play ends and irreversible purpose begins. Only thus are guilt feelings integrated in a strong (not severe) conscience; only thus is language verified as a shared actuality. The "oedipal" stage thus not only results in a moral sense restricting the horizon of the permissible, but also directs the way to the possible and the tangible, which attract infantile dreams to the goals of technology and culture. Social institutions, in turn, offer an ethos of action, in the form of ideal adults fascinating enough to replace the heroes of the picture book and fairy tale.

That the adult begins as a playing child means that there is a residue of play acting and role playing even in what he considers his highest purposes. These he projects on a larger and more perfect historical future; these he dramatizes in the ceremonial present with uniformed players in ritual arrangements; thus men sanction aggressive initiative, even as they assuage guilt by submission to a higher authority.

Purpose, then, is the courage to envisage and pursue valued and tangible goals guided by conscience but not paralyzed by guilt and by the fear of punishment.

School Age (Industry Versus Inferiority—Competence)

Before the child, psychologically a rudimentary parent, can become a biological parent, he must begin to be a worker and potential provider. Genital maturation is postponed (the period of latency). The child develops a sense of industriousness, i.e., he begins to comprehend the tool world of his culture, and he can become an eager and absorbed member of that productive situation called "school," which gradually supersedes the whims of play. In all cultures, at this stage, children receive systematic instruction of some kind and learn eagerly from older children.

The danger of this stage lies in the development of a sense of inadequacy. If the child despairs of his skill or his status among his tool partners, he may be discouraged from further learning. He may regress to the hopeless rivalry of the oedipal situation. It is at this point that the larger society becomes significant to the child by admitting him to roles preparatory to the actuality of technology and economy. Where he finds, however, that the color of his skin or the background of his parents rather than his wish and his will to learn will decide his worth as an apprentice, the human propensity for feeling unworthy (inferior) may be fatefully aggravated as a determinant of character development.

But there is another danger: If the overly conforming child accepts work as the only criterion of worthwhileness, sacrificing too readily his imagination and playfulness, he may become ready to submit to what Marx called a "craft-idiocy," i.e., become a slave of his technology and of its established role typology.

This is socially a most decisive stage, preparing the child for a hierarchy of learning experiences which he will undergo with the help of cooperative peers and instructive adults. Since industriousness involves doing things beside and with others, a first sense of the division of labor and of differential opportunity—that is, a sense of the technological ethos of a culture—develops at this time. Therefore, the configurations of cultural thought and the manipulations basic to the prevailing technology must reach meaningfully into school life.

Competence, then, is the free exercise (unimpaired by an infantile sense of inferiority) of dexterity and intelligence in the completion of serious tasks. It is the basis for cooperative participation in some segment of the culture.

Adolescence (Identity Versus Identity Confusion—Fidelity)

With a good initial relationship to skills and tools, and with the advent of puberty, childhood proper comes to an end. The rapidly growing youths, faced with the inner revolution of puberty and with as yet intangible adult tasks, are now primarily concerned with their psychosocial identity and with fitting their rudimentary gifts and skills to the occupational prototypes of the culture.

The integration of an identity is more than the sum of childhood identifications. It is the accrued confidence that the inner sameness and continuity gathered over the past years of development are matched by the sameness and continuity in one's meaning for others, as evidenced in the tangible promise of careers and life-styles.

The adolescent's regressive and yet powerful impulsiveness alternating with compulsive restraint is well known. In all of this, however, an ideological seeking after an inner coherence and a durable set of values can be detected. The particular strength sought is fidelity—that is, the opportunity to fulfill personal potentialities (including erotic vitality or its sublimation) in a context which permits the young person to be true to himself and true to significant others. "Falling in love" also can be an attempt to arrive at a self-definition by seeing oneself reflected anew in an idealized as well as eroticized other.

From this stage on, acute maladjustments caused by social anomie may lead to psychopathological regressions. Where role confusion joins a hopelessness of long standing, borderline psychotic episodes are not uncommon.

Adolescents, on the other hand, help one another temporarily through much regressive insecurity by forming cliques and by stereotyping themselves, their ideals, and their "enemies." In this they can be clannish and cruel in their exclusion of all those who are "different." Where they turn this repudiation totally against the society, delinquency may be a temporary or lasting result.

As social systems enter into the fiber of each succeeding generation, they also absorb into their lifeblood the rejuvenative power of youth. Adolescence is thus a vital regenerator in the process of social evolution, for youth can offer its loyalties and energies to the conservation of that which it feels is valid as well as to the revolutionary correction of that which has lost its regenerative significance.

Adolescence is least "stormy" among those youths who are gifted and well trained in the pursuit of productive technological trends. In times of unrest, the adolescent mind becomes an ideological mind in search of an inspiring unification of ideas. Youth needs to be affirmed by peers and confirmed by teachings, creeds, and ideologies which express the promise that the best people will come to rule and that rule will develop the best in people. A society's ideological weakness, in turn, expresses itself in weak utopianism and in widespread identity confusion.

Fidelity, then, is the ability to sustain loyalties freely pledged in spite of the inevitable contradictions of value systems. It is the cornerstone of identity and receives inspiration from confirming ideologies and "ways of life."

Young Adulthood (Intimacy Versus Isolation—Love)

Consolidated identity permits the self-abandonment demanded by intimate affiliations, by passionate sexual unions, or by inspiring encounters. The young adult is ready for intimacy and solidarity—that is, he can commit himself to affiliations and partnerships even though they may call for significant sacrifices and compromises. Ethical strength emerges as a further differentiation of ideological conviction (adolescence) and a sense of moral obligation (childhood).

True genital maturity is first reached at this stage; much of the individual's previous sex life is of the identity-confirming kind. Freud, when asked for the criteria of a mature person, is reported to have answered: *"Lieben und Arbeiten."* ("love and work"). All three words deserve equal emphasis.

It is only at this stage that the biological differences between the sexes result in a full polarization within a joint life style. Previously established strengths have helped the two sexes to converge in capacities and values which enhance communication and cooperation, while divergence is now of the essence in love life and in procreation. Thus the sexes first become similar in consciousness, language, and ethics in order then to be maturely different. But this, by necessity, causes ambivalences.

The danger of this stage is possible psychosocial isolation—that is, the avoidance of contacts which commit to intimacy. In psychopathology isolation can lead to severe character problems of the kind which interfere with "love and work," and this often on the basis of infantile fixations and lasting immaturities.

Man, in addition to erotic attraction, has developed a selectivity of mutual love that serves the need for a new and shared identity in the procession of generations. Love is the guardian of that elusive and yet all-pervasive power of cultural and personal style which binds into a "way of life" the affiliations of competition and cooperation, procreation and production. The problem is one of transferring the experience of being cared for in a parental setting to an adult affiliation actively chosen and cultivated as a mutual concern within a new generation.

The counterpart of such intimacy, and the danger, are man's readiness to fortify his territory of intimacy and solidarity by exaggerating small differences and prejudging or excluding foreign influences and people. Insularity thus aggravated can lead to that irrational fear which is easily exploited by demagogic leaders seeking aggrandizement in war and in political conflict.

Love, then, is a mutuality of devotion greater than the antagonisms inherent in divided function.

Maturity (Generativity Versus Stagnation—Care)

Evolution has made man the teaching and instituting as well as the learning animal. For dependency and maturity are reciprocal: mature man needs to be needed, and maturity is guided by the nature of that which must be cared for.

Generativity, then, is primarily the concern with establishing and guiding the next generation. In addition to procreativity, it includes productivity and creativity; thus it is psychosocial in nature. From the crisis of generativity emerges the strength of care.

Where such enrichment fails, a sense of stagnation and boredom ensues, the pathological symptoms of which depend on variations in mental epidemiology: certainly where the hypocrisy of the frigid mother was once regarded as a most significant malignant influence, today, when sexual "adjustment" is in order, an obsessive pseudo intimacy and adult self-indulgence are nonetheless damaging to the generational process. The very nature of generativity suggests that the most circumscribed symptoms of its weakness are to be found in the next generation in the form of those aggravated estrangements which we have listed for childhood and youth.

121

Generativity is itself a driving power in human organization. For the intermeshing stages of childhood and adulthood are in themselves a system of generation and regeneration given continuity by institutions such as extended households and divided labor.

Thus, in combination, the basic strengths enumerated here and the structure of an organized human community provide a set of proven methods and a fund of traditional reassurance with which each generation meets the needs of the next. Various traditions transcend divisive personal differences and confusing conditions. But they also contribute to a danger to the species as a whole, namely, the defensive territoriality of the pseudo species, which on seemingly ethical grounds must discredit and destroy threateningly alien systems and may itself be destroyed in the process.

Care is the broadening concern for what has been generated by love, necessity, or accident—a concern which must consistently overcome the ambivalence adhering to irreversible obligation and the narrowness of self-concern.

Old Age (Integrity Versus Despair—Wisdom)

Strength in the aging and sometimes in the old takes the form of wisdom in its many connotations—ripened "wits," accumulated knowledge, inclusive understanding, and mature judgment. Wisdom maintains and conveys the integrity of experience, in spite of the decline of bodily and mental functions. Responding to the oncoming generation's need for an integrated heritage, the wisdom of old age remains aware of the relativity of all knowledge acquired in one lifetime in one historical period. Integrity, therefore, implies an emotional integration faithful to the image bearers of the past and ready to take (and eventually to renounce) leadership in the present.

The lack or loss of this accrued integration is signified by a hidden fear of death: fate is not accepted as the frame of life, death not as its finite boundary. Despair indicates that time is too short for alternate roads to integrity: this is why the old try to "doctor" their memories. Bitterness and disgust mask such despair, which in severe psychopathology aggravates senile depression, hypochondria, and paranoiac hate.

A meaningful old age (preceding terminal invalidism) provides that integrated heritage which gives indispensible perspective to those growing up, "adolescing," and aging. But the end of the cycle also evokes "ultimate concerns," the paradoxes of which we must leave to philosophical and religious interpreters. Whatever chance man has to transcend the limitations of his self seems to depend on his full (if often tragic) engagement in the one and only life cycle permitted him in the sequence of generations. Great philosophical and religious systems dealing with ultimate individuation seem to have remained (even in their monastic establishments) responsibly related to the cultures and civilizations of their times. Seeking transcendence by renunciation, they remain ethically concerned with the maintainance of the world. By the same token, a civilization can be measured by the meaning which it gives to the full cycle of life, for such meaning (or the lack of) cannot fail to reach into the beginnings of the next generation and thus enhance the potentiality that others may meet ultimate questions with some clarity and strength.

Wisdom, then, is a detached and yet active concern with life in the face of death.

Social Strength and the Life Cycle

From the cycle of life such dispositions as faith, will power, purposefulness, efficiency, devotion, affection, responsibility, and sagacity (all of which are also criteria of ego strength) flow into the life of institutions. Without them, institutions wilt; but without the spirit of institutions pervading the patterns of care and love, instruction and training, no enduring strength could emerge from the sequence of generations.

We have attempted, in a psychosocial frame, to account for the ontogenesis not of lofty ideals but of an inescapable and intrinsic order of strivings, which, by weakening or strengthening man, dictates the minimum goals of informed and responsible participation.

Psychosocial strength, we conclude, depends on a total process which regulates individual life cycles, the sequence of generations, and the structure of society simultaneously, for all three have evolved together.

Each person must translate this order into his own terms so as to make it amenable to whatever kind of trait inventory, normative scale, measurement, or educational goal is his main concern. Science and technology are, no doubt, changing essential aspects of the course of life, wherefore some increased awareness of the functional wholeness of the cycle may be mandatory. Interdisciplinary work will define in practical and applicable terms what evolved order is common to all men and what true equality of opportunity must mean in planning for future generations.

The study of the human life cycle has immediate applications in a number of fields. Paramount is the science of human development within social institutions. In psychiatry (and in its applications to law), the diagnostic and prognostic assessment of disturbances common to life stages should help to outweigh fatalistic diagnoses. Whatever will prove tangibly lawful about the cycle of life will also be an important focus for anthropology insofar as it assesses universal functions in the variety of institutional forms. Finally, as the study of the life history emerges from that of case histories, it will throw new light on biography and thus on history itself.

Development Occurs in a Series of Cognitive Stages

JEAN PIAGET

Swiss psychologist Jean Piaget's genius was recognized at a young age. At the age of ten, after publishing his first article on a rare sighting of the Part-Albino Sparrow, he was offered the job of museum curator for the Geneva Museum of Natural History. The curators later rescinded their offer after finding that Piaget was only a child and instead he took a job as curator's apprentice in the Museum of Natural History in Neuchâtel where he was responsible for labeling the museum's mollusk collection two days a week after school. In his early teens Piaget began to study philosophy. While reading works by Immanuel Kant and Henri Bergson he developed an affinity for epistemology (the study of how we know what we know). After receiving his doctorate in biology he dabbled very briefly in psychoanalysis, then, in 1919 he moved to Paris to work in the laboratory of Alfred Binet standardizing a test for children's intelligence. It was there, through first-hand observations of children, that he began to combine the teachings of biology, epistemology, and psychology to explain child development.

Reprinted from Jean Piaget, "The Attainment of Invariants and Reversible Operations in the Development of Thinking," *Social Research*, vol. 30, no. 3, 1963, by permission of *Social Research*, New York, New York.

1. What is an "operation" according to Piaget?
2. How does Piaget's training in biology and philosophy influence his theory?
3. How would Piaget's theory explain gifted or developmentally disabled children?
4. What is "conservation" according to Piaget?

■ ■ ■

Basically, to solve a problem is to coordinate operations while focusing on the solution. An operation is, first of all, an action. We shall see that at its inception intelligence begins with simple actions on the sensori-motor level, actions which then become interiorized and come to be represented symbolically. Moreover, operations are basically actions which can be performed in either direction, that is, actions which are reversible. This is really the remarkable thing about intelligence, if one compares intelligence with other mental functions, for instance habits. Habits are not reversible, they are oriented in one direction only. Thus, we have learned to write from left to right, and if we wanted to write from right to left we could not do so on the basis of our previous habits, we would have to start learning a new habit. By contrast, once we can handle an operation, for instance the operation of adding in the arithmetical sense, or in its more general logical sense, we can reverse that specific action. From the moment when the child understands what it means to add, that is, to bring together two groups to form one, he implicitly knows also what it means to separate the groups again, to dissociate them, to subtract. It is of the same operation; he can work it one way, in one direction, and also the other way, in the opposite direction. This reversibility is not a primitive matter; it is progressively built up as a function of the same complex structures mentioned above. From the psychological point of view, one of the most fruitful terrains for the analysis of this reversibility is the problem of conservation.

In any system of reversible actions there results the construction of certain invariants, certain forms of conservation analogous to those subserving scientific reasoning. In the young child we can observe the development of these invariants, and the evolution of concepts of conservation. For instance, we can ask a child whether, when a given liquid is being poured from a container A into another container B of a different shape, the quantity of the liquid remains the same. For us that is self-evident, as it is for children above a certain age. But we shall see that for the younger children it is not self-evident at all. In fact, they will say that the quantity has increased because the height of the new container is greater, or that it is less because container B is thinner. They have not yet attained the logically relevant concept of conservation and the pertinent invariants, and they cannot grasp these until some time later when their thinking becomes capable of reversible operations, and when these operations become coordinated structures. The immediate result of the achievement of such structures is not only the affirmation of certain forms of conservation, but, at the same time, the insight that this conservation is self-evident, logically necessary, precisely because it arises from the coordination of operations. Let us trace now, step by step, the development of this reversibility, of these forms of conservation and also of certain complex structures.

I shall distinguish four stages in this development: 1) the pre-language sensori-motor stage; 2) the pre-operational stage from 2–7 years; 3) the stage of concrete operations between the approximate ages of 7 and 12; 4) finally the stage of propositional operations with their formal characteristics which are attained at the pre-adolescent and adolescent stage.

The Pre-Language Stage

We need to say only a few words about the sensori-motor stage. This period is important because during it are developed substructures essential for later operations. At the present time everybody agrees that there is intelligent action prior to language. The baby demonstrates intelligent behavior before he can speak. Interestingly, we note, the earliest forms of intelligence already aim at the construction of certain invariants—practical invariants to be sure, namely invariants of the concrete space of immediate action. These first invariants are already the result of a sort of reversibility but it is a practical reversibility embedded in the very actions; it is not yet a constituent of thought proper. Of the invariants which arise at the sensori-motor stage perhaps the most important one is the schema of the permanent object. I call the permanent object that object which continues to exist outside of the perceptual field. A perceived object is not a permanent object in that sense. I would say that there is no schema of a permanent object if the child no longer reacts once the object has disappeared from the perceptual field, when it is no longer visible, when it can no longer be touched, when it is no longer heard. On the other hand I would say that there is already an invariant, a schema of the permanent object, if the child begins to search for the vanished object. Such a schema is not present from the very beginning. When, at about $4^{1}/_{2}$ months of age, a child starts to reach for the things he sees in his visual field and, when he begins to coordinate vision and prehension to some extent, one can observe that he does not yet react to a permanent object. For instance, I may show the infant a watch, dangling it in front of him. He reaches out to take the watch, but at the very moment when he has already extended his hand, I cover the watch with a napkin. What happens? He promptly withdraws his hand as if the watch had been absorbed into the napkin. Even though he can very well remove the napkin if it is put over his own face, he does not lift it in order to look for the watch underneath. You might say that the watch is perhaps of no great interest to the infant; however, the same experiment can be made with a nursing bottle. I have done this with one of my children at the age of 7 months. At the time of his feeding I show him the bottle, he extends his hand to take it, but, at that moment, I hide it behind my arm. If he sees one end sticking out he kicks and screams and gives every indication of wanting to have it. If, however, the bottle is completely hidden and nothing sticks out, he stops crying and acts for all we know as if the bottle no longer existed, as if it had been dissolved and absorbed into my arm.

Towards the end of the first year the infant begins to search for the vanished object. Already at 9 to 10 months he looks for it behind a screen. If we place the child between two screens, for example, a cloth or a pillow on his right and another one at his left, we can make a very curious observation concerning the locus of the hiding place. With the child in that position I now show him, for instance, a watch. As soon as he evinces interest in the watch I place it under the cloth at his right. Thereupon the child will promptly lift the cloth and grasp the watch. Now I take it from him and, very slowly, so that he can follow with his eyes, move the watch over to his left side. Then, having made sure that he has indeed followed the movement, I cover the watch in its new position. I have observed this in my three children over varying periods of time, and we have repeated this experiment frequently since. There is a stage when, at the moment the child sees the watch disappear at the left, he immediately turns back to the right and looks for the watch there. In other words, he looks for the object where he has found it before. The object is not yet a mobile thing, capable of movements and correlated displacements in an autonomous system in space. Rather, the object is still an extension of the action itself, an action that is repeated where and how it was successful the first time around.

Finally, towards the end of the first year the object comes to have a degree of independent existence. Its disappearance elicits search, and that search is guided by the observed displacements. Now we can speak of a structure of coordinated displacements or, indeed, a group of displacements in the sense in which the term is used in geometry with the implication of the possibilities of movement in one direction and in reverse as well as of detours by means of which the same goal can be reached over a variety of alternate pathways. A long time ago Henri Poincaré advanced the hypothesis that primitive sensori-motor space must originate from such groups of displacements. Without entering into the details of that discussion, I should like to point out that this group structure—which is already a reversible structure—is not an *a priori* given, as Poincaré would have us believe. Instead, it develops gradually during the first year. The attainment of the notion of the permanent object is the exact correlate of the emerging organization of reversible movements that constitute the groups of displacements. You could say that the permanent object is the first group invariant, provided it is understood that a group at this level is not yet a system of operations but merely a system of practical actions in the immediate space. This system enables the individual to take account of successive displacements, to order them, then reverse them, and so forth.

The Pre-Operational Stage

Let us turn now to the development of representational thinking proper. We observe it first in play, in imaginary games with their fictitious qualities and symbolic aspects, play in which one thing comes to be represented by means of another thing. Differentiated imitation, for instance of various people in the child's environment, and a variety of other symbolic acts belong to this stage. Such representational thinking greatly enlarges the range of intellectual activity. The latter no longer pertains only to the nearby space, the present moment and the action in progress. Thanks to representational thought such activity can now be applied with reference to far away space, to events outside the immediate perceptual sphere, to the past which can be recovered and recounted, and to the future in the form of plans and projects. In other words the universe of representation is obviously much wider than the universe of direct action. Consequently, the first tools that have already been developed at the sensori-motor level cannot be applied immediately to this wider sphere, they cannot be generalized immediately in their broader relevance. The child must now reconstruct on an ideational plane the invariants, the forms of coordination whose beginnings we observed at the sensori-motor level. All this takes place in the period which extends from the beginning of language at one end to the age of about seven or eight years at the other end. During this period we can already speak of thought, of representation, but not yet of logical operations defined as interiorized reversible action systems. In children within this age range we have studied all sorts of problems of conservation and invariants, and we have found quite systematically that these notions of conservation begin to develop only at about the age of seven or eight years.

I shall not come back to the problem of liquids being poured from one container into another, but we can make the same experiment with beads. We can ask the child to put blue beads into container A and red beads into container B, and we make sure that each time he places a blue bead into container A he also places a red bead into the other container B, so that there will be the same number of beads in each of the two containers. The child is then told to pour the beads from container B into a new container, C; thereupon we ask him if there are the same number of beads in C as in A—those in A having remained there and those from B having been poured into C. Now a curious thing happens. Until approximately the age of 6½ years the child believes that the number of beads has changed, that there are more beads in container C because it is higher than B, or that there are fewer beads in container C because it is thinner than B. If you ask him "Where do these extra beads come from?" or "What happened to the beads that are no longer there?" he is very much surprised at your question. He is totally uninterested in the mechanism of the transformation. What interests him is the gross perceptual configuration which is different in the two situations; even in the case of these discrete entities there is no conservation of absolute quantities. . . .

The Stage of Concrete Operations

Towards the age of seven or so the problems of conservation become resolved. There are a few exceptions that concern complex quantities, for instance weight or volume, but simple quantities such as collections or lengths are no longer problematical. How have they been resolved? They have been resolved as a function of three arguments which children always give you, irrespective of the experimental problem. The first argument is: the quantity, or the number is the same—for example, in the bead problem, nothing has been added and nothing has been taken away. I call this the identity argument, because it takes place entirely within the single, self-contained system without any attempt at transcending the boundaries of that system. This argument is certainly not the true root of the attainment of conversation, because the younger children also know very well that nothing has been added or taken away. The real problem is to know why this becomes an argument for the child at a given moment, when it was not an argument for him before.

The child's second argument tells us the reason. I call this the argument of simple reversibility. The child says: "You have done nothing except to pour the beads in the other container, so it looks different, but all you have to do is to pour them back and you will see that they are the same." In other words, it is no longer the perceptual configuration which is interesting, it is their displacement and the resultant transformation. This transformation is apprehended as something that can take place in both directions, that is reversible. Now we understand the first argument concerning the identity of the beads. Identity is precisely the product of the original operation and its reversal; it has attained the status of a system as a function of this simple reversibility.

The third argument used by the children is again based on a kind of reversibility, but now in the form of a pattern of relationships. The child tells you: "Here is more height but a little less width; what you gain in height you lose in width; that evens it out." This implies a pattern of relationships, a multiplication of relationships and their mutual compensation; it is once more a type of reversibility. In other words these three arguments, that of identity, that of simple reversibility and that of patterned relationships show you the beginnings of operations as we have defined them. These operations, that can be observed between the ages of seven years and eleven or twelve years, are already logical operations. Their structure is essentially logical, even though the available implications of that logic are still rather limited. They are only operations of classes and relations and are not yet operations of the logic of propositions. They do not even contain all the operations possible with classes and relations, but only certain rather elementary systems that can be understood by the child as they relate to concrete *manipulanda*. These operations always center around an action or an application to specific objects. For this reason we call them "concrete operations." We use the term "operational groupings" to designate those elementary and immediate systems of action which are patterned as they occur in spatial and temporal contiguity; these simple systems do not yet include all of the logic of classes and relations.

Here is another example of such an operational grouping. The problem is one of inclusion, that is, the inclusion of a class A in a class B with the complement of A', of inclusion of class B in a class C with the complement of B' etc. In this case you have a very simple system in which the addition of two classes results in a new class from which substraction of one leads back to the first class, a tautology with rather limited possibilities. This structure first appears at about age seven and, it seems to me, is basic for the notion of conservation. It is impossible to conduct such operations without invariants and without conservation, precisely because the necessary invariant of these operations is the conservation of the total system. We can experimentally show that this is the case by testing the relationship of inclusion of A in B. You present the child with an open box that contains wooden beads. The child knows they are all wooden because he handles them, touching each and finding that it is made of wood. Most of these beads are brown, but a few are white. The problem we pose is simply this: are there more brown beads or more wooden beads? Let us call A the brown beads, B the wooden beads: then the problem is simply that of the inclusion of A in B. This is a very difficult problem before the age of 7 years. The child states that all the beads are wooden, states that most of them are brown and a few are white, but if you ask him if there are more brown beads or more wooden beads he immediately answers: "There are more brown ones because there are only two or three white ones." So you say: "Listen, this is not what I am asking, I don't want to know whether there are more brown or more white beads, I want to know whether there are more brown beads or more wooden beads." And, in order to make it easier, I take an empty box and place it next to the one with the beads and I ask: "If I were to put the wooden beads into that box would any remain in this one?" The child answers: "No, none would be left because they are all wooden." Then I say: "If I were to take the brown beads and put them into that box, would any be left in this one?" The child replies: "Of course, two or three white ones would remain." Apparently he has now understood the situation, the fact that all the beads are wooden and that some are not brown. So I ask him once more: "Are there more brown beads or more wooden beads?" Now it is evident that the child begins to understand the problem, sees that there is indeed a problem, that matters are not as simple as they seemed at first. As we watch him we observe that he is thinking very hard. Finally he concludes: "But there are still more brown beads; if you take the brown ones away, only two or three white beads remain."

Why does this answer recur? Because the child can reason about the whole as long as it is not broken up into parts or, if we force him to break it up, he can reason about the parts, but he cannot reason simultaneously about the whole and the parts. If he is pushed to deal with the brown beads, then the whole no longer exists, it is divided into the two components, the brown beads and the white beads. In order to reunite one part with the whole, the child must not only be capable of the reasoning involved, he must at the same time understand that one part is always the whole minus the other part, and that presupposes conservation of the whole, conservation which results here from simple grouping operations involving classes. This system is psychologically so interesting because it is one of the basic systems which mediate the notions of conservation.

The Stage of Propositional Operations

Let us proceed to the last stage which begins approximately at the age of 12 years and which is characteristic of the whole adolescent development. This is the period during which new logical operations appear: propositional operations, the logic of propositions, implication, and so forth. These are superimposed onto the earlier concrete operations. The adolescent is no longer limited to concrete reasoning about objects, he begins to reason hypothetically. Starting from a theoretical assumption he can reason that if it is true, then certain consequences must follow. This is the hypothetico-deductive method that presupposes implication, disjunction, compatibility, and all the other operations of the logic of propositions. The psychological problem here is first of all to discover how the logic of propositions develops, how it arises out of the concrete operations discussed above. Moreover, at the same stage—that is, starting at about the age of 12 years, there appear not only propositional operations but also, and very strikingly a host of other types of new operations which, at first glance, have no relationship to the propositional operations.

There are for instance what the mathematicians call combinatorial operations. Let me illustrate these by the results of another experiment. We present the child with piles of red, blue, green, and yellow poker chips and set him the task to make all possible combinations of pairs, or all possible combinations of three or four colors. At the level of concrete operations, up to age twelve or so, the child can produce a number of such groups and combinations, and can do so correctly, but he is unable to find a systematic method by means of which he can arrive at all possible combinations. By contrast, around age twelve the child begins to find a practical method that will permit him to make all possible combinations, even though he has not had any instruction concerning combinatorial operations nor learned the proper mathematical formula.

More or less simultaneously we observe at the same stage the appearance of operations which involve proportions. This too we can study experimentally, for instance by means of balance problems where weights and distances can be varied. Here the child discovers that a given weight A at distance B from the fulcrum is equal to weight B at distance A, and he thus comes to establish proportions between weights and distances. Also at approximately the same time operations involving probabilities first appear, operations which involve the consideration of probable and possible events. Finally, certain additional types of operations also enter during this stage, operations which we shall leave aside in the present discussion.

Two fundamental psychological questions arise in connection with this last stage. The first concerns the nature and development of the logic of propositions. Secondly, we must ask why the logic of proposition appears at the same time as such other systems of operation as combinations, proportions, and so forth, that have at first sight no particular relationship either among each other or to the logic of proposition. Here the concept of complex structures appears to me to be especially valuable. Let us take, for instance, the well known sixteen basic operations of the logic of propositions. If you compare their structure to the structure of concrete operations you see immediately that there are marked differences. The former is a lattice-type structure in the usual mathematical meaning of that term, a complete lattice, while the latter has an incomplete lattice structure, with a join for any two positions, but lacking meets for classes of the same rank.[1] It is a semi-lattice, and so are all the groups of concrete operations: they may have joins and lack meets, or they may contain meets but lack joins. As soon as you deal with propositional logic, however, you have the basic four-fold table[2] which, to be sure, looks as if it might represent simply the multiplication of classes, that is, which apparently resembles one of the systems already available at a more concrete level.

The great new achievement at this level is the fact that the sixteen binary operations of two-valued propositional logic are systematically derived from the four basic conjunctions. In other words, the attainment of propositional logic presupposes a lattice structure which has evolved from the semi-lattice structures implied by the operations at the earlier, more concrete level, and which is the direct result of the generalization of classification. The lattice is the schema of all possible classifications which can be derived from its elements but, at the same time, the lattice has combinatorial characteristics. From the psychological point of view it is very striking to find the simultaneous appearance of propositional operations on the one hand, operations which pre-

[1]In the introduction to Piaget's *Logic and Psychology* (New York, Basic Books, 1957) W. Mays gives the following definitions (p. xv): "Boolean algebra may be considered as a special case of certain abstract mathematical systems called lattices. A lattice has certain limiting conditions—*join* and *meet*. In the case of any two classes X and Y, the *join* is the smallest of the classes in which X and Y are both included, and the *meet* is the largest class included both in X and Y." (Italics in original.)

[2]Note 2, pp. xi–xiv and p. 34. For details the reader may consult any good introductory text, for example, S. K. Langer, *An Introduction to Symbolic Logic*, 2nd revised edition (New York: Dover, 1953). The interested reader is referred also to the treatment by the author of *Alice in Wonderland*, Lewis Carroll, in his *Symbolic Logic, Part I Elementary* (London: Macmillan, 1897).

suppose a lattice structure and thus combinatorial operations and, on the other hand, combinatorial operations applied to mathematical problems. The child is of course not aware of the identity of the structure of these apparently different operations, an identity which our analysis has convincingly demonstrated.

Now as to proportions—how are we to explain the appearance of proportions at the same stage? Let us remember that propositional operations do not only constitute a lattice, they also constitute a group. If you take any operation, such as implication, you can reverse it—that is, state its negative, and you can determine its reciprocal, as well as the negative of the reciprocal. The latter I would like to call its correlative. Here we have a group of four transformations, logical transformations to be sure, but transformations from which you can nevertheless derive a system of proportions. This system results from the application of simple operations to a single proposition.

Perhaps this seems a very abstract explanation. Let us go back, therefore, to concrete observations, and let us find out how the child comes to discover proportions. He discovers proportions through experience, for instance as he finds out that adding weight on a balance produces the same result as increasing a constant weight's distance from the fulcrum, and, vice versa, that he can lighten the load by decreasing either weight or distance. In this way he learns the equivalence of two transformations. At the same time he discovers reciprocals—that is, if he increases the weight he must decrease the distance, if he increases the distance he must decrease the weight in order to maintain equilibrium. The child does of course not know these special terms, he expresses himself in simple, everyday language, but his language describes his reasoning exactly. He states that increasing the weight while decreasing the distance gives the same result as decreasing the weight and increasing the distance, and this is a statement of proportions.

Conclusion

I suggest that the structure of propositional operations is a complex structure which comprises both lattices and groups.

Such a structure has many possibilities and implications. These may remain potentialities only, or they may be realized when there arises a problem requiring propositional operations. Let me add that this hypothesis is not only of psychological interest but also has physiological relevance. In recent years the models of cybernetics have begun to give us some understanding of how operations are combined in the solution of problems. A formal analysis of these models reveals that their operations are also the outcome of group structures and lattice structures. Even at the very outset you find simple regulatory mechanisms, feedbacks, which may be understood as the most elementary form of reversibility, and which derive from as well as result in a complex structure. At the present time we are engaged in the study of these structures. They have a twofold interest: first by analogy with mathematical operations, which are, after all, operations of thought; and secondly by analogy with the physiological structures, or, if you will, with the cybernetic models of hypothesized physiological structures.

VIEWPOINT

4

Development Occurs in a Series of Moral Stages

LAWRENCE KOHLBERG AND RICHARD HERSH

Lawrence Kohlberg and Richard Hersh have both published generously in learning and moral development. The following viewpoint provides an excellent review of Kohlberg's theory of moral development. Unlike other theories of development, Kohlberg refrains from the rigidity often present in stage theories and concedes that stages are not prewired to occur at exact ages. According to Kohlberg, the speed at which one passes through each of the six stages of moral development has more to do with the experiences he or she encounters and the cognitive integration of those experiences than on a set number of accumulated years.

QUESTIONS

1. According to the authors, how do individuals pass from one moral stage to another?
2. What role does "justice" play in Kohlberg's theory?
3. Is Kohlberg's theory truly a "stage theory"—can an argument be made for either side?

Lawrence Kohlberg and Richard Hersh (1977), "Moral Development: A Review of the Theory," *Theory Into Practice* 16 (2):53-58. (Theme issue on "Moral Development.") Copyright 1977, College of Education, The Ohio State University. Reprinted with permission.

■ ■ ■

Moral development, as initially defined by [Jean] Piaget and then refined and researched by [Lawrence] Kohlberg, does not simply represent an increasing knowledge of cultural values usually leading to ethical relativity. Rather, it represents the transformations that occur in a person's form or structure of thought. The content of values varies from culture to culture; hence the study of cultural values cannot tell us how a person interacts with his social environment, or how a person goes about solving problems related to his/her social world. This requires the analysis of developing structures of moral judgment, which are found to be universal in a developmental sequence across cultures.

In analyzing the responses of longitudinal and cross-cultural subjects to hypothetical moral dilemmas it has been demonstrated that moral reasoning develops over time through a series of six stages. The concept of stages of cognitive development refers to the structure of one's reasoning and implies the following characteristics:

1. Stages are "structured wholes," or organized systems of thought. This means individuals are consistent in their level of moral judgment.
2. Stages form an invariant sequence. Under all conditions except extreme trauma, movement is always forward, never backward. Individuals never skip stages, and movement is always to the next stage up. This is true in all cultures.
3. Stages are "hierarchical integrations." Thinking at a higher stage includes or comprehends within it lower stage thinking. There is a tendency to function at or prefer the highest stage available.

The stages of moral development are defined by the following characteristics:

Definition of Moral Stages

I. Preconventional Level

At this level, the child is responsive to cultural rules and labels of good and bad, right or wrong, but interprets these labels either in terms of the physical or the hedonistic consequences of action (punishment, reward, exchange of favors) or in terms of the physical power of those who enunciate the rules and labels. The level is divided into the following two stages:

Stage 1: The punishment-and-obedience orientation. The physical consequences of action determine its goodness or badness, regardless of the human meaning or value of these consequences. Avoidance of punishment and unquestioning deference to power are valued in their own right, not in terms of respect for an underlying moral order supported by punishment and authority (the latter being Stage 4).

Stage 2: The instrumental-relativist orientation. Right action consists of that which instrumentally satisfies one's own needs and occasionally the needs of others. Human relations are viewed in terms like those of the marketplace. Elements of fairness, of reciprocity, and of equal sharing are present, but they are always interpreted in a physical, pragmatic way. Reciprocity is a matter of "you scratch my back and I'll scratch yours," not of loyalty, gratitude, or justice.

II. Conventional Level

At this level, maintaining the expectations of the individual's family, group, or nation is perceived as valuable in its own right, regardless of immediate and obvious consequences. The attitude is not only one of conformity to personal expectations and social order, but of loyalty to it, of actively maintaining, supporting, and justifying the order, and of identifying with the persons or group involved in it. At this level, there are the following two stages:

Stage 3: The interpersonal concordance or "good boy-nice girl" orientation. Good behavior is that which pleases or helps others and is approved by them. There is much conformity to stereotypical images of what is majority or "natural" behavior. Behavior is frequently judged by intention—"he means well" becomes important for the first time. One earns approval by being "nice."

Stage 4: The "law and order" orientation. There is orientation toward authority, fixed rules, and the maintenance of the social order. Right behavior consists of doing one's duty, showing respect for authority, and maintaining the given social order for its own sake.

III. Postconventional, Autonomous, or Principled Level

At this level, there is a clear effort to define moral values and principles that have validity and application apart from the authority of the groups or persons holding these principles and apart from the individual's own identification with these groups. This level also has two stages:

Stage 5: The social-contract, legalistic orientation, generally with utilitarian overtones. Right action tends to be defined in terms of general individual rights and standards which have been critically examined and agreed upon by the whole society. There is a clear awareness of the relativism of personal values and opinions and a corresponding emphasis upon procedural rules for reaching consensus. Aside from what is constitutionally and democratically agreed upon, the right is a matter of personal "values" and "opinion." The result is an emphasis upon the "legal point of view," but with an emphasis upon the possibility of changing law in terms of rational considerations of social utility (rather than freezing it in terms of Stage 4 "law and order"). Outside the legal realm, free agreement and contract is the binding element of obligation. This is the "official" morality of the American government and constitution.

Stage 6: The universal-ethical-principle orientation. Right is defined by the decision of conscience in accord with self-chosen ethical principles appealing to logical comprehensiveness, universality, and consistency. These principles are abstract and *ethical* (the Golden Rule, the categorical imperative); they are not concrete moral rules like the Ten Commandments. At heart, these are universal principles of *justice*, of the *reciprocity* and *equality* of human *rights*, and of respect for the dignity of human beings as *individual persons*.

Given that people have the psychological capacity to progress to higher (and therefore more adequate) stages of moral reasoning, the aim of education ought to be the personal development of students toward more complex ways of reasoning. This philosophical argument is based on the earlier contributions of John Dewey:

> The aim of education is growth or development, both intellectual and moral. Ethical and psychological principles can aid the school in the greatest of all constructions—the building of a free

and powerful character. Only knowledge of the order and connection of stages in psychological development can insure this.
Education is the work of supplying the conditions which will enable the psychological functions to mature in the freest and
fullest manner.

Like Piaget, Dewey's idea of development does not reflect an
increase in the content of thinking (e.g., cultural values) but
instead, a qualitative transformation in the form of the
child's thought or action. This distinction has been elaborated elsewhere by D. Boyd and Kohlberg:

What we examine in our work has to do with form rather than
content. We are not describing or classifying what people think is
right or wrong in situations of moral conflict, for example,
whether draft-evading exiles should be given amnesty or thrown
in prison if and when they return to this country, or even changes
in what individuals think as they grow older. Nor are we assuming that we can specify a certain behavioral response as necessarily "moral" (in the descriptive or category sense, as distinguished
from non-moral), for example, "cheating," and then discuss
moral-development in terms of the frequency with which individuals engage in this behavior as they grow older, perhaps in
different kinds of situations ranging from spelling tests to income
tax. As distinguished from either of these two avenues of research that might be said to be dealing with moral content, our
work focuses on the cognitive structures which underlie such
content and give it its claim to the category "moral," where
"structure" refers to "the general characteristics of shape, pattern
or organization of response rather than to the rate of intensity of
response or its pairing with particular stimuli," and "cognitive
structure" refers to "rules for processing information or for con-
necting experienced events." From our point of view it is not any
artificially specified set of responses, or degree of intensity of
such responses, which characterizes morality as an area of study.
Rather, it is the cognitive moral structurings, or the organized
systems of assumptions and rules about the nature of moral-
conflict situations which give such situations their meaning, that
constitute the objects of our developmental study.

Based on this crucial difference between form and content, the
aim of moral education should be to stimulate people's thinking ability over time in ways which will enable them to use

more adequate and complex reasoning patterns to solve moral problems. The principle central to the development of stages of moral judgment, and hence to proposals for moral education, is that of *justice*. Justice, the primary regard for the value and equality of all human beings and for reciprocity in human relations, is a basic and universal standard. Using justice as the organizing principal for moral education meets the following criteria: It guarantees freedom of belief; it employs a philosophically justifiable concept of morality, and it is based on the psychological facts of human development. The stages may be seen as representing increasingly adequate conceptions of justice and as reflecting an expanding capacity for empathy, for taking the role of the other. And in the end the two are the same thing because the most just solution is the one which takes into account the positions or rights of all the individuals involved. The expansion of empathy thus, in turn, leads to an expansion of points of view and this expansion defines the three levels of moral judgment into which the six stages subdivide.

At the first or preconventional level the individual sees moral dilemmas in terms of the individual needs of the people involved. Situations of moral conflict are seen as situations in which needs collide and are resolved either in terms of who has the most power in the situation (Stage 1) or in terms of simple individual responsibility for one's own welfare (Stage 2) except where bound by simple market-place notions of reciprocity.

These formulations are perfectly consonant with the child's experience. For a young child power is perhaps the most salient characteristic of his social world (Stage 1) and as he learns to see conflicts between conformity to power and individual interests, he shifts to a notion of right as serving individual interests. However, as the child becomes increasingly involved in mutual relationships and sees himself as a sharing and participating member of groups, he sees the individual point of view toward morality as inadequate to deal with the kinds of moral conflicts which confront him. He has then two choices: he can hold on to his preconventional philosophy and simplify experience, or he can expand his philosophy so that it can take into account the expanding complexity of his experience.

The second two stages of moral development are termed "conventional" in that moral conflicts are now seen and resolved in group or social terms rather than in individual terms. Right or justice is seen to reside in interpersonal social relationships (Stage 3) or in the community (Stage 4). At the conventional levels there is an appeal to authority but the authority derives its right to define the good not from greater power at Stage 1, but from its social sharedness and legitimacy.

However, if society defines the right and the good, what is one to think when one recognizes that different societies choose differently in what they label as good and bad, right and wrong? Eskimos think it is right to leave old people out in the snow to die. When abortions were illegal in this country, they were legal in Sweden. With the increasing exposure of everyone to how others live, there is a greater recognition of the fact that our way is only one among many.

If one cannot simply equate the right with the societal and the legal, then what is one to do? We have found that adolescents may go through a period of ethical relativism during which they question the premises of any moral system. If there are many ways to live, who can presume to say which is best? Perhaps everyone should do as he or she chooses.

The way out of this moral relativism or moral nihilism lies through the perception that underneath the rules of any given society lie moral principles and universal moral rights, and the validity of any moral choice rests on the principles that choice embodies. Such moral principles are universal in their application and constitute a viable standard against which the particular laws or conventions of any society can and should be judged. When obedience to laws violates moral principles or rights, it is right to violate such laws.

At the last two stages, then, choice is based on the principles that supercede convention, just as previously the claims of society or convention were seen as the grounds for adjudicating differences between individuals. This, then, is the sequence of moral development.

What spurs progress from one stage to another and why do some individuals reach the principled stages while others do not? Moral judgment, while primarily a rational operation, is influenced by affective factors such as the ability to empathize and the capacity for guilt. But moral situations are defined cognitively by the judging individual in social interactions. It is this interaction with one's environment which determines development of moral reasoning.

Social interaction requires the assumption of a variety of roles and the entering into a variety of reciprocal relationships. Such relationships demand that one take others' perspectives (role-taking). It is this reworking of one's role-taking experiences into successively more complex and adequate forms of justice which is called moral development. Thus moral development results from the dialogue between the person's cognitive structure and the complexity presented by environment. This interactionist definition of moral development demands an environment which will facilitate dialogue between the self and others. The more one encounters situations of moral conflict that are not adequately resolved by one's present reasoning structure, the more likely one is to develop more complex ways of thinking about and resolving such conflicts.

We have stressed in this "theory" the concern for what is right, what is just or fair. To ask "what is right?" or "what ought I do in this situation?" presumes that notions of what is "good" are in conflict. But, according to Boyd and Kohlberg,

> We are not describing how men formulate different conceptions of the good, the good life, intrinsic value, or purpose. Nor are we discussing how men develop certain kinds of character traits and learn to recognize these traits in judgments of approbation and disapprobation. Instead, we are concentrating on that aspect of morality that is brought to the fore by problematic situations of conflicting claims, whether the conflict is between individuals, groups, societies, or institutions, and whether the source of the conflict lies in incompatible claims based on conceptions of the good, beliefs about human purpose, or character assessments. In short, we intend the term "moral" to be understood in the restricted sense of referring to situations which call for judgments involving denotological concepts such as right and wrong, duty and obligation, having a right, fairness, etc., although such judgments may (or may not) involve either or both of the other two basic concepts or their derivatives.

This is not to say that questions of "good" are less important or need not to be asked. Rather it is an acknowledgement that the cognitive developmental approach is limited in scope and requires that attention be paid to such issues in the development of any moral education program.

The relationship between moral judgment and moral behavior is not fully defined. That is, moral judgment is a necessary but not sufficient condition for moral action. Other variables come into play such as emotion, and a general sense of will, purpose or ego strength. Moral judgment is the only distinctive *moral* factor in moral behavior but not the only factor in such behavior. Educators who are looking for answers as to how to "get children to behave" often meaning to rid themselves of discipline problems will not find *the* answer in one theory. We hypothesize that behavior when informed by mature moral judgment is influenced by level of moral development. Further research in this crucial area is needed.

Development Occurs Through Imitation

ALBERT BANDURA

Stanford psychologist Albert Bandura began his career as a clinical psychologist but quickly changed his career direction to research and studying the role of imitation in child development. Bandura's Social Learning Theory has been referred to by a variety of different titles including vicarious or observational learning, modeling, or imitation. Regardless of the labels, Bandura's basic theory posits that a child develops by way of interaction and social and cognitive forces. That is, children learn by watching the actions of others and the end results of those actions. Bandura is best known for his research on imitative behavior of children exposed to aggressive models. He showed that children who watched a model attack an inflated "Bobo Doll" imitated that behavior with the doll later. Bandura's research has generated many studies on the transference of dysfunctional family patterns across generations and the effects of television violence on children.

QUESTIONS
1. How do consequences of a model's behavior influence the acquisition of such behaviors in children, according to Bandura?

Abridged from "The Role of Imitation in Personality Development" by Albert Bandura, *The Journal of Nursery Education* 18 (no. 3, April 1963):207-15. Reprinted with permission of the author.

2. What evidence does Bandura offer to support his notion of imitation?

3. How do the behaviors acquired through imitation differ from those acquired through more traditional learning theories (i.e., operant theories of reinforcement and punishment or classical theories of association)?

4. If Bandura's theory is correct, what implications would it have on current styles of child rearing? What implications would it have on our criminal justice system? On the media?

■ ■ ■

I remember reading a story reported by Professor Mowrer about a lonesome farmer who decided to get a parrot for company. After acquiring the bird, the farmer spent many long evenings teaching the parrot the phrase, "Say Uncle." Despite the devoted tutorial attention, the parrot proved totally unresponsive and finally, the frustrated farmer got a stick and struck the parrot on the head after each refusal to produce the desired phrase.

But the visceral method proved no more effective than the cerebral one, so the farmer grabbed his feathered friend and tossed him in the chicken house. A short time later the farmer heard a loud commotion in the chicken house and, upon investigation, found that the parrot was pommeling the startled chickens on the head with a stick and shouting, "Say Uncle!" "Say Uncle!"

While this story is not intended as an introduction to a treatise on parrot-training practices, it provides a graphic illustration of the process of social learning that I shall discuss in this paper.

One can distinguish two kinds of processes by which children acquire attitudes, values, and patterns of social behavior. First, the learning that occurs on the basis of direct tuition or instrumental training. In this form of learning, parents and other socializing agents are relatively explicit about what they wish the child to learn, and attempt to shape his behavior through rewarding and punishing consequences.

Although a certain amount of socialization of a child takes place through such direct training, personality patterns are primarily acquired through the child's active imitation of parental attitudes and behavior, most of which the parents have never directly attempted to teach. Indeed, parental modeling behavior may often counteract the effects of their direct training. When a parent punishes his child physically for having aggressed toward peers, for example, the intended outcome of this training is that the child should refrain from hitting others. The child, however, is also learning from parental demonstration how to aggress physically, and this imitative learning may provide the direction for the child's behavior when he is similarly frustrated in subsequent social interactions.

Research on imitation demonstrates that, unlike the relatively slow process of instrumental training, when a model is provided, patterns of behavior are rapidly acquired in large segments or in their entirety. The pervasiveness of this form of learning is also clearly evident in naturalistic observations of children's play in which they frequently reproduce the entire parental role-behavior including the appropriate mannerisms, voice inflections and attitudes, much to the parents' surprise and embarrassment. Although the process whereby a person reproduces the behavior exhibited by real-life or symbolized models is generally labeled "identification" in theories of personality, I shall employ the term imitation because it encompasses the same behavioral phenomenon, and avoids the elusiveness and surplus meanings that have come to be associated with the former concept.

Let us now consider a series of experiments that both illustrates the process of learning through imitation, and identifies some of the factors which serve to enhance or to reduce the occurrence of imitative behavior.

One set of experiments was designed primarily to determine the extent to which aggression can be transmitted to children through exposure to aggressive adult models. One group of children observed an aggressive model who exhibited relatively novel forms of physical and verbal aggression toward a large inflated plastic doll; a second group viewed the same model behave in a very subdued and inhibited manner, while children in a control group had no exposure to any models. Half the children in each of the experimental conditions observed models of the same sex as themselves, and the remaining children in each group witnessed opposite sex models.

This investigation was later extended in order to compare the effects of real-life and film-mediated or televised aggressive models on children's behavior. Children in the human film-aggression group viewed a movie showing the same adults, who had served as models in the earlier experiment, portraying the novel aggressive acts toward the inflated doll. For children in the cartoon-aggression groups, a film in which the female model costumed as a cartoon cat exhibiting the aggressive behavior toward the plastic doll was projected on a glass lenscreen in a television console.

After exposure to their respective models all children, including those in the control group, were mildly frustrated and tested for the amount of imitative and non-imitative aggression.

The results of these experiments leave little doubt that exposure to aggressive models heightens children's aggressive responses to subsequent frustration. . . . Children who observed the aggressive models exhibited approximately twice as much aggression than did subjects in the non-aggressive model group or the control group. In addition, children who witnessed the subdued non-aggressive model displayed the inhibited behavior characteristic of their model and expressed significantly less aggression than the control children.

Some evidence that the influence of models is partly determined by the sex appropriateness of their behavior is provided by the finding that the aggressive male model was a more powerful stimulus for aggression than the aggressive female model. Some of the children, particularly the boys, commented spontaneously on the fact that the female model's behavior was out of character (e.g., "That's no way for a lady to behave. Ladies are supposed to act like ladies . . .").

In contrast, aggression by the male model was generally viewed as appropriate and approved by both the boys ("Al's a good socker, he beat up Bobo. I want to sock like Al.") and the girls ("That man is a strong fighter. He punched and punched, and he could hit Bobo right down to the floor and if Bobo got up he said, 'Punch your nose'. He's a good fighter like Daddy.").

The data furthermore reveal that aggressive models are highly influential not only in reducing children's inhibitions over aggression, but also in shaping the form of their behavior. Children who observed the aggressive models displayed a great number of precisely imitative aggressive acts, whereas, such responses rarely occurred in either the non-aggressive model group or the control group. . . .

Although the children were somewhat less inclined to imitate precisely the cartoon character than the real-life aggressive model, all three experimental conditions—real-life, film-mediated, and cartoon aggressive models—produced equivalent increases in overall aggressive behavior based on a variety of measures of both imitative and non-imitative aggression.

The finding that film-mediated models are as effective as real-life models in eliciting and transmitting aggressive responses indicates that televised models may serve as important sources of behavior and can no longer be ignored in conceptualizations of personality development. Indeed, most youngsters probably have more exposure to prestigeful televised male models than to their own fathers. With further advances in mass media and audiovisual technology, pictorially presented models, mainly through television, are likely to play an increasingly influential role in shaping personality patterns, and in modifying attitudes and social norms.

It has been widely assumed on the basis of psychoanalytic theory and other hydraulic energy models of personality, that children's vicarious participation in film-mediated aggression or the direct expression of aggressive behavior will serve to discharge "pent-up energies" and affects. Guided by this catharsis hypothesis, many parents, educators and mental health workers encourage hyperaggressive children to participate in aggressive recreational activities, to view highly aggressive televised programs, and to aggress in psychotherapeutic playrooms and other permissive settings.

In contrast to this "drainage" view, social learning theory would predict that the provision of aggressive models and the inadvertent positive reinforcement of aggression, which inevitably occurs during the encouragement of cathartic expressions, are exceedingly effective procedures for enhancing aggressive response tendencies. It is not surprising, therefore, that studies in which children or adolescents have been exposed to film-mediated aggressive models have uniformly demonstrated that vicarious participation in aggressive activity increases, rather than decreases, aggressive behavior.

On the other hand, providing aggressive children with examples of alternative constructive ways of coping with interpersonal frustration has been found to be highly successful in modifying aggressive-domineering personality patterns. Additional comparisons of social theory and the traditional approaches to personality development will be presented later.

It is apparent that children do not reproduce the personality characteristics of every model with whom they come into contact, nor do they imitate every element of behavior exhibited even by models whom they may have selected as their primary sources of social behavior. The experiments that I shall discuss in the remaining sections of this viewpoint are mainly concerned with some of the psychological variables determining the selection of models, and the degree to which their behavior will be imitated.

Response Consequences to the Model and Imitation

The manner in which rewarding or punishing consequences to the model's behavior influences imitation is demonstrated in an experiment in which nursery school children observed either an aggressive model rewarded, an aggressive model punished, or had no exposure to the models. The models were two adults presented to the children on film projected into a television console.

In the aggression-rewarded condition, Rocky, the aggressive model appropriates all of Johnny's attractive play possessions and tasty food stuffs through aggressive-domineering means. The film shown to the children in the aggression-punished condition was identical with that shown to the aggression-rewarded group except for a slight rearrangement of the film sequence so the aggression exhibited by Rocky resulted in his being severely punished by Johnny. Following exposure to the models the children were tested for the incidence of post-exposure aggressive behavior.

Children who observed Rocky's aggressive behavior rewarded readily imitated his physical and verbal aggression, whereas, children who saw him punished exhibited relatively little imitative behavior and did not differ from a group of control children who had no exposure to the models.

At the conclusion of the experiment each child was asked to evaluate the behavior of Rocky and Johnny, and to select the character he preferred to emulate. These data yielded some interesting and surprising findings. As might be expected, children who observed Rocky's aggressive behavior punished both failed to reproduce his behavior and rejected him as a model for emulation.

On the other hand, when Rocky's aggression was highly successful in amassing rewarding resources, he was chosen by most of the children as the preferred model for imitation. The surprising finding, however, is that without exception these children were highly critical of his behavior (e.g., "Rocky is harsh" . . . "Rough and bossy" . . . "Mean" . . . "Wicked" . . . "He whack people" . . .).

It was evident from the children's comments that the successful payoff of aggression rather than its intrinsic desirability served as the primary basis for emulation (e.g., "Rocky beat Johnny and chase him and get all the good toys" . . . "He came and snatched Johnny's toys. Get a lot of toys . . ."). The children resolved the conflict by derogating the unfortunate victim, apparently as justification for Rocky's exploitive-assaultive behavior. They criticized Johnny for his inability to control Rocky ("He's a cry baby. Didn't know how to make Rocky mind."), for his miserliness ("If he'd shared right in the beginning, Rocky might have played nice."), and generally described him as, "Sulky," "Mean," and "Sort of dumb."

This study clearly demonstrates the way rewarding consequences to the model's behavior may outweigh the value systems of the observers—children readily adopted successful modeling behavior even though they had labeled it objectionable, morally reprehensible, and publicly criticized the model for engaging in such behavior.

In many televised and other mass media presentations antisocial models amass considerable rewarding resources through devious means but are punished following the last commercial on the assumption that the punishment ending will erase or counteract the learning of the model's antisocial behavior.

The findings from a recently completed experiment reveal that, although punishment administered to a model tends to inhibit children's performance of the modeled behavior, it has virtually no influence on the occurrence of imitative learning. In this experiment children observed a film-mediated aggressive model who was severely punished in one condition of the experiment, generously rewarded in a second condition, while the third condition presented no response-consequences to the model.

Consistent with the findings cited earlier, a post-exposure test of imitative behavior showed that children who observed the punished model performed significantly fewer imitative responses than children in the model-rewarded and the no-consequence groups. Children in all three groups were then offered attractive incentives contingent on their reproducing the model's behavior. The introduction of the rewards completely wiped out the previously observed performance differences, revealing an equivalent amount of learning among the children in the model-rewarded, model-punished and the no-consequences groups. Similarly, girls exhibited approximately as much imitative aggression as did the boys.

It might be concluded from these findings that exposure of children to punished antisocial or other types of models is likely to result in little overt imitative behavior. Nevertheless, the observed behavior is learned and may be exhibited on future occasions given the appropriate instigations, the instruments necessary for performing the imitative acts, and the prospect of sufficiently attractive positive rewards contingent on the successful execution of the behavior. . . .

Laboratory data have failed to support predictions derived from several widely accepted psychoanalytic principles of personality development. Research generated by modern social learning theory also raises some questions about the validity of stage theories that typically depict the developmental process as involving a relatively spontaneous emergence of age-specific modes of behavior as the child passes from one stage to another. According to Piaget's theory of moral development, for example, one can distinguish two clear-cut stages of moral orientations demarcated from each other at approximately seven years of age.

In the first stage, defined as objective morality, children judge the gravity of a deviant act in terms of the amount of material damages, and disregard the intentionality of the action. By contrast, during the second or subjective morality stage, children judge conduct in terms of its intent rather than its material consequences. The sequence and timing of these stages are presumably predetermined and, consequently, young children are incapable of adopting a subjective orientation while objective moral judgments are rarely encountered in older children.

However, in an experiment designed to study the influence of models in transmitting and modifying children's moral judgments, objective and subjective moral judgments were found to exist together rather than as successive developmental stages. The vast majority of young children were capable of exercising subjective judgments and most of the older children displayed varying degrees of objective morality.

Children who exhibited predominantly objective and subjective moral orientations were then selected and exposed to adult models who consistently expressed moral judgments that ran counter to the children's orientations. The provision of models was highly effective in altering the children's moral judgments. Objective children modified their moral orientations toward subjectivity and, similarly, subjective children became considerably more objective in their judgmental behavior. Furthermore, the children maintained their altered orientations in a new test situation in the absence of the models. It is highly probable that other personality characteristics generally viewed as predetermined age-specific phenomena can also be readily altered through the application of appropriate social learning principles.

Despite the voluminous clinical and theoretical literature pertaining to child development, the available body of empirically verified knowledge is comparatively meagre. The recent years, however, have witnessed a new direction in theorizing about the developmental process, which has generated considerable laboratory research within the framework of social learning theory. These studies are beginning to yield relatively unambiguous statements about the influence of particular antecedent events on the behavior and attitudes of children. This approach evidently holds promise of providing both more reliable guidelines for educational practice, and the type of evidence necessary for discarding procedures that prove to be ineffective in, or even a hindrance to, the successful realization of desired developmental, educational and psychotherapeutic objectives.

Does Nurture or Nature Drive Psychological Disorders?

Chapter Preface

A single debate lies at the center of the study of abnormal behaviors: Are psychological disorders environmental or biological in origin? This debate, sometimes termed the nurture or nature debate, is likely the oldest and most controversial topic in the field of psychology in general and with psychological disorders specifically. The debates are set in terms of questions. Are gender roles a product of nurture or nature? Is depression biological or psychological? Should we use psychotherapy or drug therapy to treat certain illnesses? Is homosexuality genetic or environmental? And the list continues. Most often the debate is heated and both sides can provide "proof" of their respective stance. Generally most scholars believe that a complex calculus of both environmental and biological forces is to blame. But for the most part, the argument continues to question the relative weight of each. The viewpoints in this chapter are examples of the continuing controversy in the nurture/nature area.

Alcoholism Is a Disease

IRVING MALTZMAN

Irving Maltzman, a professor from the University of California at Los Angeles, has done extensive research on alcoholism. Here, Maltzman presents the typical argument for the medical model of alcoholism. He contends, like so many others who do work in this area, that alcoholism is a disease characterized by inability to control excessive drinking patterns. Maltzman argues that controlled drinking programs for alcoholics have been unsuccessful in their efforts to treat alcoholism and that the only appropriate treatment for this syndrome is abstinence based treatment programs.

QUESTIONS

1. According to Maltzman, how does the characterization of alcoholism as a disease differ from characterization of alcoholism as hereditary?
2. What requirements must a behavior meet in order for it to be characterized as a disease?
3. Does Maltzman give support for his depiction of alcoholism as a disease?

Irving Maltzman, "Is Alcoholism a Disease?" *Integrative and Behavioral Science* 26 (no. 3, 1991): 200-210. Copyright 1991, Transaction. Reprinted by permission of the publisher.

4. According to Maltzman what are the problems with treatment programs that emphasize controlled drinking?

■ ■ ■

The concept of alcoholism as a disease can be profitably considered in the light of bio-behavioral research that has enlarged the view of disease from the limited focus on cellular and tissue pathology to include disturbances of function in the whole biopsycho-social range.

Conditions Necessary for Classification as "Disease"

1. There must be a syndrome, a lawful pattern of observable recurring signs and symptoms. Ascriptions of "disease" have been applied to syndromes in the absence of a known etiology for centuries. Malaria was considered a disease before it was known that it is caused by a parasite transmitted by the bite of a mosquito and before its treatment by quinine was known. Cancer is considered a disease despite a lack of knowledge of the etiology of many cancers. The same has been true of AIDS. Knowledge of etiology and an effective treatment are not preconditions for labelling a syndrome a disease. The lawful pattern of observed signs and symptoms *is* the disease. The ontological status of disease, the notion that there is a process with an independent existence that causes the observed signs and symptoms was rejected by Pyrrho the skeptic in approximately 300 B.C.

2. The syndrome must represent a significant deviation from a norm, standard, or ideal of health. If a syndrome is life-threatening, it is a disease. If a syndrome is judged not to be a serious threat to health, it is not labelled a disease. Malaria, cancer, AIDS, alcoholism, are serious, life-threatening diseases, as well as syndromes.

Genetic influences do not necessarily make a syndrome a disease. For example, eye color is genetically determined. But it is not a disease, for two reasons. It is not a syndrome and it is not injurious to health. That alcoholism or certain forms of alcoholism may have genetic influences does not by itself make it a disease. It must constitute a syndrome and the clinical evidence must lead to the judgment that the syndrome is injurious.

E.M. Jellinek, who began his career as a biometrician, apparently arrived at his disease concept of alcoholism after examining the questionnaire results obtained from 2000 members of Alcoholics Anonymous (AA).

Jellinek defined alcoholism as a condition where the ingestion of alcohol causes damage to oneself or to others. Damage may be interpersonal, social, as well as bio-behavioral. Alcoholism is distinguished from other kinds of behavior that may deviate from the average by the fact that it is destructive to all aspects of a person's well being and that it occupies a central part of one's life. Herbert Fingarette, in considering alcoholism nothing more than a central way of life no different from an absorbing hobby, misses this critical characteristic that distinguishes the alcoholism syndrome from other, mainly benign, lifestyles.

Implicit in Jellinek's definition is the notion that alcoholism is a bio-psychosocial disease. For years, diseases have been recognized as having psychosocial determinants. In recent years this view has flowered, as evidenced, for example, in the new discipline of psychoneuroimmunology.

Jellinek distinguished problem drinkers or simply alcohol abusers from alcoholics. He found that alcoholism, as distinct from alcohol abuse, was characterized by a progression of alcohol consumption and by signs and symptoms of tolerance, withdrawal, craving, and inability to consistently control the initiation of drinking, as well as inability to consistently refrain from drinking to a state of inebriation once starting to drink. The latter characteristics are especially critical in differentiating the onset of the disease syndrome from problem drinking.

Ground for Classifying Alcoholism as a Disease Syndrome

The signs and symptoms:

Jellinek (1952), from a questionnaire applied to approximately 2000 alcoholics who were members of Alcoholics Anonymous, listed 43 symptoms that appeared with regularity in four progressive phases: (a) the prealcoholic phase of social drinking, (b) the prodromal phase of preclinical symptoms, that is, the phase of problem drinking, of alcohol abuse, (c) the crucial phase marked by the loss of control over drinking, and finally, (d) the chronic phase of alcoholism marked by extended periods of continuous inebriation.

Jellinek's sequence has been confirmed by systematic studies by Piazza and Wise, in 1988; and Pokorny and Kanas, in 1980. The latter investigators administered Jellinek's questionnaire as well as additional items to 53 male non-alcoholic but drinking control patients who had never been treated for alcoholism as well as a group of 102 male patients in an inpatient alcoholism treatment program in the same VA hospital as the control group. Upon review, 19 of the original comparison group patients were reclassified as a borderline group as distinguished from the remaining "pure" control group of 34 men. However, they found that following conversion of "mean age of onset (of a symptom) and Jellinek's order to ranks (1 to 27), the rank order correlation coefficient between the two was .74". The authors further note:

> The idea of a progression, a typical succession of symptoms is certainly a familiar one in relation to diseases. Even acute illnesses typically have an incubation period, prodromal or early signs of symptoms, an acute phase, perhaps a crisis or turning point, resolution phase and a convalescent phase, possibly ending with residuals . . . but it is not expected that every patient will have all of them or that they will always follow a particular order.

Criticisms of the Disease Concept

Conceptual. Denials by some that alcoholism is a disease on the basis that its cause is not known and that there is no generally effective treatment, have no merit since some of the most deadly diseases fail to meet those criteria.

Empirical. Critics have cited three kinds of evidence purportedly contrary to the treatment implication of the alcoholism syndrome and loss of control, the necessity of abstinence for alcoholics.

1. They assert that considerable evidence indicates that alcoholics revert to social drinking in appreciable numbers following treatment for abstinence, and there is good evidence

that alcoholics can be trained to attain a goal of moderate, controlled drinking.

2. They deny that there is good evidence that treatment with abstinence as a goal works for appreciable numbers of alcoholics.

3. They report experimental laboratory studies examining implications of the loss of control with purportedly superior methodological features and a currently popular "expectancy" interpretation of alcohol-related behaviors. These studies purportedly show that "psychological" factors are more important than the pharmacological properties of alcohol in influencing the ingestion of alcohol. More importantly, they purport to demonstrate that alcoholics show no loss of control over drinking as the result of the ingestion of alcohol.

We will briefly examine each of these criticisms of the alcoholism disease syndrome in turn.

A paper by D. L. Davies was the first widely cited study apparently contradicting the concept that abstinence was the only viable treatment goal and outcome for alcoholics. Davies followed up seven men from a group of 93 who had undergone behavioral therapy for seven to eleven years. At the time of his study, those seven were reported as able to engage in moderate, asymptomatic drinking. There was no further follow up until Edwards restudied the original seven patients. He found that five of the seven "experienced significant drinking problems both during Davies' original follow-up period and, subsequently, that three of these five at some time also used psychotropic drugs heavily, and that the two remaining subjects (one of whom was never severely dependent on alcohol) engaged in trouble-free drinking over the total period." It is now apparent that success for one out of 93 alcoholic patients cannot provide the basis for proposing moderate drinking as a viable treatment goal for alcoholics.

A similar reassessment has been suffered by Sobell and Sobell. The Sobells' study initially had enormous impact because it purported to be a carefully controlled experiment with subjects randomly assigned to experimental and control groups and with follow-up interviews every three to four weeks providing detailed quantitative outcome results for two full years. Each interview purportedly determined the daily drinking disposition of the subject since the last interview. The Sobells reported striking success for controlled-drinking training: 85% of the subjects functioning well 85% of the days in the last six months of the second-year follow up.

However, an independent follow up of these patients found that the original results could not be sustained. Patients who had purportedly engaged in controlled drinking were found not to have been functioning well five to ten years later or even at the time of the original assessment. A study by Foy, Nunn, and Rychtarik, later followed up by Rychtarik, Foy, Scott, Lokey, and Prue, is the best designed experimental study of controlled drinking in chronic alcoholic patients to date. They assigned patients in an alcoholism treatment unit at random either to traditional abstinence treatment or the traditional treatment plus controlled-drinking skills training. A double-blind follow up was performed by an independent team of assessors. After five to six years, there was no evidence of effective controlled-drinking training. An interesting sidelight of this study is the frequency with which the results have been misinterpreted as indicating the equal effectiveness of abstinence and controlled-drinking training. This interpretation is faulty because both groups of similar patients had received abstinence training, but only one of them had received controlled-drinking skills in addition. Results were the same in both groups.

The first Rand Report is in many ways the best known study purporting to show that large numbers of individuals treated for alcoholism can return to moderate drinking. This work attracted a great deal of attention because it reported an unusually high success rate for treatment—70%. It also purported to show that a surprisingly large percentage of patients treated at alcoholism facilities supported by government funds returned to normal drinking following treatment. As many patients relapsed at eighteen months who had been drinking normally at six months as the number of patients who had been abstaining at six months. Abstention, the traditional treatment goal, showed no advantage over normal drinking. But Armor, Polich and Stambul, defined normal drinking as the average daily consumption of approximately six shots of whiskey or a six-pack of beer and less than approximately ten shots on a typical day. In addition, there must be no tremors and less than three frequently occurring symptoms.

The criterion employed by Armor, Polich, and Stambul is too high. Someone without a high degree of alcohol tolerance, someone without a drinking problem, could not function effectively, maintain good health, and be drinking the large amounts defined by Armor, et al., as normal. Cala, for example, reports that CT scans show that regular alcohol consumption of little more than two drinks per day over the long term may, in an appreciable number of people, produce evidence of brain atrophy on CT scan that is only partially reversible. These and other shortcomings in the Rand Report have generally been ignored by its supporters.

Carefully conducted studies by others have found that dependent, chronic alcoholics revert to moderate drinking so infrequently that it cannot be taken as a viable treatment goal. Taylor, Helzer, and Robins reviewed outcome studies of the occurrence of moderate drinking in ex-alcoholics published since the 1976 Rand Report. They concluded that in large studies with a large evaluation window, approximately 3% is the rate of return to moderate drinking.

Walker randomly selected 100 cases from among 1000 consecutive admissions for alcoholism inpatient treatment directed toward abstinence in a New Zealand hospital. Follow-up time varied from 8 to 12.5 years.

Forty were recovered clinically and socially. Twenty-eight had total sobriety for $2\frac{1}{2}$-12 years. Twelve had lapses of less than seven days in any year but had maintained their health and social situation. Their self assessment for happiness and achievement was eight on a scale of 0-10.

This study group of survivors shows a 40% recovery rate if it is assumed that none of the unknown and overseas group have recovered—although it is possible that some have. Some of the dead were known to be recovered at the time of death so that the recovery rate actually exceeded 40%.

With respect to controlled-drinking outcomes, "Considering all the multiple reports it is unlikely that more than . . . two people (2%) had in fact become moderate stable drinkers".

Walker concludes, "A return to social drinking for alcoholics is so rarely an achievable goal that it has no place in a normal treatment plan". This conclusion is in keeping with the similar results reported by Helzer, et al., who found that 1.6% of 1289 alcoholics followed up 5.7 years after treatment were engaged in stable moderate drinking.

Abstinence Treatment Outcomes

Successful treatment outcomes will vary greatly with the treatment facility for many reasons, including the severity of dependence of the patient population and the socioeconomic class of the patients. Following treatment, will patients return to a family, job, school, a support system, or are they homeless and will return to the street? How extensive and intensive is the treatment program, aftercare, and involvement of the family? Many of the treatment outcome evaluations and surveys do not characterize the facilities evaluated or the nature of the treatment—whether it is any more than detoxification, for example. Most reviews of treatment outcome deal only with public facilities that vary greatly in the above characteristics. Such surveys do not include private treatment facilities such as Hazelden which has served as a benchmark for treatment in North America. Facilities of this kind usually employ the "12-step" programs incorporating precepts of Alcoholics Anonymous, but are also multimodal, often including individual, group, and family counseling, problem-solving skills training, assertion training and relaxation training, etc. Treatment outcome evaluations of such facilities conducted by "an independent evaluation service reported 58%, 55%, and 71% abstinence rates with samples of 2452, 398, and 390 cases, respectively". High abstinence rates for treatment outcomes are not limited to "12-step" programs. Shick Shadel Hospital, which employs classical counter-conditioning of nausea, aversion conditioning, as part of a multimodal treatment program, has also obtained a relatively high rate of abstinence; 63% for one year when noncontacted subjects are included as failures. These private programs, some of which have been in existence for many years, report a higher success rate than the few demonstration projects that have attempted to train comparable socially stable middle class clients to return to moderate drinking. The superiority of abstinence over controlled-drinking training when North American patient populations are of comparable socioeconomic class and social stability needs to be noted.

Experimental Evaluations of Loss of Control

It is difficult to obtain field data relevant to the critical characteristic of loss of control over drinking because of the large time interval and the intimate knowledge of the behavior of the participant needed in order to test the hypothesis that alcoholics cannot consistently refuse to drink or refrain from inebriation if they start to drink. An alternative approach is to obtain indirect evidence from different sources which confirms or refutes implications of the hypothesis that loss of control is a crucial characteristic of alcoholics as distinguished from nonalcoholic problem drinkers and others. One such attempt has been the use of priming or preloading experiments. Provide a small amount of alcohol to participants and determine whether or not the initial dose stimulates—primes—excessive drinking when further alcohol is provided.

Marlatt, Demming, and Reid employed a double balanced-placebo design where half the subjects received alcohol and half received tonic water in an attempt to test the loss of control hypothesis. Half of each of these two groups were told they received alcohol and half were told they received only tonic water. These treatments were administered to a group of social drinkers and a group of purported alcoholics. In other words, it was a 2×2×2 design, a double balanced-placebo design. For both groups of subjects an instruction effect was obtained but not an alcohol effect. Subjects who were told they drank alcohol subsequently drank more alcohol than subjects who were told they drank tonic—regardless of what they initially drank.

There are several serious inadequacies in this widely cited study.

1. There is no measure of severity of dependence for the subjects classified as alcoholics; we do not know whether they are problem drinkers who would not be expected to lose control over alcohol or alcoholics who would. Insufficient criteria were used for selecting "alcoholics," for example,

drunk driving arrests. Problem drinkers as well as alcoholics may be arrested for drunk driving, etc.

2. It is an analogue experiment. It presents no evidence that subjects told they received alcohol actually drank to a stupor in the experiment or that subjects given alcohol in the experiment did not drink to stupor after they left the experiment.

3. There is an alternative, reasonable interpretation of the results. The obtained results can be interpreted as due to demand characteristics. Because of the difference in status between experimenter and subject there is a tendency on the part of the subject to please the experimenter. Subjects try to produce the results ostensibly desired by the experimenter.

4. Results and interpretation of the Marlatt, Demming, and Reid study have been contradicted by other experiments that many authors have failed to cite in this connection.

Contrary evidence is provided by Hodgson, Rankin, and Stockwell who administered no dose, a low dose, or a high dose to alcoholics in the morning and then made alcohol available to them three hours later. Each subject participated in each of the conditions on different days. Prior to the start of the experiment the patients had been independently evaluated as either moderately or severely dependent upon alcohol. Qualitatively different effects were obtained between the groups judged as severely dependent and moderately dependent. An "appetizer" effect was obtained with the severely dependent alcoholics. The larger the priming dose in the morning, the more they drank three hours later. In contrast, a satiation effect was obtained with the moderately dependent alcoholics. The larger the priming dose of alcohol in the morning, the less they drank in the afternoon. Severity of dependence is not on a continuum, as some claim. Results obtained by Hodgson, Rankin, and Stockwell support Jellinek's interpretation that there is a qualitative difference between problem drinkers and alcoholics, between moderately and severely dependent alcoholics. It must be noted that both groups were in treatment for alcoholism. Status as a patient in treatment is not limited to gamma alcoholics. Independent measures of severity of dependence, diagnosis, is critical to establishing the necessary conditions providing a test of the loss of control hypothesis. Marlatt, Demming, and Reid did not provide these necessary conditions.

Another experiment was conducted, this time employing the balanced-placebo design. Results demonstrated that amount of alcohol ingested by severely dependent alcoholics in the test situation was only affected by alcohol in the priming dose, not by instructions; drinking in the test situation by moderately dependent alcoholics, in contrast, was affected by instructions—not by alcohol—in the priming situation. Results by Stockwell, et al. contradict the expectancy notion as it pertains to gamma alcoholics and supports Jellinek's hypothesis that loss of control is a characteristic of (gamma) alcoholics and not problem drinkers.

The above two experiments provide striking confirmation for Jellinek's distinction between problem drinkers and alcoholics as qualitatively different groups of drinkers. At the same time, the results contradict an expectancy notion as applied to gamma alcoholics and also contradicts the notion that problem drinking and gamma alcoholism lie on a continuum, differing only in the amount of alcohol consumed.

Another experiment that has been inadequately evaluated is the double balanced-placebo study by Berg, Laberg, Skutle, and Ohman. In a design similar to Marlatt, Demming, and Reid, a balanced-placebo procedure was employed with patients in treatment for alcoholism and a normal control group consisting of friends and acquaintances of the experimenters. The experiment was conducted in a social setting in the lounge of the hospital while the participants watched a soccer game on television. Results were that the patients showed an instructional, "expectancy," effect, but nonpatients from the community—friends of the experimenters—did not show an instruction, "expectancy," effect.

Our interpretation of their results is that hospital patients were susceptible to the demand characteristics of the experimental situation, whereas the control subjects—friends and acquaintances of the experimenters—were not.

Studies that have explicitly investigated demand vs. expectancy interpretations of the effects of instructions demonstrate that it is demand characteristics that can best account for the results. Demand interpretations are limited to the confines of the experiment and do not have the generality of an expectancy hypothesis which extrapolates these laboratory studies to the world beyond the laboratory. Implications of all of this is that the enormous significance attributed to the Marlatt, et al. experiment is misplaced.

Evidence Supporting the Loss of Control Hypothesis

But, if it is not a simple matter to experimentally investigate and explain "loss of control" drinking, and clinical observations require a large "window" and close observation of behavior—extremely difficult in a follow up—how can evidence be accumulated to test the hypothesis that loss of control is a characteristic of alcoholics? There are several indirect sources of evidence that are relevant. They provide considerable support for the loss of control conception as well as illuminating other aspects of alcoholic behavior.

Lemere made several astute observations in this regard. He states:

> Courville has recently published an excellent book on the neuropathologic findings in chronic alcoholics. . . . One of the more common, noteworthy effects of repeated alcoholic episodes or of chronic alcoholism from constant excessive drinking is a progressive atrophy of the cortex of the frontal lobes. This change affects specifically the convolutions of the dorsolateral surface of this lobe. This reaction to chronic alcoholism seems to be one resulting from the toxic effects of ethanol rather than malnutrition . . . irreversible cerebral pathology can be found in even young alcoholics in their thirties. . . . It is my opinion that brain damage from alcoholism is not only more common than is supposed, but that it also explains to a large extent the essential pathology of alcoholism, namely, the permanent loss of control over drinking. . . . It is also my belief that the gradual loss of control over alcohol, that is the history of most alcoholics, is often the result of a gradual whittling away of brain cells by excessive drinking. . . . It is interesting that the part of the brain which suffers the most from alcoholism is that part which subserves the highest cerebral functions of will power, judgment and control, namely the frontal lobes.

For example, Cala found that only 5% of alcoholics, patients in treatment for alcoholism, had a normal CT scan. The remainder all showed atrophy greater than that of control subjects of comparable age. Atrophy was generalized. But the frontal lobes were the most severely affected, followed by the temporal, parietal, and occipital lobes. Abstinence resulted in partial reversal of the atrophy. Even "normal" drinking of little more than one drink a day resulted in some atrophy, brain damage, which was partially reversed with abstinence, partial in that atrophy reversed to varying degree from complete to no reversal in different individuals. There were marked individual differences for which there is no current explanation. Some individuals drank large amounts of alcohol regularly, but still maintained a normal CT scan and normal psychometric results. Some light, social drinkers had more extensive atrophy than much heavier drinkers. There was overlap among different categories of drinkers. Amount of alcohol consumed was neither perfectly correlated with atrophy, reversal of atrophy or psychometric deficits, as compared to matched control subjects of comparable age.

Harper, Kril, and Daly obtained quantitative data from a human necropsy study which showed that the number of neurons in the superior frontal cortex of chronic alcoholic patients was significantly reduced compared to control subjects matched for age and gender. Patients with Wernicke's disease or cirrhosis of the liver showed greater loss of neurons in the frontal cortex than alcoholic patients without these diseases. But the latter also showed significant loss of neurons compared to matched controls. There were no differences between controls and the alcoholic subgroups in neuron counts in the motor cortex.

There are now methods of assessing activity in the frontal lobes—neuropsychologically and physiologically. Research by Weinberger and his colleagues have combined these different techniques by simultaneously recording regional cerebral blood flow (rCBF) during performance on the Wisconsin Card Sorting Test (WCST).

They show that a variety of learning and problem solving tasks, for example, Raven's Progressive Matrices and number matching, do not selectively or differentially involve the frontal lobes. Only the WCST has such an effect among the tasks investigated. The research literature indicates that increased percent perseverative errors on the WCST are related to dysfunction in the dorsolateral prefrontal cortex, a specific

171

region in the frontal lobes. Techniques are therefore now available to test the hypothesis that alcohol—which would affect the entire cortex—in addition, disproportionately or selectively, affects the dorsolateral prefrontal cortex.

Research in my laboratory demonstrated that a moderate dose of alcohol yields effects on the WCST that are consistent with an interpretation that alcohol may produce a differential disruption of frontal cortical inhibitory functions as well as possible nonspecific effects independent of beverage instructions or "expectancies." A selective increase in percent perseverative errors occurred in social drinkers under the influence of a moderate dose of alcohol. Reduced inhibition of perseverative tendencies may reflect disruption of more general functions mediated by the frontal cortex. Such "executive functions" include a wide range of behaviors related to planning, the verbal regulation of behavior, and the anticipation of future consequences of one's actions.

Implications of the above studies are that frontal lobe dysfunction may mediate some of the significant behavioral consequences of acute alcohol intoxication. Chronic frontal lobe dysfunction may be the basis for loss of control drinking central to the alcoholism disease syndrome. "Once an alcoholic always an alcoholic" may be true of those alcoholics in remission who have irreversible frontal lobe atrophy. They will always remain at risk for loss of control over drinking because of their vulnerable frontal lobes. Abstinence is clearly the treatment goal for such people. Methods for accurate diagnosis and prognosis are currently lacking. It is possible that brain imaging techniques might meet this need.

Loss of control does not explain alcoholism. It is itself part of the syndrome that constitutes alcoholism. Growing evidence, however, suggests a biobehavioral explanation for the phenomenon—dysfunctional frontal lobes. Acute and chronic alcohol effects upon selected regions of the frontal lobes may produce an "environmental dependency syndrome", loss of control, which may be only partially reversible in many alcoholics. Extent of damage, degree of reversibility, individual differences, relation to consumption amounts and patterns, are important questions. These are all problems that await further detailed biopsychosocial research on the disease syndrome of alcoholism.

Alcoholism Is Not a Disease

STANTON PEELE

Stanton Peele is a zealous advocate of behavioral approaches to alcoholism. Here, Peele argues that the current conceptualization of alcoholism as a disease is a product of a historic inability to effectively treat alcohol problems in the United States. Peele argues that the disease concept of alcoholism, and its accompanying abstinence based treatment programs, are not supported by social science research and ignore the cultural components of alcoholism. He contends that the success of controlled drinking treatment programs based on behavioral theories implicates an environmental determinant of alcoholism.

QUESTIONS

1. According to Peele, what are some of the historic influences on the development of the concept of alcoholism as a disease?
2. What support does Peele provide for a cultural component to alcoholism?

Reprinted from "The Cultural Context of Psychological Approaches to Alcoholism" by Stanton Peele, *American Psychologist*, December 1984. Copyright 1984 by the American Psychological Association. Adapted by permission.

3. What is the prognosis for alcoholism treatment programs according to Peele?

■ ■ ■

Styles of drinking and attitudes toward alcohol vary tremendously across cultures. The United States has been a battleground of warring conceptions of drinking. Such diversity is not as apparent in contemporary American views of alcoholism, because alcohol problems are now widely considered to be primarily the result of an uncontrollable response to alcohol among those who are classified as alcoholic. This modern disease theory has deep historical roots and represents the experiences of particular groups of drinkers. The disease theory disagrees with social scientific research that finds responses to alcohol to be based on a range of cognitive and environmental factors and thus to be more variable than the disease theory describes. Conflict has been especially intense between the disease theory and behavioral approaches in which abstinence is not seen as essential for the treatment of alcoholism. Despite efforts to accommodate to the disease position—efforts that have significantly influenced psychological theorizing about alcoholism—controlled-drinking approaches are now endangered by dominant treatment attitudes in the field.

Disagreements also exist among social scientific conceptions of alcoholism. For example, there are differences between social-learning and control-of-supply views of the cultural variability in alcoholism rates. Important aspects of social-learning concepts of alcoholism include the extent to which drinkers doubt their own ability to control their drinking and believe that alcohol is a potent and efficacious mood modifier. All social-scientific viewpoints are overridden, however, by a larger cultural ethos that agrees with the disease viewpoint. Yet this ethos, including its emphasis on abstinence and on the potency of alcohol's effects, is one that is often found to coexist with high levels of drinking problems. There is a need for social-psychological examination of our culture's drinking dispositions at the same time that psychologists must maneuver within the reality of this cultural context in dealing with alcoholism.

Social scientists have traditionally been concerned with cultural recipes that distinguish between socially disruptive and socially integrated drinking. Moderate drinking is notable in ethnic and cultural groups such as the Chinese, the Greeks, the Jews, and the Italians, where such drinking is modeled for the young and maintained by social custom and peer groups. Children are gradually introduced to alcohol in the family setting; drinking is not presented as a rite of passage into adulthood and is not associated with masculinity and social power. Adult drinking is controlled by group attitudes both toward the proper amount of drinking and proper behavior when drinking. Strong disapproval is expressed when an individual violates these standards and acts in an antisocial manner.

The American experience with alcohol parallels the results of such cross-cultural findings. In colonial America, drunkenness was accepted as a natural consequence of drinking, and habitual drunkenness was not considered to be an uncontrollable disease. Despite higher per capita consumption, alcoholism was not a serious social problem, and problem drinking was less evident than it is today. Drinking was a universally accepted social activity that took place within a tightly knit social fabric; families drank and ate together in the neighborhood tavern. Between 1790 and 1830, due to expanding frontiers and other social changes, the male-oriented saloon became the typical setting for drinking. Here alcohol was consumed in isolation from the family (the only women likely to be present were prostitutes), and drinking came to symbolize masculine independence, high-spiritedness, and violence. Alcoholism rates rose dramatically.

The temperance movement arose in response to the explosion of alcohol problems in 19th century America. It propagated the view that habitual inebriates were unable to control their drinking, the early version of the disease theory that originated with physician Benjamin Rush. Large numbers of Americans came to view alcohol as "demon rum" and regarded drinking as frequently—or inevitably—leading to uncontrolled drunkenness. The solution they proposed was national abstinence. There were regional, social class, religious, sex, and ethnic variations in these views and in the composition of the wet and dry forces that battled throughout the century. In 1920—at a point when, paradoxically, drinking patterns had moderated substantially—national prohibition was enacted. When prohibition was repealed in 1933, the goal of universal abstinence died with it. The disease theory became transmuted at this time to the view that chronic drunkenness was not an inescapable property of alcohol but was rather a characteristic of a small group of people with an inbred susceptibility to alcoholism.

This was the modern disease theory, and it was spread effectively by the Alcoholics Anonymous (AA) self-help movement. AA had many commonalities with 19th century temperance brotherhoods, such as the Washingtonians, an organization in which reformed drunkards took the vow of abstinence. Like members of the Washingtonians, AA members gathered in a highly charged, revival-type atmosphere to relate their struggles with alcohol and to support each other's continued abstinence (as well as to convince others to join them). There are peculiarly American features of AA that made its resounding success in the United States unique. AA's emphasis on public confession, contrition, and salvation through God has its roots in Southern and Midwestern evangelical Protestantism. In no other Western country have AA and the recovering alcoholic attained such a central role in the formulation of alcoholism policy and alcoholism treatment as in the United States.

The AA hegemony over alcoholism treatment and the ascendance of the disease theory accelerated in the second half of the 20th century. The theory was officially endorsed by the American Medical Association in 1956. Its rapid growth and wide acceptance were due to the melding of its strong ethnoreligious support with its backing as medical dogma. Following World War II, public opinion polls indicated a continuous increase in the belief that alcoholism is a disease. More recently, in August 1982, a Gallup poll found that 79% of Americans accepted alcoholism as a disease requiring medical treatment. In the 1970s, federal financing for the treatment of alcoholism shifted to service contracts and third-party payments. The primary locus for treatment changed from public institutions to private facilities and contractors. A premium was placed on aggressive marketing of alcoholism services, the early identification of those with drinking problems, and compulsory treatment. The emphasis was on the identification of new, previously unrecognized *groups* of alcoholics and others needing treatment in connection with alcoholism, such as women, functioning workers and professionals, and families of alcoholics.

The aim of the alcoholism movement since the 1940s, as embodied by the National Council on Alcoholism, has been to make people aware of the prevalence of alcoholism and the need to have it treated. The movement has been extremely successful in this endeavor, and postage stamps, media programs, and public service announcements regularly drive its points home. Room estimated that there was a 20-fold increase in the number of alcoholics in treatment between 1942 and 1976. The sense of the lurking danger of alcoholism has increased further since 1976. The 1982 Gallup poll found that one third of American families had had a problem with alcohol, a figure that had doubled over the previous $5^{1/2}$ years. Some representatives of the alcoholism industry now think there are more than 15 million alcoholics in America requiring treatment. . . .

Given the emotions it is capable of arousing, the disease theory of alcoholism is surprisingly amorphous and variable. Pattison, Sobell, and Sobell pointed out that, in order to criticize the theory, the critic must often first define it, leaving the critic open to the accusation of having created a "straw man" to attack. This is especially true because prominent defenders of the disease viewpoint acclaim the lay wisdom of AA and endorse its positions although they formally propose models of alcoholism significantly at odds with lay disease notions. The basic AA version of alcoholism as a disease is that the true alcoholic cannot control his or her drinking (unlike those who choose to get drunk), an inability that exists before the first drink is taken. The condition is irreversible and progressive and requires complete and utter abstinence.

The idea of an inherited biological mechanism is not always a part of disease theories, although it has been a major impetus for medical research. The central trait of disease theories is the alcoholic's loss of control. Jellinek and Keller, founders of the Yale Center of Alcohol Studies, have provided the scholarly underpinnings for the disease theory. Jellinek's original empirical work traced the stages of alcoholism reported by 98 respondents to questionnaires sent to about 1,600 AA members. Influenced by prevailing views of drug dependence, Jellinek's book, *The Disease Concept of Alcoholism*, presented a typology of alcoholism. It identified "gamma" alcoholism as the essential disease type and defined it in terms of physical dependence, along with loss of control. This disease model, unlike the AA version, is unclear about the inbred or irreversible nature of the condition.

Many subsequent investigations have failed to confirm either the stages or the types of alcoholism that Jellinek outlined. Disease notions have been further undermined by a series of laboratory studies that found that the drinking of chronic alcoholics is not characterized by loss of control. Even when intoxicated, these alcoholics regulated their levels of drinking and responded to external rewards. Summarizing this research, Heather and Robertson found that "alcoholics' drinking behavior is subject to the same *kind* of laws which . . . describe normal drinking behavior, or . . . goal-directed behavior of any kind". As a response to increasingly complicated findings about alcoholic behavior, Keller added a note of indeterminacy to loss of control notions. He proposed that alcoholics might be able to control their drinking on occasion but are unable to guarantee when they can do so.

Field investigations of the natural course of drinking problems have evolved separately from the behavioral models of alcoholism generated in laboratory studies. Generally sociological in nature, such field research has agreed with laboratory studies in finding alcoholism to be malleable and situationally determined. In this view, people's alcohol-related problems are so diverse, fluctuate so much with time, and are so strongly influenced by social context that such problems are best conceived of as problem drinking rather than as a disease state of alcoholism. Cahalan and his co-workers, along with other sociologists, have used the term *problem drinker* in a fundamentally different way from both disease- and nondisease-oriented clinicians. Problem drinking is not a less severe type of alcohol problem than gamma or addictive alcoholism. It is a *separate* dimension for classifying drinkers where loss of control is one among several kinds of drinking problems and is not necessarily the most severe or the core, defining problem.

Field studies have found demographic categories to play an important role in alcoholism. Cahalan and Room identified youth, lower socioeconomic status, minority status (black or

Hispanic), and other conventional ethnic categories (Irish versus Jewish and Italian) as predicting drinking problems. Greeley, McCready, and Theisen continued to find "ethnic drinking sub-cultures" and their relationship to drinking problems to be extremely resilient and to have withstood the otherwise apparent assimilation by ethnic groups into mainstream American values. Cahalan and Room also discovered a paradoxical tendency for drinkers from conservative Protestant sects or from dry regions to be binge drinkers. The Rand report's analysis of treated alcoholics in comparison with a Harris poll of nationwide drinking practices made the similarly anomalous discovery that alcoholism was more frequent in the South and among Protestants, demographic categories also associated with abstinence. The predictive power of demographic traits is not limited to problem drinking or alcoholics seeking treatment. Vaillant found Irish Americans in his Boston sample to be alcohol dependent (i.e., alcoholic) seven times as often as those from Mediterranean backgrounds (Greeks, Italians, and Jews), and those in Vaillant's working class sample were alcohol dependent more than three times as often as those in his college sample.

Group differences in alcoholism are not readily explained in disease or biological terms. Indeed, even Oriental groups such as Native Americans and Chinese Americans, which are noted for their shared, exaggerated metabolic reaction to alcohol, show widely divergent alcoholism rates connected with different socially regulated styles of drinking. Such findings provide a powerful argument against a genetic basis for alcoholism. For disease proponents, the idea that social norms control drinking problems translates into the notion that some groups have a greater tendency to *deny* alcoholism. Efforts in the alcoholism movement are generally directed toward uncovering hidden numbers of alcoholics in groups, such as Jews or women, that have traditionally measured low in alcoholism rates. Yet investigators emphasizing genetic contributions to alcoholism or seeking to identify secret alcoholics have continued to note substantially lower alcoholism rates for such groups.

The most powerful predictor of drinking problems for Cahalan and Room was not social background, however, but current social environment. The potency of social drinking contexts has been identified not only as a key to causing drinking problems but as a force in socializing moderate drinking and modifying alcohol problems. The idea of using drinking environments to prevent the development of unhealthy drinking styles in the young remains a strong thrust in social learning approaches to alcoholism, one that has continued to exist despite a rising tide of disease conceptions. Social context analyses at the macro level, which point to shifting historical alcoholism rates and changing cultural conceptions of alcohol problems, have viewed alcoholism as a social construction rather than an actual disease entity. This viewpoint is as far from the disease conception as it is possible to get and has come in for a kind of criticism from disease proponents that is ordinarily directed at radical political groups.

Social "constructivist" approaches notwithstanding, the full fury of the disease movement has been reserved for studies showing that some alcoholics moderate their drinking. Abstinence has been the fundamental treatment precept in the disease approach as it was with temperance. However, nearly every outcome study has uncovered a return to moderate drinking by alcoholics. Despite the frequency of these discoveries and their often matter-of-fact reporting by researchers, several key studies of this sort have been ferociously attacked. The most significant of these were the two Rand studies. The first, originally released in 1976, found that 22% of alcoholics treated at National Institute of Alcoholism and Alcohol Abuse (NIAAA) treatment centers were drinking without problems at 18 months after treatment (compared to 24% who were stably abstaining). The National Council on Alcoholism (NCA) organized an immediate, concerted assault on this study.

Among a host of often wildly distorted accusations, genuine methodological and theoretical issues were raised about the Rand study. The Rand investigators conducted a second study that included a 4-year follow-up period, breathalyzer tests, reconstructed criteria for moderate drinking, and a careful analysis of drinking outcomes against levels of alcohol dependence shown by clients on admission. Close to 40% of the subjects who were free of drinking problems at 4 years were still drinking, including a substantial minority of those who had been most dependent on alcohol. Peer evaluations of both reports, but particularly the second, were highly positive as reflected in the statement "this four year follow-up study is one of the best outcome studies in the alcoholism field." Yet the two Rand studies have simply been buried by most in the alcoholism field. Vaillant typified this response by consistently dismissing the first study's findings on methodological grounds and generally ignoring the second study. . . .

The Rand studies reported outcomes of standard abstinence-oriented treatment at NIAAA centers. Their findings confirm those of Cahalan and Room—albeit with a treated and more severely alcoholic population—in indicating that the status of people's drinking problems varies considerably over time. The standard disease theory criticism of the Rand studies—that there was no guarantee that nonproblem drinking outcomes would be permanent—does not contravene the picture they present of alcoholics regularly shifting from alcoholic drinking to abstinence or moderation and back again. In addition, there has been a tradition of behavioral research dating from the early 1970s that has aimed at *moderating* alcoholic drinking. In 1982, the prestigious journal *Science* published a reinvestigation by Pendery, Maltzman, and West of a study by Sobell and Sobell that had claimed such techniques produced better outcomes for a group of alcoholics than had the standard hospital abstinence-oriented therapy used with a comparison group. Pendery and her colleagues found that most controlled-drinking subjects in the experiment reported instances of severe relapse soon after treatment and were not moderate drinkers 10 years later. The *Science* article was highly publicized and was often accompanied by accusations from its authors that the Sobells had falsified their results.

The Pendery report was an unusual one. It questioned only subjects in the experimental, controlled-drinking group in the original study without reporting follow-up data for the abstinence comparison group. The data were primarily recollections by subjects of events up to nine years in the past and descriptions of individual episodes of relapse. The only summary data the paper presented were the amount of hospitalization controlled-drinking subjects underwent after treatment. A report by an independent committee convened by the Addiction Research Foundation of Toronto, which employs the Sobells, noted that the original articles by the study's authors actually reported more hospitalizations for controlled-drinking subjects than did Pendery et al. The committee was frankly critical of the Pendery group's approach for its failure to reexamine subjects treated with abstinence techniques, its reliance on testimony from subjects emotionally involved in the controversy, and the lack of consideration of the larger body of evidence about controlled drinking.

The *Science* article has been invested with significance beyond its own questionable validity because of the cultural context in which it appeared. The article, although agreeing with the near-unanimous portrayals by the media of the disease nature of alcoholism, is one of the few answers to an avalanche of studies contradicting disease notions. The dispute is impossible to understand without considering the history of the controlled-drinking controversy in this country, as even an APA *Monitor* article on the controversy failed to do. For example, the senior author of the *Science* paper was a primary spokesperson in the NCA campaign against the Rand studies, including an effort to have the first report delayed so that its results could be reanalyzed.

How Does a Culture Cause Alcoholism?

The need to incorporate cultural factors has also confused alcohol dependence theorizing. Similarly, Vaillant's early reports on his natural history research noted separate and significant genetic and cultural causality in alcoholism. His final report was more guarded about inherited factors, however. Marc Vaillant did not find the distinct differences in alcoholism that Goodwin and Schuckit have traced to genetically related compared to adoptive relatives and to inheritance over environment. Vaillant also found that return to moderate drinking versus abstinence was not a function of having alcoholic relatives but was related to the cultural group of the alcohol abuser. This finding is reminiscent of the higher incidence of binge drinking alternating with abstinence among conservative Protestants and others from dry regions in the national survey by Cahalan and Room and the coincidence of high rates of alcoholism and abstinence for both Protestants and Southerners detected in the first Rand study. As Vaillant explained his finding, "It is consistent with Irish culture to see the use of alcohol in terms of black or white, good or evil, drunkenness or complete abstinence".

182

Although "the existence of cultural differences [in drinking problems] is an undoubted 'social fact,'" sociocultural explanations for these differences have been challenged. Indeed, the current thrust from social scientists in public policies for preventing alcoholism is on controlling the supply of alcohol, on the principle that there is a constant relationship between overall consumption and the amount consumed by drinkers at the extreme end of the drinking continuum. This control-of-supply approach has itself been challenged. A supply hypothesis is inadequate to explain subcultural differences in alcoholism for groups for whom alcohol is equally available. It also cannot explain historical changes, such as those in America, where per capita alcohol consumption during the colonial period was two to three times its current rate, but problem drinking was below its current level. There is a strong parallel here with 19th century developments in attitudes toward addiction and narcotics in England and America. In both countries, although 19th century opiate use was widespread and massive, modern conceptions of narcotic addiction developed only at the turn of the century when general consumption rates declined.

A social-cognitive dimension in alcoholism and addiction is evident in Levine's startling discovery that the idea of loss of control was uniformly absent from first-person descriptions of drunkenness in colonial America. In contrast, by 1835, loss of control was the unifying thread in the public confessions of reformed drunkards. If loss of control defines alcoholism, such alcohol abuse as there was took an entirely different form in the earlier era. Criteria such as violent and other aberrant behavior when intoxicated are central to the *Diagnostic and Statistical Manual of Mental Disorders* (DSM-III; American Psychiatric Association, 1980) definitions of alcohol abuse and alcohol dependence. Similarly, disease proponents concede that "the most sensitive instruments for identifying alcoholics and problem drinkers are questionnaires and inventories of psychological and behavioral variables". Yet in their classic work, *Drunken Comportment*, MacAndrew and Edgerton showed that how alcoholic disinhibition is interpreted and enacted—for example, whether it leads to violence—is socially conditioned and takes completely different forms in different cultures.

Bales provided an early effort to synthesize cultural and individual attitudes about alcohol. He proposed that the incidence of alcoholism in a society depended upon the degree of cultural arousal of inner tensions, attitudes in the culture about the effectiveness of drinking for relieving such tensions, and the presence or absence of alternate societal means of satisfaction. McClelland, Davis, Kalin, and Wanner developed a model of alcoholism predicated on a society's ambivalence about power, alcohol's association in that society with displays of power, and the absence of alternate means for an individual to realize a need for power. Later social learning models have expanded the realm of the individual's expectations of desired effects from alcohol—or other substances—to include feelings of sexual potency, personal control, tension relief, lessened self-awareness, and so on. These beliefs about alcohol's efficacy as an experience modifier may underlie the effects of parental and cultural attitudes on drinking behavior. At the same time, "virtually all the studies that use adequate control groups have found that alcoholics and problem drinkers are more external in locus of control than nonproblem drinkers are". Thus, those who cannot control their drinking may invest alcohol with the power both to bring about otherwise unattainable emotional states and to control their behavior.

Where Is Our Society Headed with Alcohol?

The indications are that the United States is abandoning its former, culturally pluralistic attitudes toward alcohol to create a dominant attitude toward alcohol as having the supreme power to corrupt and control. That is, the attitudes that characterize both ethnic groups and individuals with the greatest drinking problems are being propagated as a national outlook. This approach may work to help those who already hold this view of their drinking, but it carries dangers as a therapeutic policy for others and as a model of drinking for the young. Annual measurements have revealed in the latter half of the 1970s and the beginning of the 1980s that 40% of high school seniors (50% of male seniors) reported drinking at least five drinks in one sitting in the prior two weeks. This behavior has been accompanied by a growth in the endorsement of binge drinking over mild, regular drinking.

Social context and learning approaches have tried to deal with these trends in the young by creating moderate drinking atmospheres on campuses and by encouraging attitudes toward health that are incompatible with excessive drinking. In a household survey of drug and alcohol use, Apsler found that problem drinking was associated with the drinker's reliance on alcohol to bring about desired feelings as opposed to drinking in line with social or personal norms. Furthermore, the problematic style was more associated with youthful drinking, suggesting that emphasizing social standards in drinking over alcohol's ability to modify feelings would have a beneficial impact for youthful drinkers. On the other hand, consistent findings of the tremendous malleability of drinking behavior with age indicate it is an error to label youthful drinkers as alcoholics, even when they display major drinking problems. However, the policy goal of altering culture-wide attitudes toward drinking and drinking patterns has proved elusive. What is clear is that a range of cultural forces in our society *has* endangered the attitudes that underlie the norm and the practice of moderate drinking. The widespread propagation of the image of the irresistible dangers of alcohol has contributed to this undermining.

Alcoholism is a primary example of how political and social forces blunt and even reverse the thrust of social-scientific research and psychological conceptions. The alcoholism field is one particularly prone to drive social scientists to announce a paradigm shift. What may make one less than hopeful about such a shift in conceptions is that prevailing notions about alcoholism have gained popularity despite a lack of empirical support from the beginning. Disease conceptions may be alluring to our contemporary society because they are congruent with general ideas about the self and personal responsibility. Alcoholism viewed as an uncontrollable urge is after all part of a larger trend in which premenstrual tension, drug use and drug withdrawal, eating junk foods, and lovesickness are presented as defenses for murder. It may be that contesting disease imagery will remain an unpopular, but necessary, effort for some time.

Criminal Behavior Is Influenced By Heredity

SARNOFF MEDNICK

Sarnoff Mednick is an ardent proponent of the idea that criminal behavior is biological. Mednick, a longtime researcher on the biological correlates of abnormal behavior in general and antisocial behavior specifically, argues that the increased rate of criminal behavior in children born to criminally convicted parents supports a genetic component to criminality. To a greater degree than some psychobiologists, Mednick recognizes that environmental variables also play a limited role in the likelihood of an individual to manifest criminal behavior. However, Mednick contends that heredity, not environment, is the best predictor of criminal activity.

QUESTIONS

1. How much of a role does biology play in criminality, according to Mednick?
2. What mitigating factors does Mednick believe affect the manifestation of criminal behaviors?
3. If Mednick is correct and criminality has an origin in biology what are the prospects for intervention?

Sarnoff Mednick, "Crime in the Family Tree," *Psychology Today*, March 1985. Reprinted with permission from *Psychology Today* magazine. Copyright © 1985 (Sussex Publishers, Inc.).

■ ■ ■

During a lecture to a group of social workers and nurses in the late 1960s, I mentioned that almost all responsible researchers would agree that schizophrenia was, in part, the result of genetically transmitted biological factors. A colleague sprang to his feet and announced, "Even if it is true, I will never accept the possibility that environmental circumstances do not totally account for the existence of the schizophrenic condition." When I asked why he felt compelled to take that position, he said, "If we once admit that genetic factors are involved, our attitude toward treatment of the schizophrenic will become pessimistic; we will lock them up and throw away the keys!"

Some people still defend that position, but for the most part such resistance has died out. Evidence from numerous studies has convincingly demonstrated the importance of genetic influences in the development of schizophrenia. Similar evidence is beginning to make a solid case for the involvement of genes in another form of deviant human behavior—criminality.

The three basic ways of investigating the inheritance of human behavior are family, twin and adoption studies; in the past decade a number of such studies have linked genetic factors with criminal behavior. It has long been suspected, for example, that antisocial parents tend to have antisocial children. (Criminologists define antisocial behavior as a variety of irresponsible, aggressive or criminal types of behavior that usually begin in childhood or adolescence and persist into adult life.) Now there is good evidence from family studies that this is the case. One of the best predictors of antisocial behavior in a young boy, for example, is his father's criminality. This suggests a genetic link, but it is difficult to disentangle hereditary from environmental influences in family studies. The child may have been born with antisocial tendencies or may have learned them from the parents.

One way to distinguish the effect of nature and nurture is to compare identical with nonidentical, or fraternal, twins. If behavioral traits are largely inherited, then identical twins, whose genetic makeup is exactly the same, are more likely to have similar traits than are fraternal twins, who share on average half of their genes. Since 1929, nine studies of criminality among twins have been reported, and all have found that identical twins are approximately twice as likely as fraternal twins to be similar with regard to criminal activity.

The largest of these studies was conducted by Karl O. Christiansen of the University of Copenhagen, who used the Danish national register of criminal behavior to investigate the fates of 7,172 twins born in Denmark. He reported, in 1978, that 35 percent of the identical twins, compared with only 13 percent of the fraternal twins, were similar as far as criminal activity (or lack of it) was concerned.

These findings point out the importance of both the environment and genes in the development of criminality. The fact that 65 percent of the identical twins did not have similar records of criminality suggests that the environment is critically important. But the identical twins were almost three times as likely as the fraternal twins to be alike, suggesting that there is some shared, genetically controlled characteristic that is some as yet unknown way increases their risk of eventually becoming criminals.

Twin studies go a long way toward demonstrating the possible heritability of criminal behavior, but they too can be criticized. One problem is that identical twins are treated more alike than are fraternal twins and, therefore, are more likely to develop similar behavior patterns. Since they have more similar environments than do fraternal twins, there is a less than ideal separation of genetic and environmental influences.

Adoption studies avoid this problem by comparing children adopted at birth with their biological parents, with whom they share no environment. If both the biological parents and the adopted-away children have similar records of criminality, it suggests that the parents have passed on some characteristic that increases the risk of conviction.

At the 1974 meeting of the American Psychopathological Association, my colleague Barry Hutchings and I reported our findings from a study of 5,483 adoptions in Copenhagen. The rate of criminal behavior in the adopted-away sons of criminal fathers was considerably higher than the rate in boys whose fathers were not registered in the police files. At the same meeting, Raymond Crowe of the University of Iowa reported on the psychopathology of 46 adopted-away children in Iowa who had been born to imprisoned women. He found that six of these children, but only one of a similar group of adoptees born to noncriminal women, had antisocial personality disorders. In 1978, Remi Cadoret of the University of Iowa reported on a study of 246 Iowans adopted at birth. He found a close relationship between the antisocial behavior of the adoptees and that of their biological parents. Other researchers have found similar correlations for psychiatric hospitalization and convictions for property crime between adopted-away children and their biological parents.

These studies all suggest that we should take seriously the idea that some biological characteristics that can be genetically transmitted may be involved in causing a person to become involved in criminal activity. To investigate this possibility further, Hutchings, William F. Gabrielli Jr. and I followed up on our earlier study by launching a full-scale investigation of the parents and children involved in all 14,427 adoptions registered in Denmark between 1927 and 1947. We hypothesized that court convictions for the biological parents would be associated with similar convictions for the adoptees. We also used this larger group to explore more detailed questions, such as repeat offenses, social status and the types of crimes.

We examined criminal court records for all adoptees and their biological and adoptive parents and found 65,516 convictions. In families in which neither a biological nor an adoptive parent had been convicted, only 13.5 percent of the sons had criminal records. (We concentrated on sons in our analysis because of the low conviction rate among women.) In families in which an adoptive but not a biological parent had been convicted, 14.7 percent of the sons had criminal records—not a significant difference from the first group. But if a biological parent rather than an adoptive parent had been convicted, 20 percent of the sons had criminal records. And the rate was even higher—24.5 percent—if both an adoptive and a biological parent had court convictions.

Furthermore, we found that 4 percent of our adoptees accounted for almost 70 percent of the convictions. And these chronic offenders were more likely than the others to have biological parents with more than one conviction. Those whose biological parents had three or more convictions, for example, made up only 1 percent of the group that accounted for 30 percent of the criminal convictions. This extremely high rate of convictions among the very small number of the adoptees whose parents were multiple offenders suggests that a genetic predisposition plays an especially important role in their criminality.

Exactly what that role may be remains unknown, but our results suggest that it does not involve a tendency toward any particular kind of crime. Instead, any biological predisposition the adoptee inherits must be of a general nature, perhaps related to the capacity to learn to conform to family and social rules.

When we looked at the social and economic status of the family into which the child was adopted, we found support for the genetic theory. But we also found further proof of the interplay between nature and nurture in the development of criminality. Gabrielli, Katherine Van Dusen of the Psychological Institute Kommunehospitalet in Copenhagen and I found that children born to parents from the lowest social classes had the highest rates of criminality, no matter what type of family they were adopted into; however, those adopted by families of the lowest social and economic status were almost 40 percent more likely to have criminal convictions than the children adopted by families of the highest social class. Regardless of genetic background, improved social conditions seem to reduce criminality.

Our basic research goal was to determine whether genetically influenced characteristics play a role in the development of antisocial behavior. But we could only address this question indirectly. Our measure of antisocial behavior consisted of a decision by the courts that our subjects had committed crimes. However, we know that there is far more crime than is detected, charged or brought to trial or that results in convictions. Many of these uncounted crimes may have been committed by persons we identified as having no convictions and others by chronic offenders convicted of only one or two crimes in our records. This undercounting reduced the likelihood that we would detect any genetic effect, yet we still found a significant one.

Our study, like others, strongly suggests that genetic influences can lead to the development of criminal behavior. And because genetic transmission can involve only biological factors, we conclude that biological characteristics must be responsible for some criminal behavior, especially that of multiple offenders.

If this is so, then ways of preventing criminal behavior might grow out of studies of its biological components, and the best place to start would be with the chronic offender. Attempts to identify potential multiple offenders early in their criminal careers generally are based on environmental factors, such as social and economic status, neighborhood, family circumstances and parenting practices. Our work suggests that biological factors should also be included, and certain biological markers have been identified that might be useful in predicting who is most likely to become a chronic offender. These include measures such as an extremely unresponsive autonomic system, slow brain-wave activity, neuropsychological deficits, biochemical abnormalities and a number of psychological and behavioral signs—impulsivity, aggressiveness and poor school performance.

Using such information, researchers could undertake a pilot project to help prevent the development of criminal behavior. They would begin by rating a large group of first offenders, perhaps 2,000 to 3,000 youths, on a carefully selected battery of environmental and biological measures. The findings would then be put aside until some of these youths began to become multiple offenders. The researchers would then go back to the original measures and see which combination best predicts chronic offending. With this list as a guide they would examine a new group of youthful first offenders and identify those most likely to become chronic offenders. They and their families would then be invited into a treatment program.

Participation would be entirely voluntary. The program probably would include a heavy emphasis on educational planning and occupational guidance and training. What we already know about chronic offenders suggests that they should not be guided into boring, repetitive, low-status positions. Instead, they should be directed toward relatively challenging, varied and demanding occupations that have the element of excitement that most chronic offenders seem to crave. The promise of such interesting jobs could make education more meaningful and give them a stake in society.

Critics of genetic theories of criminality have charged that the ability to predict criminal behavior would be abused, and that innocent people would suffer. But if we could accurately identify people likely to become criminals and develop programs to help them, it is much more probable that we would be opening the door to a better life for them, rather than locking them up and throwing away the keys.

Note: Some treatment programs designed to prevent the development of antisocial behavior and delinquency already exist.

VIEWPOINT

4

Criminal Behavior Is Influenced by Society

WALTER C. RECKLESS

Unlike biological theories, the sociological study of crime emphasizes the role of the environment on criminal behavior. Here, Walter Reckless advocates that society contributes to criminal conduct by showing that external factors can influence crime rates and patterns. Reckless argues that family discord, peer pressure and community factors aid in the creation of juvenile delinquents and criminals alike. He emphasizes the role of society in both the definition and socialization of criminal behaviors and advocates increased focus on these to predict and prevent criminality.

QUESTIONS

1. How does Reckless's familial influence on crime differ from that of Mednick?
2. How do companions influence criminal behaviors, according to Reckless?
3. What role does society play in defining crime, according to the author? In socializing crime?

Walter C. Reckless, "The Sociologist Looks at Crime," *The Annals of the American Academy of Political and Social Science* 217 (Sept. 1941):76-83. Reprinted with permission (footnotes omitted).

■ ■ ■

It is now pretty generally recognized among sociologists that crime and delinquency are violations of a behavior code of a state and are not fundamentally different from violations of behavior codes of other social groups, as for example the church, the school, the family, the lodge, the labor union. Some of the violations of the latter codes overlap the violations of the criminal code and are covered by the criminal code.

Volume of Crime

The volume of violations of the criminal code is therefore only a small part of the total volume of violations of all behavior codes in a modern, complex society. Only a small part of the violations of the criminal code become officially known, whereas varying proportions of crimes known to the police actually lead to arrest. From arrest on through execution of sentence, there are drastic drop-outs of cases, i.e., great mortality of cases.

Such considerations apply also to the volume of juvenile delinquency. The juvenile delinquent is the misbehaving youth who gets acted upon officially—the one who gets caught. But the volume of known cases is just a small fraction of the total volume of violation of the junior criminal code and a still smaller fraction of the total volume of violations of all behavior codes applying to children.

In both adult crime and juvenile delinquency, there are several extraneous social and administrative considerations, other than the particular nature of the behavior, which determine what violation is going to become known and acted upon officially.

Definitions of Crimes Vary

There is still another salient fact about criminal and delinquent behavior which has gained wide recognition. It is that the definitions of what is criminal and delinquent vary in time and place. Sociologists have discovered that the definition of what is a violation is contained in the behavior codes or conduct norms of a society, which include a recognizable rating of behavior along a scale of approval-disapproval. Behind the specific conduct norms is a set of social values which the society or the dominant elements in it are seeking to perpetuate and to protect. Hence, rape does not fall at the same point of the scale in several different societies, due to the existence of differing sets of social values which give significance and point to behavior.

In view of these prefacing remarks, it is understandable why the sociologist rejects the idea that crimes are natural and universal, and why he is skeptical of claims for the existence of a criminal constitution which is prepotently prepared to violate rules of behavior. It is understandable also why the sociologist looks at criminal behavior pretty much as other kinds of violating behavior, and views criminals and delinquents pretty much as violators of behavior codes who are not caught, and not as a special constitutional order of human creature.

When violation depends upon so many variables in the social matrix and is not dependent primarily upon the nature of the behavior and the nature of the violator, one also realizes that it is difficult to work out the causes of a phenomenon such as crime and delinquency. Nevertheless, valiant efforts have been made to determine the causes. Sociologists, quite naturally, have been principally interested in the environmental influences, and have made about as good progress in etiological studies as have the representatives of other fields; which is not saying much, because progress in isolating causes has been beset with grave difficulties. In some areas of scientific research, the notion of causation has been abandoned.

Reconsideration of Environment

In the classical age of criminology, criminal sociology was identified with one and all environmental influences on crime. American sociologists soon dropped consideration of the physical and paid attention more strictly to the social aspects of environment. Still later, after analysis of causative factors from case studies came into vogue, the social environment was reduced still farther to those social conditions which could be shown to have a reasonably direct effect on conduct. Later still, when case studies included the person's own story, the environment became not the conditions around the person but rather the particular set of objects and individuals to which he responded.

Just about the time that this individualized conception of environment was dawning, sociologists, psychologists, and other students of behavior problems began emphasizing the importance of the social situation in the determination of behavior. The total situation was conceived to be the person interacting in his life situations. The total situation and the social world of the person became heirs in sociological thinking to the old conception of environment.

Looking at the immediate environment rather than at the larger one led American sociologists to narrow their coverage on causative factors considerably. Certain family, community, and companionship factors received special attention.

Family Factor in Delinquency

Workers in the field have been impressed with the frequency with which delinquents and criminals come from broken homes. But it soon became apparent to critical observers that nondelinquents and noncriminals might come from broken homes quite as frequently as court cases. Shideler estimated, probably without justification, that the proportion of broken homes among correctional school populations is almost twice as high as that among the general population. Slawson found that the proportion of correctional school boys from New York City was over twice as high as the proportion among children in three New York public schools. It has been claimed that this was not a fair comparison. Sheldon and Eleanor Glueck likewise found that the percentage of Massachusetts young adult male and female reformatory cases coming from broken homes was several times higher than an estimated proportion of one out of seven broken homes in the family population of Chicago.

Clifford Robe Shaw and Henry D. McKay, by more scientifically justifiable methods, discovered that the percentage of broken homes among male juvenile court cases in Chicago stood to the percentage of broken homes among the male school population of comparable age and comparable district as 1.18 to 1. They discovered also that there was no tendency for juvenile delinquency rates in local areas to increase as the percentage of broken homes among the school boys increased. It was found, too, that the ratio of broken homes among the delinquents to that of the school population was greatest for the youngest ages and decreased markedly as age increased. Shaw and McKay concluded that it is not so much the formal break in the family as the cumulative discord between family members that operates as a causative factor in delinquent behavior.

More recently, Weeks, using Spokane data, indicated that the broken home factor is connected much more frequently with juvenile delinquency cases charged with ungovernability, running away, and truancy than with cases charged with property offenses, traffic violations, and misdemeanors. The former are offenses in which girls are much more involved than boys, and the latter are offenses in which boys are much more involved than girls. The latter type of offenses are those referred to court mainly by the police, while the former are referred to court principally by sources other than police, such as parents, relatives, neighbors, and school. Hence, the proportion of broken homes among delinquents is acted on selectively by sex, type of offense, and source of referral. Such a discovery signifies that the broken home is more important as a risk factor in referral than a causative factor of behavior problems.

Unsatisfactory member-to-member relationships in the family, including parent-child relationships, have been suspected of having a direct bearing on misconduct and delinquency. The assumption is that the individual falls into delinquent activity as an escape from discomfort and unpleasantness. This is the family tension or family discord factor in behavior. One finds much evidence for the operation of it in individual cases of both delinquents and criminals. Healy and Bronner found that unhappiness and emotional disturbances, resulting from jangled family relationships, were present in 92 percent of a sample of cases undertaken for treatment. The belief is that family tensions are more prevalent in the family relationships of delinquents than those of nondelinquents, but this point has not been proven.

The presence of demoralizing conditions or demoralized persons in the home has been cited as an important causative factor in the breeding of delinquents and criminals. It is realized that an immoral mother or a drunken father may produce intolerance of vice and alcohol in offspring. But it is also realized that children exposed to lewdness, immorality, criminality, gambling, and drunkenness in the home have a good chance of becoming infected by such social viruses. Studies of delinquent and criminal samples indicate the frequent presence of one or more vicious and criminal persons in the family situation prior to arrest or incarceration of the subjects. One imagines that, if the coverage on the gross moral faults of family members of delinquent and criminal cases was more adequate in investigations, the percentage of inimical home environments would be even greater than is now indicated. But we do not know the extent to which comparable groups of nonoffenders have family members who are lewd, alcoholic, immoral, and criminal, and we cannot tell at present how much more, if at all, we should expect delinquents than nondelinquents to issue from such circumstances.

The Companionship Factor

The role of accomplices and associates in criminal activity has been recognized from time immemorial. In recent years notice has been taken of the occurrence of associated crime and lone-wolf offenses, particularly at the juvenile level. We are justified in saying that companionate crimes among juvenile offenders in American cities should be expected to outweigh the lone-wolf offenses two to one and better. The proportion of companionate crime among boys is expected to be much higher than among girls. It is expected also that the property crimes will show a higher amount of companionate activity than will other crimes.

The sex differential in regard to companionate crime might be explained in terms of greater gregariousness in street play and roving activities among boys and girls—a fact which in turn reflects the influence of custom on activity. The preponderance of companionate delinquency among boys in American cities gives rise to the thought that delinquency might be in large measure group activity and that one is unable to tell where group play ends and delinquency begins. Thrasher discovered that gang life of American city boys veered easily toward delinquency and crime.

When various samples of delinquents have been studied by the case study method, the companionship factor has stood out as important. Even in Healy's pioneer work on the individual delinquent, bad companions were found to have been a causative factor in 34 per cent of the cases. But from such simple enumerations as this, one cannot tell whether bad companions are more characteristic of the associative life of delinquents than of nondelinquents. One might think so, but we do not actually know.

There are indications that delinquents are more active in social participation and more gregarious in play than nondelinquents. Atwood and Shideler found that a small sample of Indiana reformatory boys had a greater degree of group participation than a matched group of nondelinquent boys. The inference is that the delinquents, by having more contacts than nondelinquents, are in a better position to get into trouble and to get caught. The inference is, also, that delinquents are thereby more likely to get exposed to criminal patterns of behavior.

Further evidence along the same line comes from Healy and Bronner's comparison of 105 delinquents with 105 nondelinquent siblings of the same sex and nearest age. Only 16 of the delinquents were fairly solitary in interests, while only 11 of the nondelinquents participated in gang activities. Twenty-three of the nondelinquents avoided companionship as a way of keeping out of trouble, while many of them busied themselves with activities at home which removed them from association on the streets.

Tracing the companionship affiliations in acts of delinquency through the records of five brothers as a starting point, Shaw discovered that there seemed to be carriers of delinquent behavior patterns from one companionship association over to another. The carriers, so to speak, had been infected by the virus of crime in previous delinquency situations and were in turn infecting their associates in current situations. If a boy was exposed to a carrier he usually succumbed, that is, became implicated in delinquency, almost regardless of personality and background factors. Such a conclusion implies either that infection is virile or that the companionship situation weakens resistance, both of which could be true. It also implies that the personality and social background factors prepare the way for the exposure but do not explain the infection.

The jail, reformatory, or prison situation provides the means for contact of the less with the more criminally sophisticated inmates and hence gives the opportunity for passing along criminal ideas, attitudes, and skills. In spite of the development of institutional programs which are aimed in part at the prevention of contamination, the penal institutions are still schools for crime for a large proportion of inmates—how large, no one knows. On the outside, there is the job affiliation of former cell mates or prison mates. It has been observed many times that one of the great stumbling blocks in reformation is the meeting up with ex-convicts. Exposure to criminal sophistication in the institution and association with ex-inmates on release are factors which do not explain initial delinquency, but they do help to explain continuation in crime and the furtherance of a criminal career.

Community Factors

Community disorganization has been found to be related to several social problems, including crime and delinquency. However, it has been impossible to show that there is a one-to-one connection between personal and social disorganization. Many, perhaps most, individuals in a disorganized community may not be delinquent, whereas some persons, not very many, will be violators even in a well-organized social environment. Reckless has suggested that, while no direct causality between social disorganization and criminal behavior can be established, there is more opportunity to become a violator in a disorganized than in an organized environment.

The same line of argument must be used in the evaluation of the studies which have uncovered the tendency for crime and delinquency to decrease in rate with the distance from the center of the city. Such gradient tendency has been demonstrated for several cities of the United States. It was found to exist for concentric zones in the metropolitan area of Detroit, and even for counties of Kansas arranged on a tier basis according to size of the largest city or town. The reputed greater per capita volume of crime in cities as compared with rural areas is also in line with the general gradient tendency. The point is that there are more opportunities to commit crimes, to get demoralized, to pursue criminal careers, and to get caught in the areas of highest delinquency and crime rates. The gradient indicates spatial risks rather than causality.

The areas of highest crime and delinquency rates in American cities, namely, those around the center, are likewise areas of the greatest amount of disorganization as is indicated by the encroachment of business and industry on former residential neighborhoods, by the physical deterioration of residential property, by the declining population, and by the heavy concentration of other social problems. As we proceed outward from the center, we move more and more away from disorder and more and more toward order in American cities. But this means that we are moving away from greater to fewer opportunities for resident and nonresident individuals to become delinquent and criminal.

Special community institutions or enterprises have been singled out for their delinquency and crime-producing potency, such as saloons, poolrooms, criminal fences, junk yards, cheap dance halls, dens of vice and gambling, and so forth. These agencies of moral risk present opportunities to be exposed to delinquent and criminal patterns of behavior or to pursue a criminal career. Some of them are even the locus for carriers of criminal virus.

As in the case of the companionship or gang infection, these agencies of moral risk do not constitute a great risk for everyone, but they do constitute a risk for those whose personality and background factors have paved the way for individuals to respond to their wares.

The movies, the newspapers, magazines, the radio, and other agencies of mass impression have been suspected of infecting some individuals with criminal virus. In routine clinical case studies of delinquents, this factor has not assumed a position of grave importance. On the other hand, when delinquents are asked to indicate whether or not movies had any direct effect on misconduct, it appears that the movies play a more important role—more so for girls than for boys. It is safe to say that the significant patterns of behavior conveyed by movies, press, or radio must fall on prepared ground, that is, must reach individuals whose behavior resistance is low, in order to be influential, much the same as propaganda needs prepared soil upon which to work most effectively.

Operation of Sociological Factors

One can readily surmise that there is really nothing positive which can be said about the workings of the sociological factors in crime and delinquency. In making this confession, we should hasten to say that this status of affairs applies to the workings of biological and mental factors also. Causation is difficult to work out for behavior which must be socially defined in the first place and acted on officially in the second place.

Nevertheless, it may not be too unwarranted to point out that there seem to be two very important ways in which sociological factors in causation operate to produce delinquent and criminal behavior. The first is that the pressure of an unsatisfactory and discordant set of social relationships often forces some persons—we do not know exactly what sorts as yet—into delinquency as an out, just as they force persons into other behaviors of social escape such as desertion, vagrancy, and drink.

The relation of an unhappy set of human relationships to deviant behavior must be considered in connection with wish blockage and frustration. But we do not know which comes first or which is the more important: unbearable relationships or emotional distress.

The second, and perhaps the more, important relationship of sociological factors to delinquent and criminal behavior applies equally as well in cases where frustration is indicated as in those where it is not indicated. Reference is made to actual inculcation or transmission of delinquent and criminal behavior patterns in the companionship situation, in families with criminal or delinquent members, at agencies of moral risk in the community, and by agencies of mass impression—all of which contain carriers of infectious patterns. Here, again, we do not know just what sorts of persons adopt the available patterns of deviation. The theory of a special trait of suggestibility to account for unresisted takeover is not particularly satisfactory. All we know is that some individuals readily adopt the delinquent and criminal patterns available to them.

Socially Processed Careers

Sometimes the confronting patterns of deviant behavior merely take the form of ordinary delinquency and crime. Other times they take the form of definite criminal skills and attitudes as may be found in professional and organized crime.

The acquisition of criminal patterns of behavior is most clearly shown in the development of individuals with criminal careers, because the acquisition is visibly cumulative and progressive. Habitual and professional offenders are verily socially processed products, although the former may take the low road in crime (the way of the derelict and the bum) and the latter, the high road (the way of the successful operators).

The processing of careers in crime is essentially no different sociologically than the processing which turns out surgeons, ministers, newspaper reporters, longshoremen, professional baseball players, and so on. The prostitute, the safecracker, the bookie, the peddler, each in his own way, has acquired progressively the skills, the attitudes, and the philosophy of life of his peculiar milieu, in spite of differences in personality and background of the individuals in any one career.

If, in the future, students of behavior finally give up the study of causation of crime as too unyielding a job, they can certainly study the behavior patterning or behavior processing which comes off the social assembly line. Sociologists might never be able to tell why a person committed his initial delinquencies, but they may be able to tell how far he has been steeped in crime. And for what purpose, one might ask. Possibly to indicate in advance of treatment an adequate prognosis of the degree of unimprovability.

The sociologist looking at crime has called attention to four important points: (1) Crime is a violation of the criminal code which is just one type of behavior code, and hence it is unreasonable to expect criminals to be essentially different from violators of other behavior codes. (2) As a form of deviating behavior, crime and delinquency have a rather small liability of being acted upon officially, that is, becoming known and the violator caught. (3) The pressure of unbearable social relationships forces some persons into delinquency as an out for themselves. (4) The impact of confronting delinquent and criminal patterns of behavior may account for much of ordinary delinquency and crime and still more for criminal careers, which are socially processed products.

Society, in setting up the norms for deviating behavior and in developing informal or formal machinery to bring deviations to light, thereby subjects the various categories of people to differential criminal liability, according to their age, sex, class, and spatial position in the social order. Individuals falling within various combinations of these sociological categories are a greater or lesser risk for becoming violators and for getting caught. By their circumscribed social position, they are more or less exposed to unsatisfactory relationships, confronting patterns of delinquency and crime, and to official police action. The chances of a middle-aged widow, living in a fashionable hotel, to commit a crime and to be acted on officially are pretty slim indeed. But the chances of a nineteen-year-old boy, living in an area of high delinquency in American cities, would be very, very much greater.

With better and more adequate reporting of information on the records of offenders acted upon officially, it should be possible to compute the categoric crime risks for any area of consistent and uniform coverage. If causative studies cannot solve the riddle of why people become violators, actuarial methods should at least be able to predict what categories of people are a high or low risk for getting involved in crime.

Genes Cause Depression

PETER McGUFFIN AND RANDY KATZ

Peter McGuffin researches genetic influences in psychological disorders. Randy Katz studies depression. Together, they have published generously on the genetics of depression. In the following piece on depression, Peter McGuffin and Randy Katz argue that genes determine the acquisition of depressive illnesses. The authors look at the relationship between life events and depression to determine if familial factors in depression could somehow be related to external events and conclude that little if any relationship exists. McGuffin and Katz contend that studies of depression within families implicate a hereditary component to particular types of both depression and adversity. Here, McGuffin and Katz review family, twin, and adoption studies on the genetic transmission of depression and conclude that genes, rather than external factors, appear to be the driving force in depression.

QUESTIONS

1. According to the authors, what are the different ways of studying the genetic transmission of depression?

Peter McGuffin and Randy Katz, "Genes, Adversity, and Depression," in *Nature, Nurture, and Psychology*, edited by Robert Plomin and Gerald E. McClearn. Washington: American Psychological Association, 1993. Copyright 1993 by the American Psychological Association. All rights reserved. Reprinted with permission.

2. What evidence do the authors present for a genetic component to depression?
3. How do the authors differentiate the role of genetics and the role of the environment?

■ ■ ■

One of the most consistent observations about the likely causes of depressive disorders is that they are more frequently found among the relatives of depressed patients than in the population at large. However, familial aggregation could imply environmental causes, a genetic etiology, or a combination of the two. Although it is true that some (mainly uncommon) disorders for which abnormal behavior is prominent are transmitted as simple mendelian traits, for example, Huntington's disease and probably some subforms of Alzheimer's disease, a more complicated pattern of inheritance is usual. Indeed, as discussed elsewhere in this book, there is a large range of behaviors for which familial resemblance can be demonstrated. This includes scores on IQ tests and paper-and-pencil tests of personality for which genes seem to play a part in family resemblance, as well as characteristics that are likely to reflect cultural transmission such as religious beliefs or political attitudes.

Although it might seem quite straightforward to decide whether it is genes or family culture that is mainly responsible for the transmission of a particular trait, the evidence, based on family data alone, can be quite misleading. The idea that certain traits that are mainly nongenetic can "simulate mendelism" is not new, but it is something that researchers constantly need to remind themselves of in an era in which dramatic advances are being made in molecular genetics and for which it is tempting to speculate that this branch of science might hold all the answers for biological or behavioral phenomena. For example, McGuffin and Huckle recently studied attendance at medical school among the relatives of first- and second-year students at the University of Wales College of Medicine. The "risk" of attending medical school in the first-degree relatives of medical students was about 60 times that of the general population and, on carrying out a complex segregational analysis, McGuffin and Huckle found that the trait showed a pattern within families that was closely similar to that of autosomal recessive inheritance. This study thus replicated the finding of Lilienfeld, who 3 decades earlier obtained the same result using a simpler method of analysis. It is clear that if researchers are to proceed from observing familial aggregation to making inferences about the role of genes rather than family environment, then other sources of information will be needed. Fortunately, such information exists for depression.

Natural Experiments

Studies of twins and individuals separated from their biological relatives early in life provide the classical methods of teasing apart the effects of genes and family environment. For depression, the results are mainly consistent in showing an important genetic contribution to at least the more severe forms of affective disturbance. Thus, for example, the concordance in monozygotic (MZ) twins for manic depression was 67% compared with 20% in dizygotic (DZ) twins in a carefully conducted study for which the index cases were systematically ascertained using the Danish National Twin Register. This was very similar to the averaged results of earlier studies for which the overall MZ concordance was 69% compared with the DZ concordance of 13%. The adoption data are less extensive and show some inconsistencies; but overall, there is only evidence for an increased rate of affective disorder in biological relatives and not in adopted relatives.

Thus, taken together, the family, twin, and adoption data provide a suggestive body of evidence for an important genetic contribution to affective disorder. So far, however, we have used the terms *affective disorder*, *manic depression*, and *depressive disorder* in a general and, more or less, interchangeable way as if these terms were all-embracing and all descriptive of the same entity. This was indeed a prevailing view from the time of Kraepelin's first description of manic-depressive insanity at the end of the 19th century through most of the 20th century. However, influential family studies coincidentally published in the same year by Angst and Perris helped bring about a change. This was a move toward the view first proposed by Leonhard that manic depression could usefully be divided into *bipolar disorder*, which presents as episodes of both mania and depression, and *unipolar* disorder, which presents as episodes of depression alone. Although Perris' study indicated that the two disorders tended to "breed true," Angst's findings were more complicated. Nearly all subsequent research has found the same pattern as that found by Angst: Family members of unipolar index cases tend toward an excess of only unipolar disorder, whereas the family members of patients with bipolar disorder have increased risk of both bipolar and unipolar disorders. Another fairly consistent finding is that, although both types of disorder are familial, the overall risk of affective disorder is greater in the relatives of bipolar cases. The findings of the twin study of Bertelsen et al. also suggest that the genetic influences on bipolar disorder are strong, with the heritability in excess of 80%; whereas in unipolar disorder, the genetic influences may be more modest, with greater room for invoking environmental effects. For this reason, and because it is the commoner form of affective disorder, most studies that have examined environmental effects in affective disorder have focused on the unipolar form. We follow this convention in dealing with only unipolar disorder. However, we will also break somewhat with convention by attempting to simultaneously consider both genes and environment and how they coact and interact to cause depression.

Genetic Diathesis, Environmental Stress?

A long-established and common view of depression among psychiatrists in Europe (although less prevalent in the United States) is that there are broadly two types of unipolar disorder with different etiologies. On the one hand, there is endogenous depression, which has prominent "biological" features such as early morning waking, diurnal variation of mood, and loss of appetite and also has a constitutional basis; whereas on the other hand, there is neurotic depression, which lacks biological feature and is mainly reactive to stress. For example, Stenstedt noted that there were psychogenic factors in 90% of his neurotically depressed subjects but other exogenous factors in the remainder. In an earlier study, he found that those patients in whom there were obvious precipitants tended to have less family loading than those who did not. Such results then would support the idea that some patients with a marked biological/genetic diathesis develop their illness "out of the blue," whereas other patients in whom there is a smaller and nonspecific constitutional predisposition develop their illness as a result of obvious stress. Unfortunately, either because such dichotomy was taken for granted or because until recently researchers with interests in both factors were uncommon, most studies considered potential stresses and genetic diathesis quite separately. One exception was the investigation by Pollitt, who found a morbid risk of depression among relatives that was particularly high (at around 21%) when precipitants for the proband's illness were doubtful or absent. The morbid risk in relatives fell to between 6% and 12% when the proband's illness was "justifiable" in the sense that it followed severe physical stress, infection, or psychological trauma.

Since then, there have been methodological advances both in the ways that "stress" and psychiatric diagnosis are assessed and in the ways that family studies are conducted. Therefore, in collaboration with colleagues at the Medical Research Council's Social Psychiatry Unit in London, we mounted a study to investigate the relationship between adversity, in the form of life events or chronic difficulties, and familial aggregation of depression in a consecutive series of depressed patients and their families. The three main hypotheses with which we set out were as follows:

1. Depression with a neurotic pattern of symptoms is more often associated with a preceding threatening life event than is depression with an endogenous pattern.
2. Depressed patients whose disorder occurs in the absence of life events more often have depression among their relatives than do patients whose onset of disorder is associated with adversity.
3. Depression associated with adversity and depression not associated with any detectable stress are definable as two different forms of disorder, with each showing a tendency to breed true within families.

All of these hypotheses proved to be incorrect. Threatening life events and chronic difficulties were as often found before the onset of endogenous depression as before the onset of neurotic disorder, which contradicts the traditional view. The frequency of depression, regardless of how the disorder was defined, was higher among the relatives of the depressed subjects than in the general population, but there was no difference between the morbid risk in relatives of index cases who had experienced life events and that in relatives of those who had not. Furthermore, among the currently depressed family members, there was no tendency for subtypes of depression (one life event associated and the other not) to breed true.

We did, however, have one strikingly positive finding that was completely unexpected. Not only did depression aggregate in families but so also did life events. In the 3-month period before the interview (or before the onset of depression if the relative was depressed), 42% of the relatives of depressed patients reported one or more threatening life events compared with only 7% of a community sample studied earlier by Bebbington, Hurry, and Tennant. One possible explanation of these results might just have been that the recent onset of depression in the probands (the index cases) and their subsequent referral to a hospital caused turmoil throughout the family. However, even when all events that were in any way related to the probands were omitted, there was still a marked excess of reported adversity among family members, with 29% of them having had one or more threatening life events. Furthermore, the timing of life events of family members was unrelated to the proband's onset of depression.

Another intriguing finding was of a surprisingly weak association between recent life events and current depression among family members. Of the first-degree relatives who had recent life events, 21% were found to be current "cases" of depression on interview with the present state examination (PSE) compared with 15% among the relatives who had not experienced life events. However, this difference was nonsignificant statistically and contrasts markedly with the results of a study of a community sample, which used the same methods, for which 57% of those who had a recent life event were cases of depression compared with 7.5% of those who had not had a life event. A logistic regression that put the family and community data together showed that there was a highly significant interaction between life events and being the first-degree relative of a depressed patient in an analysis in which the proportion of affected subjects was taken as the response variable.

These results raised the question of whether the reported association between life events and depression that has been repeatedly observed in community studies is partly due to the fact that both are familial. Although this has yet to be replicated directly, recent twin study findings support the idea that life events show familial aggregation. In conclusion, the relationships between adversity, familiality, and depression turned out to be more complicated than we had originally thought, and we then attempted to explore this further in a twin study of our own.

Different Diagnostic Definitions, Different Environmental Effects

Our aims in carrying out a twin study of depression were to assess the degree of genetic determination of unipolar depression (a question that has sometimes been neglected compared with bipolar disorder), explore further the effects of different phenotypic definitions, and attempt to understand better the interplay between genes and environment in causing depressive disorder. Our sample was derived from the Maudsley Hospital twin register in London, which was established by Eliot Slater in 1948. We found that the register contained 408 probands with a primary diagnosis of depression of whom 215 fulfilled our screening criteria based on the third edition of the *Diagnostic and Statistical Manual of Mental Disorders* (*DSM-III*) and the syndrome check list of the PSE. Of these, 34 probands turned out to have had one or more episodes of bipolar disorder, and therefore, this part of the sample was set aside. The remaining 181 probands and their cotwins were closely investigated by personal interviews when possible, as well as examination of hospital case records and information from general practitioners and relatives. Case abstracts were prepared and assessed by clinicians who were unaware of the twins' zygosity and the diagnosis of the cotwin. This resulted in the elimination of 4 probands, which left us with a sample of 68 MZ and 109 DZ proband cotwin pairs.

A variety of definitions of depression were applied, and the preliminary results have been reported previously. Some of the main findings both for the preliminary analysis and a more recent assessment are summarized in Table 1. The constant finding, regardless of the definition that was applied, was of a significantly higher concordance for MZ twins than for DZ twins, which suggests a genetic effect. However, we then went on to apply a simple biometric model under which the observed phenotype could have resulted from additive gene effects, shared (familial) environment, and nonshared environment with no interactions (i.e., no nonadditive effects). Having made certain assumptions about the morbid risk of depression in the general population based on the study by Sturt, Kumakura, and Der, which was carried out in Camberwell, the old London borough in which the Maudsley Hospital is based, and about the distribution of liability to depression, we obtained two very different results for two different definitions of depression in the cotwins. The first was a narrow definition that used criteria of the revised *DSM-III* (*DSM-III-R*) for which we estimated the lifetime risk in the population to be 4.2%. The second broader definition used PSE-ID-CATEGO criteria, which we had somewhat modified so that having received hospital treatment was a necessary component and which has a population lifetime risk of about 8.9%. For the narrower definition, 79% of the variance was accounted for by additive genetic effects and the remainder by nonshared environment. Model fitting allowed no room for shared (familial) environment. By contrast, under the broad definition of depression, the additive genetic component explained only 39% of the variance, with shared environment accounting for 46%, and

TABLE 1 Concordance (Percentage) for Different Definitions of Unipolar Depression in Monozygotic (MZ) and Dizygotic (DZ) Twins

Definition	MZ		DZ	
	C	r	C	r
Broad	66	0.88[a]	42	0.66[a]
Narrow	46	0.77[b]	20	0.45[b]

Note. For MZ twins, *n* probands = 68; for DZ twins, *n* probands = 109. Broad = PSE-ID-CATEGO/hospital-treated; narrow = blind *DSM-III-R* major depression. *r* = correlation in liability. [a]Assuming a population risk of 8.9%. [b]Assuming a population risk of 4.2%.

the remainder due to nonshared environment. Attempts to remove either genes or shared environment as explanatory variables of broadly defined depression resulted in a significant worsening of the fit of each model, which led to the conclusion that all three components were necessary.

We speculate that these differences arose both because of the difference in breadth of the definition of depression and because of the incorporation of the receipt of hospital treatment in the broader definition. Thus, it might be expected that if an individual develops symptoms of depression, the probability that he or she will seek treatment and be referred to a hospital specialist is increased if he or she has a relative (such as a twin) who has already received such treatment. Therefore, our findings can be interpreted as showing that all of the familial aggregation of narrowly defined depression is explained entirely genetically, whereas treatment seeking for depressive symptoms is influenced by family environment (as in our analysis of the broad definition).

So far in our discussion of these twin results, environment—whether shared or nonshared—has been treated as a "latent variable." However, we also used some direct measures of the environment. Past environment, in particular those aspects of it that had been shared by the twins when growing up, was investigated using a questionnaire. As might be predicted, MZ twins were more alike than were DZ twins, including dressing alike during childhood. However, none of these measures appeared to influence their similarity for the later development of depression, nor did other measures of shared environment, which did not differ between MZ and DZ twins, such as the number of years spent together in the family home. But what of more immediate factors, such as recent life events, which may be of more direct relevance to the development of depression? Our next set of analyses concerned these.

Twin Similarities for Adversity and Depression

In our twin study, we used a measure of life events that was much less elaborate than, but derived from, the life events and difficulties schedule of Brown and Harris. This measure consisted of a checklist of the 12 most common categories of events associated with marked or moderate long-term threat. These included categories of events that were likely to be independent of the subject's symptoms, such as death of a first-degree relative, as well as events that might be associated with depressive symptoms, such as separation due to marital difficulties. In addition, we attempted to quantify subjective distress for each category of event on a 5-point scale ranging from 0, which signifies no event occurring in this category, to 4, which indicates that such an event occurred during this period and was severely distressing.

In general, the results supported the principal findings of our family study. The frequency of reported life events was high, with 74% of probands and 68% of cotwins having had one or more events in the 6 months before interview. Although we do not have a reliable population figure based on the checklist of 12 events with which to compare these results, other studies suggest that the frequency of reported life events for the general population is much lower. Also in keeping with the family study was an apparent lack of relationship between report of threatening life events and the presence of disorder. Although, because of our methods of ascertainment, we were less certain about time of onset than for the family material, threatening life events were actually less commonly reported by those cotwins who were current cases of depression according to PSE-ID-CATEGO than in cotwins who were not current cases. Thus, among cases, 66% had one or more life events compared with 70% in the cotwins who were not cases. Life events were similarly reported by 61% of cotwins who had a lifetime diagnosis of major depression compared with 73% of those who did not have such a diagnosis. This difference, which again is opposite to expected direction, is nonsignificant; and in fact, there was no relationship between the frequency of reported life events and any lifetime psychiatric diagnosis. In summary, the twin and family data both suggest a high frequency of reported threatening life events in individuals who have had a depressive disorder and in their relatives regardless of whether or not the relatives themselves are, or have been, depressed.

Interestingly, there was no apparent concordance for life events between probands and cotwins when the data were analyzed according to a simple dichotomy of life events reported/not reported in the past 6 months. However, when we quantified life events according to the number of different categories of events reported or by adding up the total subjective distress score, significant correlations emerged. The overall correlation for number of events was 0.35; and the correlation for MZ twins was only slightly higher at 0.37 than that for DZ twins, for which it was 0.33.

The distress scores turned out to be markedly skewed, but a reasonable approximation to normality was obtained by using the transformation $y = (1 + x)^{-1/2}$. The MZ intraclass correlation for the transformed score was 0.37, and the DZ correlation 0.33, which suggests only modest genetic effects. However, we explored this further using formal model fitting similar to that described earlier for the analysis of depression. The results are summarized in Table 2. Although the full model suggests a large common environmental effect and low heritability, it was impossible to reject reduced models with either common environment constrained to be zero or heritability similarly constrained. The only model that could be rejected with $x^2 = 54.7$ ($df = 2$) was the null model with no familial effects. We conclude that the subjective distress associated with life events is familial, but we are unable to differentiate whether this is due to family environment, genes, or a combination of the two. We suggest that family environment has the larger effect, but the results of the analysis are inconclusive.

As mentioned earlier, two other recent twin studies also found positive correlations for life events in twins. In both of these studies, a differentiation was made between *controllable* events (those likely to have been influenced by the subject's own actions) and *uncontrollable events* (those that were not conceivably influenced by the subject). Only controllable events

TABLE 2 Model Fitting Based on Subjective Distress Score Following Life Event

Model	h^2	c^2	x^2
Additive genes and family environment	0.06	0.30	0.0
Additive genes only	0.37	[0.0]	0.74
Family environment only	[0.0]	0.36	0.03
No familial effects	[0.0]	[0.0]	54.68

Note. Parameter values in brackets (i.e., [0.0]) are fixed.

(which by implication might be related to the subject's personality or mood state) appeared to have a genetic component.

Conclusions

Our findings strongly suggest that the syndrome of major depression when narrowly defined is highly heritable and that common family environment plays little if any part. These results are in keeping with those of other studies such as that of Torgersen, whose research was also based on a clinical sample, and that of Kendler et al., who studied a sample of female twins drawn from the general population. We found that the pattern of our results was markedly influenced by the definition of phenotype; and in particular, incorporating hospital treatment into the definition of depression resulted in a substantial family environmental contribution to the variance in liability. This may suggest that the main role of family environment in clinical depression is to influence help seeking.

The findings in relation to life events are surprising, but the familial effect is consistent with the results of our twin and family studies as well as those of two other recent twin studies. Our own studies are, as far as we are aware, the only ones to attempt to examine the familiality of both adversity and depression within the same sample. In both the family study and the twin study, there was little or no association between life events and depression in the relatives of depressed probands, which is in marked contrast to the often-repeated finding of an association between onsets of depression and preceding life events in samples of unrelated individuals. This may suggest that at least part of this association between life events and depression is due to the fact that both are familial. At present, it is impossible to say whether the familiality of life events reflects a type of behavior that is event prone or a type of thinking that is characterized by an increased awareness of perception of threat.

However, our studies contribute to an intriguing pattern of findings that are emerging in recent behavioral genetics research suggesting that genetic influences have a role in a variety of phenomena that have traditionally been regarded as indicators of the environment.

VIEWPOINT

6

Psychosocial Factors Cause Depression

ANDREW BILLINGS AND RUDOLF MOOS

Both individually and together Andrew Billings and Rudolf
Moos have written extensively on the role of stress and environment in depression. In the following viewpoint, Billings
and Moos discuss the psychosocial factors involved in the development of depressive illnesses. Their model assumes that
personal coping styles and the availability and utilization of
both personal and environmental resources can serve as miti-
gators or exacerbators of the various life stressors that promote depression. The model makes no assumptions about the
relative weight of each of the variables that determine an individual's likelihood of a depressive illness but instead develops a framework for analyzing some of the social factors related to depression.

Andrew Billings and Rudolf Moos, "Psychosocial Theory and Research on Depression," *Clinical Psychology Review* 2 (1982):213-37. Reprinted with permission of Elsevier Science Ltd., Pergamon Imprint, Oxford, England.

QUESTIONS

1. According to the authors, what are some of the environmental factors that can increase or reduce the probability of depression?
2. According to Billings and Moos, what are some of the personal factors that can increase or reduce the probability of depression?
3. According to the authors, what role do cognitions (thought patterns) play in the mediation or exacerbation of depression?

■ ■ ■

There is increasing theoretical and empirical concern about the etiology and treatment of depression. This concern mirrors recent confirmation that depressive disorders are a major health problem. Present estimates place the point prevalence of clinically significant depression at approximately five percent, with as much as 10 to 20% of the population reporting significant depressive symptomatology. A diversity of conceptual models and empirical methods have been used to explore intrapsychic, cognitive-phenomenological, social, and behavioral aspects of depression. Each of these approaches also have implications for the formulation and implementation of clinical interventions.

While psychosocial research has identified the etiologic role of stressful life events and several promising psychological treatments have been formulated, a number of important research and clinical issues have been identified. For instance, why do stressful life circumstances lead to depression among some persons but not others? How can one explain the finding that different psychosocial interventions appear to have similar affects on depression? Toward what areas should prevention efforts be targeted?

In this viewpoint we formulate a framework to organize these questions and to explore the commonalities among diverse areas of research and treatment on depression. The framework focuses on such issues as the identification of factors that determine the occurrence of stressful events and the likelihood that they will lead to depression, as well as the stress-moderating role of coping and social resource factors. Our goal here is to review and integrate research on the interplay of a set of conceptual domains, including environmental stressors, personal and environmental resources, and appraisal and coping responses. We use the framework to help understand the effectiveness of conceptually different treatment strategies, to explore the recovery process, to plan interventions that maximize the durability of treatment gains, and to develop implications for designing prevention programs and clarifying the determinants of their effectiveness.

An Integrative Framework

The framework presented in Figure 1 hypothesizes that the depression-related outcomes of stressful life circumstances are influenced by individuals' personal and environmental resources as well as by their appraisal and coping responses. These resources affect the occurrence of stressors, shape and nature of the coping responses selected to deal with them, and influence the adaptive outcome of the stressful episode. Thus the link between *environmental stressors* and depression is seen as mediated by individuals' personal and environmental resources, their cognitive appraisal and coping responses, and the interrelationships among these domains. Stressful life circumstances develop from personal and environmental factors

FIGURE 1. An integrative framework for the analysis of adaptive processes and depression

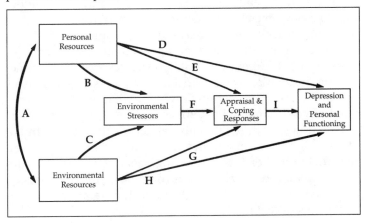

and include specific events (divorce, death of a spouse, job loss), chronic life strains associated with major social roles (a stressful job, marital discord), and medical conditions and illnesses (arthritis, cancer).

Personal resources include dispositional characteristics such as self-concept, sense of environmental mastery and attributional styles, as well as social skills and problem-solving abilities. *Environmental resources* refer to the informational, material, and emotional support provided by intimates, other family members, and nonkin social network members. It is in the context of these environmental and personal resources that individuals *appraise* particular stressors; that is, perceive and interpret specific events. Along with the appraisal process, individuals use *coping responses* that are intended to minimize the adverse effects of stress. The outcome of this process influences the individual's level of *functioning* and adaptation. From this perspective, adaptation includes those cognitive, affective, and behavioral aspects of functioning that may be disrupted in the depressive syndrome.

The model highlights the interrelationships among the domains affecting depression. For instance, the impact of environmental stressors on functioning is mediated by the other domains identified. A stressor elicits appraisal and coping responses (path F), whose nature and effectiveness determine whether the stressful event leads to depression and disruptions in functioning (path I). These processes are conditioned by personal and environmental resources. Personal resources, such as high self-esteem, may mitigate depressive outcomes by reducing the occurrence of stressors (path B), by facilitating stress-reducing coping (path E), or by fostering healthy functioning even in the absence of stress (path D). Environmental resources can affect functioning in similar ways. Furthermore, personal resources can indirectly affect depression by facilitating the development of environmental resources, such as supportive interpersonal ties (path A), that also affect functioning (path H). Finally, depressed mood and related aspects of functioning can affect each of the "preceding" sets of factors. We describe existing research in terms of these paths or processes and use the model to highlight important relationships between sets of factors. . . .

Stressful Life Circumstances

Much of the literature on stress and depression is concerned with the effects of major life events such as divorce, job loss, and death. Recent studies indicate the need to expand the concept of stress to include continuing life strains arising from major social roles, as well as more minor but frequent stresses encountered in daily living. We consider each of these factors in examining the role of stressful life circumstances in depression. This research has focused primarily on the overall association between stressors and depression without considering the mediating factors noted in our framework.

Stressful Events

Substantial evidence implicates environmental stressors in the development and maintenance of depression. The conceptual and methodological issues concerning life events are summarized elsewhere and will not be reviewed here. In brief, this line of inquiry has identified depressogenic effects of undesirable (negative) life changes in the areas of health, finances, and interpersonal relationships, particularly those representing exits or losses in the social field (such as deaths and separations). These events, which apparently have cumulative effects that may manifest themselves over several months, are three to six times more common among depressed individuals as compared to general population controls.

Another significant source of stress derives from chronic strains associated with an individual's major social roles of spouse, parent, and provider. For example, Pearlin and Schooler found that such strains as frustration of marital role expectations, children's deviations from parental standards of behavior, and difficulty affording food and clothing were associated with greater depressive symptomatology among community residents. Physical and emotional dysfunction of one's spouse or children also create strain. Recent research has focused on the work setting as an important source of such stressors. Work pressure, a lack of autonomy in decision making, and ambiguity about job roles and criteria of adequate performance have been associated with psychological distress and depression. The comparability of findings on life strains (examined primarily among community samples) and stressful events (typically explored among clinical samples) suggests an underlying commonality in the role of environmental stressors in minor and major depressive outcomes.

Microstressors

Lazarus and Cohen have noted the potential impact of daily "hassles," those comparatively minor but frequent irritants and frustrations associated with both the physical and social environment (such as noise, rush hour traffic, concerns about money, family arguments). In a short-term longitudinal study of a middle-aged community sample, indices of daily hassles were better predictors of current and subsequent depression than were indices of major life events. Hassles may have "direct" effects on adaptation and may also be the functional subunits that comprise the stressful aspects of major life events.

Despite these conceptual and methodological advances, stressful life circumstances provide only a partial explanation for the development of serious depression or for the prevalence of depressive mood and reactions among essentially "normal" individuals. While up to three-quarters of depressed patients may have experienced a provoking stressful event or strain recently, only one person in five in a nonpatient sample will become clinically depressed after facing a severe stressor. Among general community samples, typically less than 10% of the variance in depressive symptoms can be "accounted for" by life stressors. Stressors may act "directly" on depression or they may have "indirect" effects by reducing social resources and leading to maladaptive appraisals and ineffective coping responses. We turn our attention now toward factors that may help to explain individual variability in response to stressful circumstances.

Personal Resources

Personal resources include relatively stable dispositional characteristics that affect functioning and provide a "psychological context" for coping. We focus here on several aspects of personal resources that are particularly relevant to depression: sense of environmental mastery, attributional styles relating to environmental stressors, and interpersonal orientation and skills. These resources are thought to be consistent across situations; specific appraisal and coping responses that vary according to the nature of the stressor are discussed subsequently. These stable personal resources accrue from the outcomes of previous coping episodes and may be shaped by demographic factors which we consider later.

Personal resources can affect depression in several related ways. They may have "direct" effects on functioning (path D), as supported, for instance, by the finding that individuals who enjoy high self-esteem are less likely to become depressed. In fact, there is often some conceptual overlap in measures of personal resources and depression, since low self-esteem may be considered to be one aspect of a depressive syndrome. Personal resources may have indirect effects on depression by reducing stressors (path B) and by fostering social resources (path A) and coping responses (path E) that can attenuate the effects of stress.

Sense of Environmental Mastery

A lack of global personal resources such as perceived competence and a sense of mastery is common in many disorders, particularly depression. A focal construct in this area is an internal locus of control, that is, a generalized belief in one's ability to affect the environment so as to maximize rewards and minimize unpleasant outcomes. An external locus of control, a perceived inability to master one's environment either by controlling important events or in managing the consequences of events that are not controllable, has been directly associated with depression. For example, an external locus of control is associated with serious depression as well as greater frequency of dysphoria among college students.

An internal control orientation may afford some resistance to the effects of stress. For instance, Johnson and Sarason found that negative life events were less likely to be associated with depression among college students with an internal locus of control than among those with an external locus. Similarly, in comparison to externally oriented corporative executives, internally oriented executives were more likely to remain healthy while under high stress. A sense of environmental mastery, along with high self-esteem and freedom from self-denigration, has also been found to attenuate the depressive effects of life strains among members of a community group.

The development and maintenance of this sense of mastery has been a focus in the work of several important theorists including Bandura, Beck, and Seligman. For example, Bandura's model of adaptational behavior suggests that an internal control orientation and feelings of self-efficacy are related to the generalized expectancy of being able to cope successfully with prospective stressors. Self-efficacious persons will typically persist in active efforts to reduce stress, while those who see themselves as less efficacious tend to lack persistence and to utilize avoidance responses (path E). Active coping responses should reduce exposure to stress (path F') as well as moderate the effects of stress when it occurs (path I). Mastery of previous stressful circumstances can increase feelings of self-efficacy and reduce the use of defensive and avoidance-oriented coping styles. The effects of a sense of mastery may also extend to the development and use of social-environmental resources (path A), which themselves affect coping and depression (paths G and H).

Attributional Styles

Cognitive styles that are thought to be relatively stable and to affect perceptions of stressful circumstances have received considerable attention. Much of this work centers on the issue of perceived controllability and personal attribution of causality of the outcomes of stressful situations. The learned helplessness model hypothesizes that the lack of contingency between an individual's coping responses and environmental outcomes produces a generalized belief in the uncontrollability of the environment which relates to depression directly (path D) and indirectly by inhibiting active coping responses (path E). This belief, with its associated behavioral passivity (path E) and depressive affect (paths D and I), insulates the individual from future counteractive experiences of environmental control.

Beck's cognitive theory holds that persons with a strong predisposition to assume personal responsibility for negative outcomes are prone to depression. Such individuals are filled with self-blame that may cause depression (path D) and their pessimistic view of their future effectiveness can adversely affect their coping responses (path E). Beck postulates that depressives' cognitive appraisals are characterized by several distortions: arbitrary inferences—conclusions unwarranted by the situation; selective abstractions—not considering all elements of a situation; magnification/minimization—distortions of the significance of an event; and overgeneralization—drawing inappropriate conclusions given minimal evidence. Such appraisals are thought to promote attributions of failure in mastery situations to personal rather than environmental factors, thereby reinforcing depressive cognitive schemas (path E').

The learned helplessness and cognitive self-blame theories have been viewed as complementary. However, Abramson and Sackeim point out that these two theories have conceptually contradictory positions on the role of perceived controllability of stressful events. Merging these models could create "the paradoxical situation of individuals blaming themselves for outcomes they believe they neither caused nor controlled". In exploring such a paradox, Peterson found that depressives do have a tendency toward contradictory attributions, viewing stressful events as externally controlled yet blaming themselves for unsuccessful resolutions of such events. Additional theory development has suggested that depressives view themselves as personally incompetent in handling stressful situations which they perceive as being handled adequately by other persons (i.e., who are internally controlled).

While research has indicated an association between certain attributional dispositions and depression, we know little of how such factors shape the appraisal of specific environmental stressors (path E). Thus, the consistency with which these attributions will be observed across different stressful situations is unclear. We later consider specific attributional responses that have been measured within the context of particular events in discussing the appraisal and coping domain of our framework. We also explore the mechanisms whereby treatment procedures that focus on these styles may alleviate or prevent depression. . . .

Environmental Resources

Supportive interpersonal relationships are a major component of a person's social-environment resources. These social resources provide companionship, emotional support, cognitive guidance and advice, material aid and services, and reaffirmation of normative social role expectations. Access to new sources of support may also be provided via the interpersonal relationships that characterize social networks. The development of these resources is influenced by an individual's personal resources (path A). These resources are also shaped by the physical and architectural features of community settings and by the organizational and suprapersonal characteristics (that is, average characteristics of individuals inhabiting a setting) of these interpersonal contexts. We focus here on the functional effects of environmental resources rather than on their determinants.

Social-environmental resources may have both positive and negative effects on personal functioning. Theorists have suggested that deficits in such resources may lead to depression (path H) due to the unavailability or lack of social reinforcers, or both. A direct relationship between a lack of support and depression has been noted in surveys of community samples. Social-environmental factors may also have indirect effects. For instance, impaired communication processes and friction in interpersonal relationships can indirectly promote depressive symptomatology by fostering stress or leading to ineffective coping responses (paths C and G).

Among positive effects, the stress-buffering value of social support has been most frequently noted. There is evidence that social support attenuates the relationship between depressive symptomatology and stressful life events among community and depressed patient respondents, as well as among individuals experiencing such stressors as pregnancy and childbearing, job strain and job loss, and bereavement. The presence of social support may positively influence stressor-related appraisals and provide the resources necessary for effective coping that underlie the "buffering" effect (path G). Although there are many different sources of support, we focus here on family and work settings as two primary sources of environmental resources.

Family Support

Family members are a central source of emotional and material resources. Depression is associated with marital dissatisfaction as well as with disruption of the marital relationship. In a study of depressed patients, Vaughn and Leff found that the amount of criticism expressed toward the patient by family members at the time of hospitalization was a significant predictor of relapse during the posthospitalization period. In studies of a general community group, persons living in families that were less cohesive and expressive, and had more interpersonal conflict, reported more symptoms of depression than those living in more supportive families. In another community survey, Pearlin and Johnson found that married persons reported less depression than did the unmarried, even after controlling for such sociodemographic factors as gender, age, and ethnicity. In probing the determinants of this difference, persons who were married were found to be less exposed to various life strains (path C) such as occupational stress and economic hardship. Married persons were still less depressed than the unmarried after equating for levels of strain, indicating that married persons are less vulnerable to the effects of such strains, possibly because they have more sources of available support.

Work Support

The work setting is a potential source of support and stress. Work support is highest for persons who are highly involved in their jobs, have cohesive relationships with co-workers, and have supportive supervisors who encourage job involvement through work innovation and participation in decision making. In a community sample, Billings and Moos found that employees who perceived their work settings as high on these dimensions reported fewer symptoms of depression. These support factors also attenuated the depressive effects of work stress among men, but less so among women. A supportive work setting may diversify one's social resources by serving as an alternate source of interpersonal support. Conversely, work stress can erode family support (path C'). For instance,

Billings and Moos noted that men whose wives were employed in stressful job settings tended to report less family support and more depression than men whose wives had non-stressful jobs.

Indirect and Reciprocal Effects

Environmental resources may affect depression by facilitating effective coping with minor stressors, thereby circumventing the occurrence of major stressors (path G). The availability of social relationships can also provide the necessary context for certain coping responses (such as help-seeking and comparing one's situation to that of others) that may be particularly effective in preventing or alleviating stress (path C). In addition, the appraised severity of a stressor may be attenuated by the awareness that supportive resources are available to resolve a problematic situation (path G). For instance, Gore found that persons with high support perceived less financial stress due to a job loss than did those with less support, even though there were no differences between high and low support groups in their objective financial hardship.

Conversely, depression may affect environmental resources by leading to an erosion of social support (path H'). Depressed persons often elicit negative reactions from friends and family members. When friends and relatives are unsuccessful in controlling and reducing the individual's distress they may become hostile, withdraw their support, and eventually avoid interaction. Concurrent elevations in the depressive symptomatology of spouses and family members of depressed patients may reflect a cyclic process that reduces family support and exacerbates stress for all members. Depression can also reduce support by impairing future social initiative and social skills which are necessary to maintain social resources (via paths D' and A).

Clinicians who plan intervention efforts need to employ an expanded perspective to understand the varied aspects of social support and the different mechanisms of its effects. For instance, low social resources may be sufficient to induce depression in the absence of stress. Conversely, high stress and/or a lack of adaptive personal factors may be sufficient to cause depression even in the presence of supportive environmental resources. The framework suggests that environmental supports shape and are shaped by personal resources and levels of functioning, as well as by stressors and coping responses. Practitioners thus need to consider support in the context of these other domains. In addition, to understand the evolution of a depressive episode and plan effective treatment, clinicians must plan interventions to overcome the negative effects that depression can have on the individual's social resources.

Appraisal and Coping Responses

Our framework indicates that cognitive appraisal and coping responses can help an individual avoid depression by mediating the potential effects that stressors have on functioning (paths F and I), as well as by avoiding stressors (path F'). An appraisal involves the perception and interpretation of environmental stimuli. Appraisals are an iterative component of the coping process in which initial appraisals are followed by specific coping responses, and by reappraisal and possible modification of coping strategies. Our inclusion of appraisal and coping in a common domain reflects the interconnected and inseparable nature of these processes. We use appraisal and coping to refer to the particular cognitions and behaviors emitted in response to specific events. These specific behaviors are influenced by the "traitlike" attribution factors described earlier as personal resources and by the individual's environmental resources, which provide the context for coping. Current research has not always observed this distinction between personal resources and general attribution patterns and appraisal and coping responses to specific stressors.

While several attempts have been made to formulate a classification system for categorizing various appraisal and coping responses, no accepted method has yet emerged. We organize these dimensions into three sub-domains: (1) appraisal-focused coping—efforts to define and redefine the personal meaning of a situation; (2) problem-focused coping—behavioral responses to modify or eliminate the source of stress by dealing with the reality of the situation; and (3) emotion-focused coping—functions oriented toward managing stress-elicited emotions and maintaining affective equilibrium.

Appraisal of Stressors

Much of the research on the appraisal of stressful events has evolved from the self-blame and learned helplessness theories of depression. For example, among college students and depressed patients, Krantz and Hammen found a consistent relationship between depressive symptoms and scores on the *Cognitive Bias Questionnaire*, a measure of the distortions outlined by Beck. Hollon and Kendall have also shown that depressives score higher on an inventory of cognitive distortions and negative self-statements potentially triggered by stressful events. Although it is possible that depression may exacerbate "depressive" appraisals (path I), Golin, Sweeney, and Schaeffer found that such appraisals were more likely to precede than to follow an increase in depressive symptomatology (i.e., path I is stronger than path I').

The attribution of causality is an important aspect of the reformulated learned helplessness model. Abramson et al. hypothesize that individual attributions of the *causes* of a stressful event and perceived coping ability vary along three dimensions: (a) internal vs. external to self, (b) stable vs. unstable, and (c) global vs. situation- or role-specific. For example, given the stressor of unemployment and unsuccessful job search, attributions might be to either internal causes such as personal characteristics like lack of employment-related skills, or to external causes such as job discrimination. Stable causal attributions imply that future job-seeking efforts are likely to result in a similar lack of success. Global causal attributions, such as a general lack of perceived self-efficacy, would involve role performances in addition to employment and job hunting. Presumably, persons are more likely to remain free of depression if they attribute causality of negative outcomes to characteristics of stressors that are external to the self, that vary across situations, and that relate to a restricted area of performance. Operationalizing these factors with their *Scale of Attributional Style*, Seligman and his colleagues found that the appraisals of depressed and nondepressed college students differed in expected directions along these dimensions.

However, several recent studies have failed to find inconsistent relationships between these three attributional dimensions (internality, stability, and globality) and depression among college student samples. Extending research on these attributional processes to patient populations, Gong-Guy and Hammen utilized an attribution questionnaire to assess respondents' appraisals of recent stressful events as internal, stable, global, expected, and intended. Depressed and nondepressed outpatients showed expected differences along these dimensions in the appraisal of their most upsetting event, but not in their appraisals of all recent stressors. The reconciliation of these findings is complicated by divergence in the content of current measures. For example, the *Cognitive Bias Questionnaire* and the *Scale of Attributional Style* are both correlated with depressive symptoms, even though they are only moderately related to each other.

Stressor-Appraisal Specificity

Our framework indicates that the appraisal process is at least partially determined by the type of stressor (path F). In fact, studies employing heterogeneous samples of stressors have indicated that appraisal may be more closely related to event characteristics (path F) than personal characteristics (path E). Clinical theories have emphasized the interaction between personal factors and predispositions to appraise stressors in characteristic ways. Much of the laboratory research, however, has focused on the appraisals and effects of success versus failure outcomes in experimental tasks, such as solving anagram problems. Thus, there is little information on the extent to which stable attributional styles are linked to specific appraisal responses (paths E and E').

While conceptual and measurement issues have received increasing attention, we as yet know little of the actual appraisals made by depressed persons in their natural environments. Observed differences between depressed and nondepressed respondents in their appraisals of questionnaire-based scenarios of stressful events may not reflect their appraisals of actual personal stressors. Studies are needed to examine the extent to which the attributional styles of depressed individuals are related to their appraisals of real-life stressors. Current conceptualizations also need to be reviewed and elaborated. For instance, depressed persons may be "accurate" in perceiving stressors as personally uncontrollable and their personal and environmental resources as being inadequate. In this regard, there is evidence that normals have positively biased and self-serving attributions of causality, while depressives may have "accurate" perceptions rather than negative biases. During recovery, depressed persons' perceptions of their competence and control may become somewhat less realistic by moving toward the self-enhancing bias of non-depressed persons.

Coping Responses

We now consider the problem-focused and emotion-focused cognitions and behaviors that occur in response to appraised stressors. Relevant studies have examined the coping responses of depressed patients as well as the responses associated with depression among community groups. As with other domains, coping responses may attenuate the depressive effects of stress (paths F and I) or directly reduce or prevent the stressor (path F'). Coping patterns may also be influenced by the fact that depression can develop into a syndrome that requires coping efforts (path I'). For example, insomnia, weight loss and memory problems can influence current coping responses and may require additional coping efforts to alleviate the stress they themselves engender.

The interplay between appraisal and coping responses among a community group has been explored by Coyne, Aldwin, and Lazarus. They compared the coping responses of 15 persons falling within the depressed range of the Hopkins Symptom Checklist (on two occasions) with 72 persons who did not meet this criterion at either assessment. Although the depressed and non-depressed group did not differ in the type or perceived significance of stressful events encountered, there were differences in appraisal and coping responses. Depressed persons tended to appraise situations as requiring more information before they could act, and to view fewer events as necessitating acceptance and accommodation. They were also more likely to use such responses as seeking advice and emotional support and engaging in wishful thinking. However, there were no differences in the amount of problem-focused coping or use of self-blame, as might be predicted from the learned helplessness model. These findings are consistent with the idea that depressed persons find it difficult to make decisions and wish to be completely certain prior to either taking action or electing to view the objective characteristics of the stressor as outside of their control.

Billings and Moos evaluated the efficacy of various classes of coping responses among a representative community sample. Coping responses to a recent stressful event were assessed according to the method (active-behavioral coping, active-cognitive coping and avoidance coping) and focus of coping (problem-focused, emotion-focused). The use of avoidance responses, which serve to avoid actively confronting a problem or to reduce emotional tension by such behavior as increased eating or smoking, was associated with greater depressive symptomatology. In contrast, the use of active-cognitive and active-behavioral coping attenuated the depressogenic effects of stressful life events.

Some investigators have examined how individuals cope with the stress of being depressed. Funabiki and his colleagues developed a method of assessing the thoughts and behaviors college students use in coping with a depressive episode. Depressed students were more likely to be preoccupied with their stress-related emotions and to seek help from other depressed persons. However, these students also reported the use of efforts to counteract depression (tell myself things to cheer me up and try something new). Self-preoccupation may not be entirely maladaptive as it may provide an opportunity to identify environmental and intrapsychic contingencies relevant to depression. In this connection, structured self-monitoring of mood and activity can be effective in treating depressed patients.

Help-Seeking

Since social resources can be an important source of protection against the depressive effects of stressful events, help-seeking behaviors that tap or generate these resources are a key class of coping responses. Indeed, over half of the individuals who experience a troubling event will seek some help. While preliminary, there is some evidence that the nature and success of help-seeking may differentiate depressed and non-depressed groups. The nature of these differences is complex, as shown by the unexpected finding of Pearlin and Schooler that those who sought help in handling a stressful event reported more depression than those who relied on their own personal resources.

To understand the link between help-seeking responses and depression, we need to consider the impact that coping responses and depressive symptomatology may have on an individual's social resources (paths G' and H'). Help-seeking together with the expression of distress may have mixed effects on these resources. Howes and Hokanson found that undergraduates expressed more overt reassurance and sympathetic support to a "depressive" than to a normal role confederate. However, Coyne found that subjects conversing with a depressed patient were themselves more depressed and anxious, and tended to covertly reject the patient. Hammen and Peters also report results indicating the covert rejection of depressed partners, although depressive behavior was more acceptable from women than from male partners. Thus, certain patterns of help-seeking may be more intense than is appropriate for the strength, intimacy, and context of the relationship.

While help-seeking in the context of depression may elicit superficial support in brief encounters with strangers, its long-term consequences on more intimate relationships may be negative. Intimates may initially offer mollifying support to aid the depressed person and to control that person's expression of hysphoria, which intimates find aversive. Intimates may suppress the direct expression of their own negative reactions to the depressives' behavior. However, these initial responses often fail to provide the validation that depressives seek for the appropriateness of their stress reactions. This ambiguity in the "supportive" communications of others exacerbates stress (path C), and fails to provide the feedback necessary to guide the depressive's coping responses (path G) that might effectively reduce dysphoria.

Increased help-seeking and expression of depressive behaviors, so as to draw more convincing and effective support, may lead to an increase in intimates' efforts to control and minimize depressive symptomatology. The failure of social network members to control the expression of distress produces frustration and more negative attitudes toward the depressed person. It may be at this point that the negative and rejecting responses of intimates and family members are frankly expressed. Network members' expression of negative reactions and withdrawal from their relationship with the stressed individual may have adverse effects on that individual's coping and functioning (paths G and H), and may heighten susceptibility to depression by decreasing the individual's self-esteem (path A).

The effects of various help-seeking responses should be explored in the context of particular stressors. The chronicity of the stressor may be a particularly relevant dimension. For instance, obtaining help from informal sources may be most advantageous in coping with discrete, time-limited stressors. When the stressor is of a more chronic nature (e.g., long-term unemployment or physical disability), individuals may "burnout" their social resources by overreliance on an informal social network. Professional or institutionalized sources of support may be especially important in handling chronic or major stressors that surpass the individual's social resources. Similarly, normative life stage stressors, such as marriage and childbirth, elicit institutionalized support responses while unexpected events, such as divorce, have no guides for help-seeking.

Should Psychological Theory Determine Public Policy?

Chapter Preface

In recent years psychology has begun to play an increased role in the shaping of public policy in both the judicial and legislative domains. However, it is not clear whether psychological theories are, as of yet, sturdy enough to serve as a foundation for law.

Psychological issues become legal issues when, as a society, we are forced to make legal decisions based on psychological theories. The debate surrounding the accuracy of repressed memories, for example, is not just a philosophical debate over Freud's theories, rather, its result has ominous implications in the courtroom. Proof of the existence of repressed memories may open the door to tort claims of sexual abuse by tolling the statute of limitations, or it may increase the number of false accusations. On the other side of the argument dismissal of repressed memories may prevent sexual abuse survivors from pressing charges on viable claims for redress and protect their molesters.

Another area of interest for psycho-legal theorists is the debate surrounding the practice of involuntary commitment for the mentally ill. Here, the principles of personal autonomy are weighed against the needs of society and of the mentally ill individual. Psychological definitions of mental illness as well as data reflecting the prognosis of treatment and predictability of dangerousness are called to task in courtrooms and thus affect whether certain psychological disorders demand forced commitment.

The implications of psychology on public policy can be seen in the first set of articles in this chapter dealing with repressed memories. Although popular media has recently donated an incredible amount of attention to the issue of repressed memories, the controversy is as old as Freud's theory of repression itself. The idea that traumatic memories too unbearable to face may be buried in an individual's unconscious mind has endured fierce skepticism. The contemporary slant on the repressed memory debate questions the therapist's role in the creation of false memories. The media, as well as a large number of critics in the field of psychology, cite cases where clients have created false traumatic memories because of the expectations or suggestions of their therapist. The implications of this practice are threefold: First, these false memories, as vivid as actual memories, inevitably produce traumas comparable to those of actual survivors of childhood sexual abuse. If indeed this practice is occurring at the rate that its critics suggest, it would mean that a considerable number of people are leaving therapy worse off than when they entered. Second, false memories often produce false accusations of sexual abuse. Finally, assuming that some unresolved issue brought the client to the therapist in the first place, this issue remains unresolved while clients attend to their false memories. Elizabeth Loftus's article in this section explores these issues in detail.

On the other side of the repressed memory debate, as has historically been the case, adherents to the concept of repression cite case histories and research documenting the existence of repression and its link to childhood sexual trauma. They assert that the unearthing of hidden childhood traumas creates survivors out of victims and puts the client on the road to recovery. Furthermore, because one of the greatest fears of those who have suffered child sexual abuse is that their stories will not be believed, a therapist who questions the veracity of a client's repressed memories may be doing more harm than good for the client. The article by Matthew Erdelyi explores some of the methodological problems with the study of repressed memories.

The viewpoints in all of the following chapters debate psychology's usefulness in determining public policy.

Repressed Memories Are Questionable

ELIZABETH F. LOFTUS

Elizabeth F. Loftus is one of the nation's foremost authorities on memory. The veteran expert witness testifies on human memory, and is best known for her research implicating the inaccuracy of eyewitness testimony. Here, she discusses repressed memories in the context of their legal implication for delayed child sexual abuse claims. Loftus points to the paucity of research substantiating repressed memories and outlines the research on suggestibility and the creation of false memories. She ends her discussion with some suggestions and cautions for professionals working with repressed memories.

QUESTIONS

1. Does Loftus deny the existence of repressed memories?
2. According to Loftus what are some of the sources of false memories?
3. According to Loftus how do real memories differ from false memories?

4. What are some of the dangers of false memories and how can professionals guard against these?

■ ■ ■

There is little doubt that actual childhood sexual abuse is tragically common. Even those who claim that the statistics are exaggerated still agree that child abuse constitutes a serious social problem. I do not question the commonness of childhood sexual abuse itself but ask here about how the abuse is recalled in the minds of adults. Specifically, how common is it to repress memories of childhood sexual abuse? Claims about the commonness of repressed memories are freely made: It is typical to read estimates such as "most incest survivors have limited recall about their abuse" or "half of all incest survivors do not remember that the abuse occurred". One psychotherapist with 18 years of experience has claimed that "millions of people have blocked out frightening episodes of abuse, years of their life, or their entire childhood". Later, she reported that "sexual abuse is particularly susceptible to memory repression".

Beliefs about the commonness of repressed memories are expressed not only by those in the therapeutic community but also by legal scholars who have used these beliefs to argue for changes in legislation. For example, Lamm argued in favor of legislation that would ease access to the courts for victims of childhood sexual abuse. She applauded legislation, such as that enacted in California in 1991, that allows victims, no matter how old they are, to sue within three years after discovering their injuries or eight years after reaching majority, whichever date occurs later. As part of her argument that victims should have more time to file claims against their abusers, she expressed a view that "total repression of memories of abuse is common".

Despite the confidence with which these assertions are made, there are few studies that provide evidence of the extent to which repression occurs. One study sampled 450 adult clinical clients who had reported sexual abuse histories. Therapists approached their individual clients or group clients with this question: "During the period of time between when the first forced sexual experience happened and your 18th birthday was there ever a time when you could not remember the forced sexual experience?" The main result obtained in this largely female (93%) largely White (90%) sample was that 59% said yes. A yes response was more likely in cases involving violent abuse (physical injury, multiple perpetrators, and fears of death if abuse was disclosed) than nonviolent abuse. Reported amnesia was more likely with early molestation onset, longer abuse, and greater current symptomatology. The authors concluded that amnesia for abuse was a common phenomenon.

Briere and Conte's result has been taken by others as evidence for the widespread extent of repression. For example, Summit (1992) interpreted the 59% yes rate as evidence that this proportion of people "went through periods of amnesia when they were not aware of their prior abuse". He used the finding to support the commonness of childhood dissociation.

One problem with Briere and Conte's estimate is that it obviously depends on how the respondent interprets the eliciting question. A yes response to the question could be interpreted in a variety of ways other than "I repressed my memory for abuse." For example, it could mean "Sometimes I found it too unpleasant to remember, so I tried not to"; or "There were times when I could not remember without feeling terrible"; or "There were times I could not bring myself to remember the abuse because I would rather not think about it." Although no question is free of the possibility of multiple interpretations, the great potential for idiosyncratic interpretation by respondents to the particular wording used by Briere and Conte warrants a further examination of the issue with a different eliciting question.

A further problem with Briere and Conte's study is that the respondents were all in therapy. If some of their clinicians were under the belief that repression of memory is common, they may have communicated this belief to their clients. Clients could readily infer that, if repression of memory is so common, it is likely to have happened to them, thus the answer to the question is probably yes. This would, of course, inflate the estimates of the prevalence of repression.

Other studies have given much lower estimates for the existence of repression. Herman and Schatzow gathered data from 53 women in therapy groups for incest survivors in the Boston area. Of the 53 cases, 15 (28%) reported severe memory deficits (including women who could recall very little from childhood and women who showed a recently unearthed repressed memory). Severe memory problems were most likely in cases of abuse that began early in childhood and ended before adolescence. Cases of violent or sadistic abuse were most likely to be associated with "massive repression as a defense".

An even lower estimate was obtained in a study of 100 women in outpatient treatment for substance abuse in a New York City hospital. More than one half of the women in this sample reported memories of childhood sexual abuse. The vast majority of them remembered the abuse their whole lives. Only 18% claimed that they forgot the abuse for a period of time and later regained the memory. Whether the women remembered the abuse their whole lives or forgot it for a period was completely unrelated to the violence of the abuse.

Of course, the data obtained from the New York sample may include an underestimation factor because there could have been many more women in the sample who were sexually abused, repressed the memory, and had not yet regained it. In support of this hypothesis, one could point to the research of L. M. Williams, who interviewed 100 women, mostly African American, known to have been abused 17 years earlier in their lives. Of these, 38% were amnestic for the abuse or chose not to report it. Perhaps there were women in the New York sample who denied sexual abuse but who were still repressing it. Possibly there are women who were actually abused but do not remember it; however, it is misleading to assume that simple failure to remember means that repression has occurred. If an event happened so early in life, before the offset of childhood amnesia, then a woman would not be expected to remember it as an adult, whether it was abuse or something else. This would not imply the mechanism of repression. Moreover, ordinary forgetting of all sorts of events is a fact of life but is not thought to involve some special repression mechanism. For example, studies have shown that people routinely fail to remember significant life events even a year after they have occurred. One study consisted of interviews with 590 persons known to have been in injury-producing motor vehicle accidents during the previous year. Approximately 14% did not remember the accident a year later. Another study consisted of interviews with 1,500 people who had been discharged from a hospital within the previous year. More than one fourth did not remember the hospitalization a year later.

How common are repressed memories of childhood abuse? There is no absolute answer available. There are few satisfying ways to discover the answer, because we are in the odd position of asking people about a memory for forgetting a memory. For the moment, figures range from 18% to 59%. The range is disturbingly great, suggesting that serious scholarly exploration is warranted to learn how to interpret claims about the commonness of repression and what abuse characteristics the repression might be related to.

What Are the Memories Like?

The quality of the memories that filter back vary tremendously. They are sometimes detailed and vivid and sometimes very vague. Sometimes they pertain to events that allegedly happened in early childhood and sometimes in adolescence. Sometimes they pertain to events that allegedly happened 5 years ago and sometimes 40 years ago. Sometimes they include fondling, sometimes rape, and sometimes ritualism of an unimaginable sort.

Highly detailed memories have been reported even for events that allegedly happened more than 25 years earlier and during the first year of life. One father-daughter case recently tried in Santa Clara County, California, illustrates this pattern. The daughter, DC, a college graduate who worked as a technical writer, claimed that her father sexually abused her from the time she was six months old until she was 18. She repressed the memories until the age of approximately 26, when she was in individual and group therapy.

Other cases involve richly detailed allegations of a more bizarre, ritualistic type, as in a case reported by Rogers. The plaintiff, Bonnie, in her late 40s at the time of trial, accused her parents of physically, sexually, and emotionally abusing her from birth to approximately age 25. A sister, Patti, in her mid-30s at the time of trial, said she was abused from infancy to age 15. The allegations involved torture by drugs, electric shock, rape, sodomy, forced oral sex, and ritualistic killing of babies born to or aborted by the daughters. The events were first recalled when the plaintiffs went into therapy in the late 1980s.

In short, reports of memories after years of repression are as varied as they can be. One important way that they differ is in terms of the age at which the events being remembered allegedly happened. In many instances, repressed memory claims refer to events that occurred when the child was one year old or less. This observation invites an examination of the literature on childhood amnesia. It is well known that humans experience a poverty of recollections of their first several years in life. Freud (1905/1953) identified the phenomenon in some of his earliest writings: "What I have in mind is the peculiar amnesia which . . . hides the earliest beginnings of the childhood up to their sixth or eighth year". Contemporary cognitive psychologists place the offset of childhood amnesia at a somewhat earlier age: "past the age of ten, or thereabouts, most of us find it impossible to recall anything that happened before the age of four or five". Most empirical studies of childhood amnesia suggest that people's earliest recollection does not date back before the age of about three or four. One study showed that few subjects who were younger than three recalled any information about where they were when they heard about the assassination of President Kennedy, although most subjects who were more than eight at the time had some recall. Although one recent study suggests that some people might have a memory for a hospitalization or the birth of a sibling that occurred at age two, these data do not completely rule out the possibility that the memories are not true memories but remembrances of things told by others. Still, the literature on childhood amnesia ought to figure in some way into our thinking about recollections of child molestation that supposedly occurred in infancy.

Are the Memories Authentic?

Therapists' Beliefs About Authenticity

Many therapists believe in the authenticity of the recovered memories that they hear from their clients. Two empirical studies reveal this high degree of faith. Bottoms, Shaver, and Goodman conducted a large-scale survey of clinicians who had come across, in their practice, ritualistic and religion-related abuse cases. Satanic ritualistic abuse (SRA) cases involve allegations of highly bizarre and heinous criminal ritual abuse in the context of an alleged vast, covert network of highly organized, transgenerational satanic cults. Clients with SRA memories have reported vividly detailed memories of cannibalistic revels and such experiences as being used by cults during adolescence as serial baby breeders to provide untraceable infants for ritual sacrifices. If therapists believe these types of claims, it seems likely that they would be even more likely to believe the less aggravated claims involving ordinary childhood sexual abuse. Bottoms et al.'s analysis revealed that 30% of responding clinicians had seen at least one case of child sexual abuse. A detailed analysis of 200 clinicians' experiences revealed that a substantial number of cases involved amnesic periods (44% of adult survivor cases). Overall, 93% of clinicians believed the alleged harm was actually done and that the ritualistic aspects were actually experienced by the clients. The conclusion was, in the investigators' own words, "The clinical psychologists in our sample believe their clients' claims.

A different approach to the issue of therapist belief was taken by Loftus and Herzog. This study involved in-depth interviews with 16 clinicians who had seen at least one repressed memory case. In this small, nonrandom sample, 13 (81%) said they invariably believed their clients. One therapist said, "if a woman said it happened, it happened." Another said, "I have no reason not to believe them." The most common basis for belief was symptomatology (low self-esteem, sexual dysfunction, self-destructive behavior), or body memories (voice frozen at young age, rash on body matching inflicted injury). More than two thirds of the clinicians reacted emotionally to any use of the term *authentic,* feeling that determining what is authentic and what is not authentic is not the job of a therapist. The conclusion from this small study was that therapists believe their clients and often use symptomatology as evidence.

These and other data suggest that therapists believe in their clients' memories. They point to symptomatology as their evidence. They are impressed with the emotional pain that accompanies the expression of the memories. Dawes has argued

that this "epidemic" of belief is based in large part on authority and social consensus.

Are the Memories Accurate?

There are those with extreme positions who would like to deny
the authenticity of all repressed memories and those who would
accept them all as true. As Van Benschoten has pointed out, these
extreme positions will exacerbate our problems: "Denial fosters
overdetermination, and overdetermination invites denial".

If we assume, then, that some of the memories might be authentic and some might not be, we can then raise this question:
If a memory is recovered that is not authentic, where would it
come from? Ganaway proposed several hypotheses to explain
SRA memories, and these same ideas are relevant to memories
of a repressed past. If not authentic, the memories could be due
to fantasy, illusion, or hallucination-mediated screen memories,
internally derived as a defense mechanism. Further paraphrasing Ganaway, the SRA memories combine a mixture of borrowed ideas, characters, myths, and accounts from exogenous
sources with idiosyncratic internal beliefs. Once activated, the
manufactured memories are indistinguishable from factual
memories. Inauthentic memories could also be externally derived as a result of unintentional implantation of suggestion by
a therapist or other perceived authority figure with whom the
client desires a special relationship, interest, or approval.

The Memories Are Authentic

There is no doubt that childhood sexual abuse is tragically
common (Daro, 1988). Surveys reveal a large range in the estimated rates (10%–50%), but as Freyd has argued, even the
most conservative of them are high enough to support the
enormity of child abuse. A sizeable number of people who
enter therapy were abused as children and have always remembered their abuse. Even when they have severe emotional
problems, they can provide rich recollections of abuse, often
with many unique, peripheral details. Occasionally the abuse
is corroborated, sometimes with very cogent corroboration,
such as pornographic photographs. If confirmed abuse is
prevalent, many instances of repressed memory abuse cases

also could be authentic. Unfortunately, in the repressed memory cases, particularly when memories do not return for 20 or 30 years, there is little in the way of documented corroboration. This, of course, does not mean that they are false.

Claims of corroborated repressed memories occasionally appear in the published literature. For example, Mack reported on a 1955 case involving a 27-year-old borderline man who, during therapy, recovered memories of witnessing his mother attempting to kill herself by hanging. The man's father later confirmed that the mother had attempted suicide several times and that the son had witnessed one attempt when he was 3 years old. The father's confirmation apparently led to a relief of symptoms in the son. It is hard to know what to make of examples such as these. Did the son really remember back to age 3, or did he hear discussions of his mother's suicide attempts later in life? The memories could be real, that is, genuine instances of repressed memories that accurately returned much later. If true, this would only prove that some memory reports are authentic but obviously not that all reports are authentic. Analogously, examples of repressed memories that were later retracted, later proved to be false, or later proved to be the result of suggestion would only prove that some memory reports are not authentic but obviously not that all such reports are illusory.

Some who question the authenticity of the memories of abuse do so in part because of the intensity and sincerity of the accused persons who deny the abuse. Many of the thousands of people who have been accused flatly deny the allegations, and the cry of "witch hunt" is often heard. *Witch hunt* is, of course, a term that has been loosely used by virtually anyone faced by a pack of accusers. Analogies have been drawn between the current allegations and the witch craze of the 16th and 17th centuries, when an estimated half million people were convicted of witchcraft and burned to death in Europe alone. Although the denials during the witch craze are now seen as authentic in the light of hindsight, the current denials of those accused of sexual abuse are not proof that the allegations are false. Research with known rapists, pedophiles, and incest offenders has illustrated that they often exhibit a *cognitive distortion*—a tendency to justify, minimize, or rationalize their behavior. Because accused persons are motivated to verbally and even mentally deny an abusive past, simple denials cannot constitute cogent evidence that the victim's memories are not authentic.

The Memories Are Not Authentic

To say that memory might be false does not mean that the person is deliberately lying. Although lying is always possible, even psychotherapists who question the authenticity of reports have been impressed with the honesty and intensity of the terror, rage, guilt, depression, and overall behavioral dysfunction accompanying the awareness of abuse.

There are at least two ways that false memories could come about. Honestly believed, but false, memories could come about, according to Ganaway, because of internal or external sources. The internal drive to manufacture an abuse memory may come about as a way to provide a screen for perhaps more prosaic but, ironically, less tolerable, painful experiences of childhood. Creating a fantasy of abuse with its relatively clear-cut distinction between good and evil may provide the needed logical explanation for confusing experiences and feelings. The core material for the false memories can be borrowed from the accounts of others who are either known personally or encountered in literature, movies, and television. . . .

Why Would Therapists Suggest Things to Their Patients?

The core of treatment, it is widely believed, is to help clients reclaim their "traumatic past". Therapists routinely dig deliberately into the ugly underbelly of mental life. They dig for memories purposefully because they believe that in order to get well, to become survivors rather than victims, their clients must overcome the protective denial that was used to tolerate the abuse during childhood. Memory blocks can be protective in many ways, but they come at a cost: they cut off the survivors from a significant part of their past histories and leave them without good explanations for their negative self-image, low self-esteem, and other mental problems. These memories must be brought into consciousness, not as an end in itself but only insofar as it helps the survivors acknowledge reality and overcome denial processes that are now dysfunctional.

Another reason therapists may be unwittingly suggesting ideas to their clients is that they have fallen prey to a bias that affects all of us, known as the "confirmatory bias". People in general, therapists included, have a tendency to search for evidence that confirms their hunches rather than search for evidence that disconfirms. It is not easy to discard long-held or cherished beliefs, in part because we are eager to verify those beliefs and are not inclined to seek evidence that might disprove them.

The notion that the beliefs that individuals hold can create their own social reality is the essence of the self-fulfilling prophecy. How does "reality" get constructed? One way this can happen is through interview strategies. Interviewers are known to choose questions that inquire about behaviors and experiences thought to be characteristic, rather than those thought to be uncharacteristic, of some particular classification. If therapists ask questions that tend to elicit behaviors and experiences thought to be characteristic of someone who had been a victim of childhood trauma, might they too be creating this social reality?

Whatever the good intentions of therapists, the documented examples of rampant suggestion should force us to at least ponder whether some therapists might be suggesting illusory memories to their clients rather than unlocking authentic distant memories. Or, paraphrasing Gardner, what is considered to be present in the client's unconscious mind might actually be present solely in the therapist's conscious mind. Ganaway worried that, once seeded by the therapist, false memories could develop that replace previously unsatisfactory internal explanations for intolerable but more prosaic childhood trauma.

Creation of False Memories

The hypothesis that false memories could be created invites an inquiry into the important question of what is known about false memories. Since the mid-1970s at least, investigations have been done into the creation of false memories through exposure to misinformation. Now, nearly two decades later, there are hundreds of studies to support a high degree of memory distortion. People have recalled nonexistent broken glass and tape recorders, a cleanshaven man as having a mustache, straight hair as curly, and even something as large and conspicuous as a barn in a bucolic scene that contained no buildings at all. This growing body of research shows that new, postevent information often becomes incorporated into memory, supplementing and altering a person's recollection. The new information invades us, like a Trojan horse, precisely because we do not detect its influence. Understanding how we can become tricked by revised data about our past is central to understanding the hypothesis that suggestions from popular writings and therapy sessions can affect autobiographical recall.

One frequently heard comment about the research on memory distortion is that all changes induced by misinformation are about trivial details. There is no evidence, the critics allege, that one can tinker with memories of real traumatic events or that one can inject into the human mind whole events that never happened.

Can Real Traumatic Memories Be Changed?

There are some who argue that traumatic events leave some sort of indelible fixation in the mind (e.g., "traumatic events create lasting visual images . . . burned-in visual impressions," "memory imprints are indelible, they do not erase—a therapy that tries to alter them will be uneconomical,". These assertions fail to recognize known examples and evidence that memory is malleable even for life's most traumatic experiences. If Eileen Franklin's memory of witnessing her father murder her eight-year-old best friend is a real memory, then it too is a memory replete with changes over different tellings. However, there are clearer examples—anecdotal reports in which definite evidence exists that the traumatic event itself was actually experienced and yet the memory radically changed.

In the category of documented anecdotes there is the example of one of the worst public and personal tragedies in the history of baseball. Baseball aficionados may recall that Jack Hamilton, then a pitcher with the California Angels, crushed the outfielder, Tony Conigliaro, in the face with a first-pitch fastball. Although Hamilton thought he remembered this horrible event perfectly, he misremembered it as occurring during a day game, when it was actually at night, and misremembered it in other critical ways. Another example will be appreciated by history buffs, particularly those with an interest in the second world war. American Brigadier General Elliot Thorpe recalled the day after the bombing of Pearl Harbor one way in a memoir and completely differently in an oral history taken on his retirement. Both accounts, in fact, were riddled with errors.

Evidence of a less anecdotal, more experimental nature supports the imperfections of personally experienced traumatic memories. For example, one study examined people's recollections of how they heard the news of the 1986 explosion of the space shuttle *Challenger*. Subjects were questioned on the morning after the explosion and again nearly three years later. Most described their memories as vivid, but none of them were entirely correct, and more than one third were wildly inaccurate. One subject, for example, was on the telephone having a business discussion when her best friend interrupted the call with the news. Later she would remember that she heard the news in class and at first thought it was a joke, and that she later walked into a TV lounge and saw the news, and then reacted to the disaster.

Another study demonstrated the malleability of memory for a serious life-and-death situation. The subjects had attended an important high school football game at which a player on the field went into cardiac arrest. Paramedics tried to resuscitate the player and apparently failed. The audience reactions ranged from complete silence, to sobbing, to screaming. (Ultimately, fortunately, the player was revived at the hospital.) Six years later, many of these people were interviewed. Errors of recollection were common. Moreover, when exposed to misleading information about this life-and-death event, many individuals absorbed the misinformation into their recollections. For example, more than one fourth of the subjects were persuaded that they had seen blood on the player's jersey after receiving a false suggestion to this effect.

These anecdotes and experimental examples suggest that even details of genuinely experienced traumatic events are, as Christianson put it, "by no means, completely accurate".

Can One Inject a Complete Memory for Something That Never Happened?

It is one thing to discover that memory for an actual traumatic event is changed over time but quite another to show that one can inject a whole event into someone's mind for something that never happened. There are numerous anecdotes and experimental studies that show it is indeed possible to lead people to construct entire events.

Piaget's memory. Whole memories can be implanted into a person's real-life autobiography, as is best shown by Piaget's classic childhood memory of an attempted kidnapping. The false memories were with him for at least a decade. The memory was of an attempted kidnapping that occurred when he was an infant. He found out it was false when his nanny confessed years later that she had made up the entire story and felt guilty about keeping the watch she had received as a reward. In explaining this false memory, Piaget assumed, "I, therefore, must have heard, as a child, the account of this story, which my parents believed, and projected into the past in the form of a visual memory."

Loud noises at night. Although widely disseminated and impressive at first glance, Piaget's false memory is still but a single anecdote and subject to other interpretations. Was this really a memory, or an interesting story? Could it be that the assault actually happened and the nurse, for some inexplicable reason, lied later? For these reasons it would be nice to find stronger evidence that a false memory for a complete event was genuinely implanted.

An apparently genuine 19th-century memory implantation was reported by Laurence and Perry: Bernheim, during hypnosis, suggested to a female subject that she had awakened four times during the previous night to go to the toilet and had fallen on her nose on the fourth occasion. After hypnosis, the woman insisted that the suggested events had actually occurred, despite the hypnotist's insistence that she had dreamed them. Impressed by Bernheim's success, and by explorations by Orne, Laurence and Perry asked 27 highly hypnotizable individuals during hypnosis to choose a night from the previous week and to describe their activities during the half hour before going to sleep. The subjects were then instructed to relive that night, and a suggestion was implanted that they had heard some loud noises and had awakened. Almost one half (13) of the 27 subjects accepted the suggestion and stated *after* hypnosis that the suggested event had actually taken place. Of the 13, 6 were unequivocal in their certainty. The remainder came to the conclusion on basis of reconstruction. Even when told that the hypnotist had actually suggested the noises, these subjects still maintained that the noises had occurred. One said "I'm pretty certain I heard them. As a matter of fact, I'm pretty damned certain. I'm positive I heard these noises".

The paradigm of inducing pseudomemories of being awakened by loud noises has now been used extensively by other researchers who readily replicate the basic findings. Moreover, the pseudomemories are not limited to hypnotic conditions. Simply inducing subjects to imagine and describe the loud noises resulted in later "memories" for noises that had never occurred.

Other false memories. Other evidence shows that people can be tricked into believing that they experienced an event even in the absence of specific hypnotic suggestions. For example, numerous studies have shown that people misremember that they voted in a particular election when they actually had not. One interpretation of these findings is that people fill in the gaps in their memory with socially desirable constructions, thus creating for themselves a false memory of voting.

In other studies, people have been led to believe that they witnessed assaultive behavior when in fact they did not. In this study, children aged four to seven years were led to believe that they saw a man hit a girl, when he had not, after hearing the girl lie about the assault. Not only did they misrecall the nonexistent hitting, but they added their own details: Of 41 false claims, 39 children said it happened near a pond. One said it was at the girl's house, and 1 could not specify exactly where the girl was when the man hit her.

Violent false memories. People can hold completely false memories for something far more traumatic than awakening at night, voting in a particular election, or a simulation involving a man and a girl. Pynoos and Nader studied children's recollections of a sniper attack at an elementary school playground. Some of the children who were interviewed were not at the school during the shooting, including some who were already on the way home or were on vacation. Yet, even the non-witnesses had memories:

> One girl initially said that she was at the school gate nearest the sniper when the shooting began. In truth she was not only out of the line of fire, she was half a block away. A boy who had been

away on vacation said that he had been on his way to the school, had seen someone lying on the ground, had heard the shots, and then turned back. In actuality, a police barricade prevented anyone from approaching the block around the school.

The memories apparently were created by exposure to the stories of those who truly experienced the trauma.

Memories of being lost. A question arises as to whether one could experimentally implant memories for nonexistent events that, if they had occurred, would have been traumatic. Given the need to protect human subjects, devising a means of accomplishing this was not an easy task. Loftus and Coan (in press), however, developed a paradigm for instilling a specific childhood memory for being lost on a particular occasion at the age of five. They chose getting lost because it is clearly a great fear of both parents and children. Their initial observations show how subjects can be readily induced to believe this kind of false memory. The technique involved a subject and a trusted family member who played a variation of "Remember the time that . . . ?" To appreciate the methodology, consider the implanted memory of 14-year-old Chris. Chris was convinced by his older brother, Jim, that he had been lost in a shopping mall when he was 5 years old. Jim told Chris this story as if it were the truth: "It was 1981 or 1982. I remember that Chris was 5. We had gone shopping at the University City shopping mall in Spokane. After some panic, we found Chris being led down the mall by a tall, oldish man (I think he was wearing a flannel shirt). Chris was crying and holding the man's hand. The man explained that he had found Chris walking around crying his eyes out just a few moments before and was trying to help him find his parents."

Just two days later, Chris recalled his feelings about being lost: "That day I was so scared that I would never see my family again. I knew that I was in trouble." On the third day, he recalled a conversation with his mother: "I remember mom telling me never to do that again." On the fourth day: "I also remember that old man's flannel shirt." On the fifth day, he started remembering the mall itself: "I sort of remember the stores." In his last recollection, he could even remember a conversation with the man who found him: "I remember the man asking me if I was lost."

It would be natural to wonder whether perhaps Chris had really gotten lost that day. Maybe it happened, but his brother forgot. But Chris's mother was subjected to the same procedure and was never able to remember the false event. After five days of trying, she said, "I feel very badly about it, but I just cannot remember anything like this ever happening."

A couple of weeks later, Chris described his false memory and he greatly expanded on it.

> I was with you guys for a second and I think I went over to look at the toy store, the Kay-bee toy and uh, we got lost and I was looking around and I thought, "Uh-oh. I'm in trouble now." You know. And then I . . . I thought I was never going to see my family again. I was really scared you know. And then this old man, I think he was wearing a blue flannel, came up to me . . . he was kind of old. He was kind of bald on top . . . he had like a ring of gray hair . . . and he had glasses.

Thus, in two short weeks, Chris now could even remember the balding head and the glasses worn by the man who rescued him. He characterized his memory as reasonably clear and vivid.

Finally, Chris was debriefed. He was told that one of the memories presented to him earlier had been false. When asked to guess, he guessed one of the genuine memories. When told that it was the getting-lost memory, he said, "Really? I thought I remembered being lost . . . and looking around for you guys. I do remember that. And then crying. And mom coming up and saying 'Where were you. Don't you . . . Don't you ever do that again.'"

A false memory of abuse. The lost-in-a-shopping-mall example shows that memory of an entire mildly traumatic event can be created. It is still natural to wonder whether one could go even further and implant a memory of abuse. Ethically, of course, it would not be possible, but anecdotally, as it happens, it was done. It is one of the most dramatic cases of false memory of abuse ever to be documented—the case of Paul Ingram from Olympia, Washington. As described above, Ingram was arrested for child abuse in 1988 at the time he was chair of the county Republican committee. At first Ingram denied everything, and detectives told him he was in denial. After five months of interrogation, suggestions from a psychologist, and continuing pressure from detectives and advisors, Ingram began to confess to rapes, assaults, child sexual abuse, and participation in a Satan-worshiping cult alleged to have murdered 25 babies. To elicit specific memories, the psychologist or detectives would suggest some act of abuse (e.g., that on one occasion, Ingram and several other men raped his daughter). Ingram would at first not remember these fragments, but after a concerted effort on his part, he would later come up with a detailed memory.

Richard Ofshe, a social psychologist hired by the prosecution to interview Ingram and his family members, decided to test Ingram's credibility. Ofshe had made up a completely fabricated scenario. He told Ingram that two of his children (a daughter and a son) had reported that Ingram had forced them to have sex in front of him. As with the earlier suggestions, Ingram at first could not remember this. But Ofshe urged Ingram to try to think about the scene and try to see it happening, just as the interrogators had done to him earlier. Ingram began to get some visual images. Ingram then followed Ofshe's instructions to "pray on" the scene and try to remember more over the next few hours. Several hours later, Ingram had developed detailed memories and wrote a three-page statement confessing in graphic detail to the scene that Ofshe had invented. Ofshe noted that this was not the first time that a vulnerable individual had been made to believe that he had committed a crime for which he originally had no memory and which evidence proved he could not have committed. What is crucial about the Ingram case is that some of the same methods that are used in repressed memory cases were used with Ingram. These include the use of protracted imagining of events and authority figures establishing the authenticity of these events.

These examples provide further insights into the malleable nature of memory. They suggest that memories for personally experienced traumatic events can be altered by new experiences. Moreover, they reveal that entire events that never happened can be injected into memory. The false memories range from the relatively trivial (e.g., remembering voting) to the bizarre (e.g., remembering forcing one's daughter and son to have sex). These false memories, with more or less detail, of course do not prove that repressed memories of abuse that return are false. They do demonstrate a mechanism by which false memories can be created by a small suggestion from a trusted family member, by hearing someone lie, by suggestion from a psychologist, or by incorporation of the experiences of others into one's own autobiography. Of course, the fact that false memories can be planted tells nothing about whether a given memory of child sexual abuse is false or not; nor does it tell how one might distinguish the real cases from the false ones. These findings on the malleability of memory do, however, raise questions about the wisdom of certain recommendations being promoted in self-help workbooks, in handbooks for therapists, and by some therapists themselves. The false memories created in the examples above were accomplished with techniques that are not all that different from what some therapists regularly do—suggesting that the client was probably abused because of some vague symptoms, labeling a client's ambiguous recollections as evidence of abuse, and encouraging mental exercises that involve fantasy merging with reality.

Final Remarks

The 1990s brought a blossoming of reports of awakenings of previously repressed memories of childhood abuse. One reason for the increase may be the widespread statistics on sex abuse percentages that are published almost daily: "By 1980 . . . the government tallied almost 43,000 cases of child sex abuse annually"; "One in five women are 'incest victims;'" "6.8 million women nationwide would say they had been raped once, 4.7 million more than once"; "In 1972, 610,000 [child abuse cases] were reported nationally, and by 1985 the number had exceeded 1.7 million". "If it happens so often, did it happen to me?" is a question many women and some men are asking themselves now more than ever before. The appearance of abuse statistics is one battle in the war waged against an earlier tendency on the part of society to disbelieve the abuse reports of women and children—a tendency that we should all deplore. The repressed memory cases are another outlet for women's rage over sexual violence. Although women's anger is certainly justified in many cases, and may be justified in some repressed memory cases too, it is time to stop and ask whether the net of rage has been cast too widely, creating a new collective nightmare.

Repressed memories of abuse often return in therapy, sometimes after suggestive probing. Today, popular writings have been so fully absorbed by the culture that these too can serve as a source of suggestion that can greatly influence what happens in therapy and outside of it. The result is memories that are often detailed and confidently held. Despite lack of corroboration, some of these recollections could be authentic. Others might not be.

Several implications of these observations follow. First, we need a renewed effort at research on the problem of repressed memories. This should encompass, in part, a reexamination of some of the widely cherished beliefs of psychotherapists. Is it true that repression of extremely traumatic experiences is common? Do these experiences invade us despite the fact that "all the good juice of consciousness has drained out". It is common to see analogies drawn between Vietnam War veterans and the incest survivors. Do they share in common the use of "massive repression" as a mechanism for coping? If so, how do we explain findings obtained with children who witness parental murder and other atrocities? In one study, not a single child aged 5 to 10 years who had witnessed the murder of a parent repressed the memory. Rather, they were continually flooded with pangs of emotion about the murder and preoccupation with it.

Is it true that repressed material, like radioactive waste, "lies there in leaky canisters, never losing potency, eternally dangerous" and constantly threatens to erupt into consciousness? Psychotherapists have assumed for years that repressed memories are powerful influences because they are not accessible to consciousness. Is there evidence for this assumption? Is it necessarily true that all people who display symptoms of severe mental distress have had some early childhood trauma (probably abuse) that is responsible for the distress? With cutting-edge research now showing that mental distress involves neuronal and hormonal systems of a much wider scope than previously realized, should not other potential causes be at least considered?

Questions must also be examined about the well-intentioned treatment strategies of some clinicians. Is it possible that the therapist's interpretation is the cause of the patient's disorder rather than the effect of the disorder, to paraphrase Guze? Is it necessarily true that people who cannot remember an abusive childhood are repressing the memory? Is it necessarily true that people who dream about or visualize abuse are actually getting in touch with true memories? Good scientific research needs to be done to support these assumptions, or they should be challenged. Challenging these core assumptions will not be an easy thing to do, any more than it was for psychologists of the 1930s to challenge the radical subjectivity of psychoanalysis, or for psychologists of the 1980s to challenge the reliability of the clinical judgments made by psychologists and psychiatrists. Nonetheless, when we move from the privacy of the therapy session, in which the client's reality may be the only reality that is important, into the courtroom, in which there can be but a single reality, then we as citizens in a democratic society are entitled to more solid evidence.

Until we have better empirical answers, therapists might consider whether it is wise to "suggest" that childhood trauma happened, to probe relentlessly for recalcitrant memories, and then to uncritically accept them as fact. Uncritical acceptance of uncorroborated trauma memories by therapists, social agencies, and law enforcement personnel has been used to promote public accusations by alleged abuse survivors. If the memories are fabricated, this will of course lead to irreparable damage to the reputations of potentially innocent people, according to Ganaway, who discussed the problem in the context of SRA memories.

Uncritical acceptance of uncorroborated trauma memories poses other potentially dangerous problems for society. According to Ganaway, reinforcing the validity of unverifiable memories in the therapeutic setting may lead to diversionary paths in the patient's therapy away from actual childhood trauma. This could lead to interminable therapy and a total draining of the patient's financial resources as the therapist and patient collaborate in a mutual deception to pursue a bottomless pit of memories. Worse, the patient's initial wonderings supported by therapist affirmations could then become fixed beliefs, precipitating suicidal thoughts and behaviors based on the new belief system, because the patient would no longer challenge the veracity of the new memories. Like Betsy Ross sewing the first American flag, the abuse becomes a myth that was never true but always will be. Patients who are reinforced into a new belief system could develop newer, larger problems. If actual childhood sexual abuse is associated with numerous negative long-term effects, what might be the consequence of implanted childhood sexual abuse? If the memories are ultimately shown to be false, therapists may then become the targets of future ethics violations and lawsuits. They will be charged with a grave form of mind abuse—charges that have already been initiated in several states.

What should therapists do instead? As a first step, it is worth recognizing that we do not yet have the tools for reliably distinguishing the signal of true repressed memories from the noise of false ones. Until we gain these tools, it seems prudent to consider some combination of Herman's advice about probing for traumatic memories and Ganaway's advice about SRA memories. Zealous conviction is a dangerous substitute for an open mind. Psychotherapists, counselors, social service agencies, and law enforcement personnel would be wise to be careful how they probe for horrors on the other side of some presumed amnesic barrier. They need to be circumspect regarding uncorroborated repressed memories that return. Techniques that are less potentially dangerous would involve clarification, compassion, and gentle confrontation along with a demonstration of empathy for the painful struggles these patients must endure as they come to terms with their personal truths.

There is one last tragic risk of suggestive probing and uncritical acceptance of all allegations made by clients, no matter how dubious. These activities are bound to lead to an increased likelihood that society in general will disbelieve the genuine cases of childhood sexual abuse that truly deserve our sustained attention.

Repressed Memories May Be Reliable

MATTHEW ERDELYI AND BENJAMIN GOLDBERG

The following article by Matthew Erdelyi and Benjamin Goldberg discusses the methodological problems inherent in the study of repression. Erdelyi and Goldberg support the theory of repression but say that standard laboratory studies on repressed memories have failed to tax the concept of repression correctly. They say that the criticisms of repression are misdirected in that critics challenge the existence of the concept rather than the methodology of the research. Erdelyi and Goldberg present clinical as well as empirical findings on repression and call for further research on the issue.

QUESTIONS

1. What evidence do Erdelyi and Goldberg provide for the existence of repressed memories?

Excerpted from "Let's Not Sweep Repression Under the Rug: Toward a Cognitive Psychology of Repression" by Matthew Erdelyi and Benjamin Goldberg, in *Functional Disorders of Memory*, edited by John F. Kilstrom and Frederick J. Evans. Hillsdale, NJ: Lawrence Erlbaum Associates, 1979. Copyright 1979 by Lawrence Erlbaum Associates. All rights reserved. Reprinted with permission.

2. How does the methodology of research on repression to date contaminate the debate over repressed memories, according to the authors?
3. What are some of the problems with studying repressed memories, according to Erdelyi and Goldberg?

■ ■ ■

The problem of repression—and we introduce it gingerly as "the problem," since no consensus has yet emerged about whether we are dealing with an everyday "fact," a "theory," or a discredited "hypothesis"—poses some unique difficulties. These difficulties are profound as well as far-ranging, involving intractable issues of methodology, theory, and even semantics. Beyond these types of problems, which perhaps are really not that unusual but simply the burden of any truly seminal concept in psychology, there exists an additional difficulty that probably is unique to repression among major psychological constructs.

Defining the Problem

Affect and Bias Toward Psychodynamic Formulations

We might as well confront the fact at the outset: Repression is an emotionally loaded term. As the "foundation-stone on which the whole structure of psychoanalysis rests", repression is willy-nilly caught up in psychology's problematical attitude toward psychoanalysis in general, which of late (particularly among contemporary personality and clinical psychologists) has once more entered a negative phase inclined toward indiscriminate and often vitriolic rejection.

The emotional stakes are high. For the committed, whether pro or con, the fate of the repression concept may represent nothing less than a lifetime's investment in a particular psychological Weltanschauung. It may not come altogether as a surprise, therefore, given such highly charged emotional considerations, to discover certain peculiar aberrations in the conceptual treatment of repression. These are hardly novel manifestations to psychodynamicists, for they include such cognitive "vicissitudes" as regressive logic, displacement of accent, concretism, euphemistic symbolic representation, syncretism (condensation), and especially, censorship by omission.

Consider, for example, the fate of the repression concept in mainstream cognitive psychology. For a specialty that takes thought as its subject matter and information processing as its principal metaphor, one might suppose that the topic of tendentious *mis*thinking—or motivated information *mis*processing—would be of central concern. Nothing could be further from the facts. Despite a remarkably far-flung range of concerns, often on topics of a decidedly exotic nature, not a single article on repression has appeared in the 1970s in any of the major speciality journals of cognition and memory. The broader topic of defense mechanisms and indeed the whole field of psychodynamics (concerned with the interaction of motives and cognition) have similarly been relegated to silence. (An exception, a computer simulation of paranoid thinking by Faught, Colby, and Parkinson [1977], has appeared at this writing.) Recent textbooks on memory and cognition, many of them encyclopedic efforts spanning the whole history of psychology, as a rule fail even to index the term. . . .

How is this neglect to be explained? Is it really a reflection of bias against psychoanalytic notions in general and, through guilt by association, against psychodynamics in particular? Or is there perhaps some other simpler or more reasonable explanation? In the face of cognitive psychology's pervasive silence on the matter, we cannot know for sure; we would need more data to draw a defensible conclusion. At this point we have only the fact: The concept of repression in cognitive psychology is—to use the expression Freud so often borrowed from Charcot—treated as *non-arrivée.*

Definition and Development of the Repression Concept

The meaning of repression has been a subject of great and continuing confusion, both within as well as outside of psychoanalysis. Indeed, it may turn out eventually that most controversies about the existence of repression constituted not controversies in the true sense of the word, i.e., *differences in opinion,* but rather *different opinions about different things.* Although Freud, who developed the concept of repression, has deservedly gained a reputation for impressionistic, even loose, articulation of technical terms, we believe that in the case of repression he was unusually clear, certainly so by the standards of clarity associated with any fundamental psychological construct such as attention, aggression, behavior modification, intelligence, and consciousness. The key to the confusion lies in a general failure to distinguish between the phenomenon itself and theories of the phenomenon, about which it is only natural to find differences.

What, then, constitutes the phenomenon of repression? It would be difficult to put the matter any more clearly than Freud himself did: *"the essence of repression lies simply in the function of rejecting and keeping something out of consciousness."* Note that this basic definition does not stipulate the method or methods of rejection from consciousness—whether by inhibition (e.g., "counter-cathexes"), attention withdrawal, or some other single or combined set of techniques; nor does the definition stipulate that the process must be conscious or unconscious. The definition does not even commit itself to the nature of the "something" that is rejected nor to the reason or purpose behind the rejection, though in virtually all of his writings, including the article in which this quote occurs, it is made clear that repression *as a defense* seeks to eliminate or prevent some form of psychological "pain," variously conceptualized as "trauma," "intolerable ideas," "unbearable affect," "anxiety," "guilt," or "shame" ("moral anxiety"), etc. However, the irreducible essence of the phenomenon is nothing more than what Freud has stated. Extensions of the concept—e.g., that it must be unconscious, that it applies only to sexual or aggressive impulses, that it must concern infantile traumas, that it requires constant expenditures of psychic energy, that it results in symptoms, that it constitutes an ego or superego mechanism—all these, and many other notions, are theoretical elaborations, not the "essence" of the phenomenon itself.

To place too much reliance on any single quote of Freud's may not be an altogether satisfactory way of proceeding, however; Freud's proclivity toward self-contradiction is only too well known. Ultimately the best way to gain a clear conception of the meaning of repression is through an examination of the origin and development of the concept. This "genetic" (i.e., historical or developmental) approach, after all, is precisely the psychoanalytic strategy for penetrating problematical meanings.

It is generally believed, probably because Freud himself suggested it, that repression was a fortuitous discovery resulting from the abandonment of hypnosis in favor of the free-association technique. This is not really so, however, for the repression concept was clearly central to Freud's earliest psychological writings, preceding both the free-association technique and the development of psychoanalysis. In his 1892–1893 report of "A Case of Successful Treatment by Hypnotism" (a technique that antedates not only psychoanalytic therapy but also the earlier cathartic method of Breuer), Freud sets forth a conflict theory of hysteria in which one element of the conflict is intentionally barred—"suppressed," "excluded," "dissociated"—from consciousness: "the distressing antithetic idea, which has the appearance of being inhibited, is removed from association with the intention and continues to exist as a disconnected idea, often unconsciously to the patient himself". In a posthumously published letter to Breuer, written in 1892, Freud states: "an hysterical patient intentionally seeks to forget an experience, or forcibly repudiates, inhibits, and suppresses an intention or idea". In his joint "Preliminary Communication" with Breuer the term *repression—verdrängt* (repressed)—appears for the first time, casually intermixed with a number of synonyms: "it is a question which the patient wished to forget, and therefore intentionally repressed from his conscious thought and inhibited and suppressed."

In the *Studies on Hysteria*, repression comes to play a central theoretical role. It constitutes, as it did before under different labels, Freud's explanation of the psychogenesis of hysteria—"an idea must be *intentionally repressed* from consciousness." Also, repression serves to explain the ubiquitously found "resistance" encountered in "talking cures," seen with special clarity in "free associations," against openly and freely broaching painful memories. The "free" associations of the patient are thus never really free; they reflect not only a form of "outward dishonesty" in which he self-censors painful *responses* but also a form of "inward dishonesty," involving ultimately the *cognitive* counterpart of the response censorship, repression. Freud's work with free associations led him to emphasize that memory is organized not only *thematically* but *psychodynamically* as well:

I have described such groupings of similar memories into collections arranged in linear sequences (like a file of documents, a packet, etc.) as constituting "themes." These themes exhibit a second kind of arrangement. Each of them is—I cannot express it in any other way—stratified concentrically round the pathogenic [traumatic] nucleus. . . . The contents of each particular stratum are characterized by an equal degree of resistance, and the degree of resistance increases in proportion as the strata are nearer to the nucleus. . . . The most peripheral strata contain the memories (or files) which, belonging to different themes, are easily remembered and have always been clearly conscious. The deeper we go the more difficult it becomes for the emerging memories to be recognized, till near the nucleus we come upon memories which the patient disavows even in reproducing them.

Freud seems to be outlining here a notion of gradients of inhibition or avoidance, to be elaborated more formally some half a century later by Dollard and Miller. The critical point, however, is that inhibition of response and inhibition of thought are manifestations of the same process. There is no discontinuity between response processes and cognitive processes. Free associations—freely thinking aloud—constitute therefore a "microscope" for cognition in that what they reveal about overt responses presumably reflects also the covert process of thought.

It should be quite clear, then, that Freud's earliest conception of the phenomenon of repression, initially formulated under a remarkable profusion of interchangeable rubrics— "repression," "inhibition," "exclusion," "dissociation," "removal," "censorship," "defense," "resistance," "forcible repudiation," "intentional forgetting"—unmistakably corresponds to his conception of two decades later. The intervening developments in psychotherapeutic technique and the accumulation of clinical data thus served merely to corroborate the original observation. The only real change was a finer-grained articulation of the manifold ways in which it was possible to achieve the "function of rejecting and keeping something out of consciousness." As early as 1894, for example, Freud observed that a painful ideational complex might be dealt with, not through a blanket, indiscriminate inhibition of the whole complex, but through the inhibition or repression of only its *emotional* component: "[the] defense against the incompatible idea was effected by separating it from its affect; the idea itself remained in consciousness." This affective form of repression came later to be known in psychoanalysis as the defense mechanism of "isolation." With the accumulation of clinical experience, an increasing spectrum of special cognitive techniques for distorting consciousness of reality (and therefore in some sense "rejecting and keeping something out of consciousness") was delineated by Freud, sometimes formally and sometimes in passing. In just two published case histories, the "Rat Man" and the psychotic "Dr. Schreber" , Freud delves into more than a dozen such devices (though not always by actual name), including omissions and ellipses, symbolization, isolation, displacement, doubt, regression, reaction formation, undoing, rationalization, denial, and projection.

As the specific techniques or combination of techniques proliferated, Freud began to revert to the construct of "defense" (*Abwehr*) as the generic rubric for all the diverse mechanisms for rejecting painful aspects of reality from consciousness. Freud was never too consistent in this regard, however, and frequently continued using "repression," especially "repression in the broadest sense," as a synonym. This inconsistency may best be understood, perhaps, by appreciating the fact that all specific "defense" techniques involve "repression" (rejection from consciousness) in some sense, even though they may be discriminable from one another. Thus, for example, the mechanism of "projection" excludes some piece of psychological reality from consciousness by the transposition of subject and object of a proposition (e.g., "I love you"➜"you love me"), whereas "reaction formation" transposes the predicate of the proposition into its opposite (e.g., "I love you"➜"I hate you"). Since both transformations, though different, exclude the original reality from consciousness (i.e., "I love you"), they may be properly conceived of as "repression"—in the broadest sense. These specific mechanisms, however, are clearly distinct from one another and may also be distinguished from a narrower conception of "repression" as the direct inhibition of an idea's access to consciousness. It has become customary within psychoanalysis to adopt this narrower view of repression—the direct inhibition of a thought, impulse, memory, etc.—and to treat it as only one of a myriad of cognitive devices for tampering with reality for the purpose of avoiding pain.

Whether this latter, "narrow" sense of repression ultimately conveys a distinct meaning is problematical, however, despite its superficial plausibility and widespread adoption. What, after all, could we mean when we say "direct" or "inhibit" or, indeed, "thought" or "memory"? What would be the effect on the notion of "direct memory inhibition" if we adopted Tulving's distinction between episodic vs. semantic memory (conceptualization of repression as "failure of comprehension" rather than merely "memory failure"). What would "thought or memory inhibition" constitute if we emphasized the constructive, generative nature of all cognitive processes? Would not most or all specific defense mechanisms revert to being variants of this now peculiarly broad "narrow" conception of repression (based on a "broad" construction of thought or memory)?

Consider, for example, the fate of the superficially straightforward notion of "intentional forgetting" in the recent experimental literature (discussed later) that in less than a decade has spawned such varied conceptualizations as "selective rehearsal," "differential grouping," "selective search," "dumping," "erasure," "differential encoding," "differential depth of search," "blocking," "report withholding," "active inhibition," "output interference". Even at this point—and we shall no doubt witness further conceptual proliferation, perhaps even the rediscovery of some Freudian mechanisms—it would be perplexing in the extreme to propound a notion of intentional forgetting in the "narrow sense." It is no different, we believe, with "repression." The only clear meaning of repression is the general one—i.e., "the function of rejecting and keeping something out of consciousness"—with narrower formulations representing hypothesized variants, of the overall phenomenon. In our view, therefore, the expression "processes of defense" (usually known as the "mechanisms of defense," after Anna Freud) is synonymous with repression, having perhaps the nomenclatural advantage of emphasizing the multifaceted nature of the overall phenomenon and also the distinction, remarkably unappreciated in the literature, between the *mechanisms* involved and the *purpose* that they serve, i.e., defense. This latter distinction, of little immediate relevance in clinical contexts, assumes a major significance for laboratory approaches, for, as we shall see, it is much easier to prove by standard experimental paradigms the existence of mechanisms than the existence of purposes.

A last issue remains to be broached before concluding this examination of the meaning of repression. We have seen that the clearest definition of repression is the general one, namely, the overall function of rejecting something from consciousness. We now raise the question of whether the function *itself* is something that is excluded from consciousness; i.e., is repression—are the defense mechanisms—unconscious? An almost universal consensus has emerged on this issue. Probably as a result of *Anna* Freud's exceptionally influential monograph on the topic, it is believed that the mechanisms of defense, without exception, operate unconsciously. So widespread is this belief, that by now most theorists treat the notion not as a hypothesis but as an integral component of the definition of the phenomenon. The most significant exception to this rule, curiously, is *Sigmund* Freud.

The unconscious nature of repression was simply not a critical theme in Freud's treatment of the topic, certainly not before his relatively late "structural" theorizing. Although defenses were often treated as unconscious processes, there was no consistent suggestion that they had to be unconscious; indeed, repression was often portrayed as a conscious or sometimes conscious process. In "Repression" Freud specifically speaks of the "censorship of consciousness" and, in fact, feels obliged to warn the reader not to assume that repression is always a conscious undertaking ("it is a mistake to emphasize only the repulsion which operates from the direction of the conscious upon what is to be repressed"). Although it is appreciated by psychoanalytic scholars that in his very earliest writings repression was treated as a potentially conscious mechanism, it is mistakenly assumed that by 1895 Freud had shifted to the now orthodox view of repression as unconscious. There is even a regrettable tendency toward retrospective reinterpretations—secondary elaborations—of Freud's original intended meanings (the laws of psychodynamics are not suspended for psychodynamicists). Thus, for example, a lengthy editorial footnote appears in the English translation of Breuer and Freud's *Studies on Hysteria* in which the reader is warned against falsely construing terms such as *deliberate* or *intentional* as implying *conscious*. Although the logic of the point is unassailable, it nevertheless remains the case that the contexts in which the terms occur make it very clear that at least at times, repression is a conscious, deliberate act. Thus, in the case of Miss Lucy R., where Freud states that for a hysterical symptom to develop, "an idea must be *intentionally repressed from consciousness*," he goes on to quote the following exchange: "'But if you knew you loved your employer why didn't you tell me?'— 'I didn't know—or rather I didn't want to know. I wanted to drive it out of my head and not think of it again; and I believe lat-terly I have succeeded'." In the case of Katherina, Freud speaks directly of "conscious rejection." Nor do we need to restrict our-selves to the *Studies on Hysteria* for such examples, for in numer-ous subsequent articles, including "Repression", Freud implies or directly indicates that repression may be conscious. In his dis-cussion of Schreber, for example, Freud states that repression "emanates from the highly developed systems of the ego—sys-tems which are capable of being conscious." In a footnote added to *The Interpretation of Dreams* in 1914 Freud remarks: "In any ac-count of the theory of repression it would have to be laid down that a thought becomes repressed as a result of the continued in-fluence upon it of two factors: It is pushed from the one side (by the censorship of *Cs.*) and from the other (by the *Ucs.*)."

But did not Freud specifically distinguish between uncon-scious and conscious forms of consciousness rejection by using "repression" for the former and "suppression" for the latter? The answer is no. Although many psychoanalytic and nonpsy-choanalytic scholars have advanced such a distinction (though careful scrutiny reveals that "suppression" is by no means used uniformly—compare, for example, Brenner, Dollard & Miller, Holmes, the distinction is simply not one that Freud himself made. The closest he comes to so doing is in an isolated footnote in *The Interpretation of Dreams* where he suggests that repression "lays more stress" than suppression "upon the fact of attach-ment to the unconscious." Such an amorphous passing hint is not a particularly serviceable foundation on which to build a formal distinction, particularly since elsewhere, from his earliest psychological writings to his last, Freud uses "suppression" and "repression" interchangeably.

Nor is there any conspicuous theoretical need to make the distinction. Let, for example, R refer to the conscious operation of repressing something—i. Let us further consider the possi-bility that consciousness of the operation of repressing i, that is, R(i), is itself aversive; by again using the same operation R the subject need only repress R(i), that is, R(R(i)), to escape residual pain. This constitutes nothing other than an intrapsy-chic version of the "cover-up of the cover-up," hardly a novel notion in this post-Watergate era.

We have laid such emphasis on the issue of whether re-pression is, or need be, unconscious for two reasons. First, from the historical standpoint, we have here an almost universally accepted notion—a truism—that is not clearly true. Although a particular repression may indeed be unconscious, our point is that not every repression need be unconscious; moreover, a particular repression that is unconscious may have originally started out as a conscious process. For the clinician, such concerns can hardly be of major import. For the laboratory scientist, however, it may well be one of the most critical, for we believe that contemporary laboratory experimental psychology can, despite its many limitations, easily demonstrate the phenomenon of motivated forgetting; it may even be in a position to demonstrate, though this becomes immeasurably more difficult, that such motivated forgetting is used instrumentally to avoid pain, i.e., for defense. But to prove simultaneously all this and, in addition, that such a process operates unconsciously is simply beyond the scope of experimental psychology's current methodological perimeters. A laboratory attempt to demonstrate unconscious defensive processes with current techniques is foredoomed to failure. Such a failure, however (and here we radically part with Holmes and other experimentalists), may be more of a reflection on today's experimental psychology than on unconscious defensive processes.

The Evidence for Repression: Clinical and Experimental[1]

Clinical Evidence

Excepting a transitory fascination with Jung's reaction-time studies of word associations, Freud saw little need or value in laboratory demonstrations of repression. (Jung himself was later to turn against the experimental approach to complex mental processes: "whosoever wishes to know about the human mind

---

[1]Space limitations require us to be highly schematic and selective in this section. Our major purpose is not in any sense to detail the clinical and laboratory data relating to repression but rather to provide a summary overview of the major types of empirical evidence available and the kinds of problems and limitations to which these are subject.

will learn nothing, or almost nothing, from experimental psychology.") The basic phenomenon (if not its varied manifestations and consequences) was too obvious, ubiquitously observed in the clinic and outside it, partaken by all human beings (even psychologists). For this reason, Freud did not feel obliged to elaborate in any great detail the evidentiary basis of repression, viewing with alternate bemusement and incredulity the insistence of experimental psychologists to foist the ceremonial rigors of the laboratory upon the obvious. For example, responding in 1934 to reprints sent to him by Rosenzweig on attempts to demonstrate repression experimentally, Freud stated bluntly that he could not "put much value" on such confirmations because repression was based on a "wealth of reliable observations" that made it "independent of experimental verification," adding, with little apparent confidence, that the exercise could at least "do no harm".

Hypermnesia

The clinical observations supporting the notion of repression are basically of two kinds, direct and indirect. The former, the direct data, involve those not infrequent situations where the subject (in therapy, hypnosis, or with just the passage of time) manages finally to remember some heretofore inaccessible painful idea, including in many instances the original resolve to reject the material from consciousness (see, for example, the foregoing quote from the case of Miss Lucy R.) This is a direct form of what Freud sometimes referred to as "the return of the repressed" and as such, constitutes the most straightforward proof of the existence of repression. There are numerous instances of such hypermnesias (i.e., the lifting of amnesias) scattered across Freud's clinical reports. In Freud's famous case, "The Wolfman", the patient, after some premonitory dreams, suddenly recalled his sister's seduction of him ("Let's show one another our bottoms," etc.). In the case of Elizabeth von R., the patient experienced excruciating physical pain whenever she began to broach the idea that she was eventually to retrieve into consciousness, the wish that her beloved sister should die so she might marry her brother-in-law. Even before the climactic hypermnesia, Elizabeth was aware that she had "carefully avoided" certain thoughts (e.g., the possibility that her sister might die of her illness); after the hypermnesia, she was overwhelmed by excruciating guilt (psychic pain), the motive for "fending off" the idea. Getting at the painful psychological material was a "layer by layer" process, akin to "excavating a buried city," except that the patient fought the "work of recollection" at every step. We have already had occasion to cite Freud's summary of his observations of the retrieval process involving painful mentation: Memories are "stratified concentrically" about a traumatic "nucleus," the material becoming progressively more inaccessible as the subject gets closer to the traumatic nucleus.

Such hypermnesia-based evidence for repression is not, of course, limited to Freud's observations. It is a virtually standard feature of any long-term clinical interaction, whether the therapist is psychoanalytically oriented or otherwise. In Thigpen and Cleckley's famous case, *The Three Faces of Eve*, for example, the patient, with the initial help of hypnosis, achieved a remarkable array of hypermnesias of aversive memories (e.g., the terrifying experience of being forced by her mother to touch the face of her dead grandmother). Moreover, the patient was able to recall in some instances the hitherto unconscious undertaking of the repression itself, an effort experienced consciously as headaches. Similarly, there is an abundance of reports in the literature on traumatic neurosis of recoveries from amnesias of unbearable memories through hypnosis, drugs, or dynamic therapies. Gillespie, for example, reports the case of a man buried alive by an explosion. After his rescue, the man developed symptoms of cramps and bed wetting that could be neither cured nor explained until the patient recalled, under Evipan narcosis, the terrible leg cramps from which he had suffered while trapped in the debris and his desperate effort to avoid the shame of wetting his pants while thus trapped. Grinker and Speigel report the permanent cure of a patient's vomiting symptom after the patient was able to gain consciousness (under the influence of sodium pentathol) of hitherto unconscious resentment toward his superior officers (case 30). Another patient (case 43) was cured of his symptoms of depression, moodiness, and insomnia after gaining consciousness (again under sodium pentathol) of his unconscious resentments against his family, particularly his younger brother. Without hypnosis or drugs, another patient was eventually able to recall, after several years of intermittent dynamic therapy, the actual details of the airplane crash he survived, for which he had been hitherto amnesic. Typically, patients experience great anxiety in achieving hypermnesias of traumatic materials and struggle against the work of recollection.

Hypermnesias of traumatic materials in combat neurotics have been construed by some experimentalists as constituting unambiguous corroboration of "the reality of repression". Actually, experiences of this nature are by no means restricted to such recondite settings or, for that matter, to the special conditions of the clinic. It appears that the vast majority of ordinary people can recollect the past use of one form of defense or another for the purpose of avoiding "psychic pain" (anxiety, guilt, shame, etc.). In a recent informal survey of undergraduates by the senior author, virtually every subject (85 of 86) reported having used "conscious repression" ("excluding painful memories or thoughts from consciousness for the purpose of avoiding psychological discomfort"). Moreover, a remarkably high percentage of subjects were able to recall past use of unconscious defenses; that is, they were now conscious of previous unconscious use of defense techniques such as unconscious projection (72%), unconscious reaction formation (46%), unconscious displacement (86%), and unconscious rationalization (93%). Clearly, then, the direct hypermnesia paradigm of repression yields not only abundant but almost universal support for repression: Most people, inside or outside clinical settings, can recall materials they had previously excluded from consciousness in order to avoid psychic pain and can, moreover, recall the specific techniques of defense by which the rejection from consciousness was achieved.

It remains only to ask whether such broad-based evidence allows any continuing doubt about the reality of repression. There are, actually, two methodological issues that must be confronted, both related to the problem of shifting *report criteria* with pressures (demand characteristics, etc.) to retrieve initially inaccessible materials. The first of these is, in the terminology of signal detection theory, the problem of "false alarms," or in Freud's system the problem of "paramnesias" or "false recollections." It is possible that subjects purportedly recovering lost memories are in fact generating not memories of true events but fanciful guesses, fantasies, or plain confabulations. Such data would then constitute evidence not of repression but imagination.

There can be little question that clinicians have seriously underestimated this problem, no doubt because subjects will frequently generate false recollections with every sign of believing in them themselves. Freud himself fell prey to the methodological trap when, being too credulous of his early patients' apparent hypermnesias of childhood seductions, he rushed into his "infantile seduction theory" of hysteria only to be obliged to recant it in short order. Hypnotic hypermnesias are similarly suspect. Thus Bernstein has reported success in retrieving inaccessible memories not only from childhood but from previous reincarnations! Those not inclined to dismiss reincarnation out of hand may well have to contend with time travel or clairvoyance as well, for experiments have shown that subjects imaginatively responding to hypnotic suggestions will confidently recall events not only from the past but from the future as well. As Bernheim used to warn his students, "when a physician employs hypnosis with a patient it is wise always to be aware who may be hypnotizing whom." Even Penfield's dramatic hypermnesias brought on by temporal lobe stimulation may turn out, at least in some cases, to have been highly elaborate concrete fantasies.

The methodological solution to this problem is to obtain some independent verification of the accuracy of the hypermnesias produced by the subject. Unfortunately, this is not always possible; moreover, even when feasible, clinicians have not as a rule made efforts to verify their patients' hypermnesias, partly because it is difficult, partly because clinicians are not sensitized to the methodological issue, but mainly because it is of little clinical import. If the patient is cured, it matters little whether he has "worked through" traumatic memories or traumatic fantasies. Nevertheless the problem is not insurmountable. Careful search will turn up specific hypermnesias of painful materials that are consistent with already-known facts (as in the details of the air crash for which Kardiner and Spiegel's patient was amnesic) or which are independently confirmed by relatives and acquaintances.

Even if the recovered memories can be shown to be veridical (i.e., to constitute "hits" rather than "false alarms"), there remains the residual methodological issue of whether the subject is actually recalling (i.e., remembering) more or merely reporting more. For example, it is possible that Elizabeth von R. was from the beginning aware of her shameful wishes concerning her sister and brother-in-law but could not initially bring herself to acknowledge them to her therapist. This brings us to the murky frontier between deception and self-deception: report bias vs. memory bias. Despite the impressive contribution of signal detection theory, which might yet find profitable application in the clinic, the fact remains that no absolutely foolproof technique exists for resolving the problem. This is tantamount to saying that psychology—clinical or experimental—has not yet devised a fully reliable technique for reading minds. In the interim we must remain content with a Bayesian approach, involving probabilities rather than certainties. Fortunately, there are myriad clinical situations in which we are able, by virtue of our combined knowledge of the subject, the context of events, and the types of events involved, to dismiss with (virtual) certainty the possibility of gross initial withholding of eventually recovered materials. Laboratory data, moreover, with maximal controls over shifting report criteria—and total control over false-alarm effects—have confirmed the feasibility of achieving extensive hypermnesias of hitherto inaccessible materials through multitrial recall techniques. Erdelyi and Kleinbard

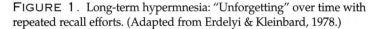

FIGURE 1. Long-term hypermnesia: "Unforgetting" over time with repeated recall efforts. (Adapted from Erdelyi & Kleinbard, 1978.)

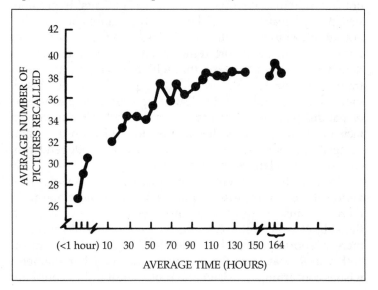

for example, repeatedly testing subjects' recall over periods of days, were able to obtain memory functions resembling upside-down versions of the classic Ebbinghaus curve of forgetting (see Fig. 1). (Curiously, for reasons not yet understood, the hypermnesias seem to be largely restricted to pictorial or imagistic materials.). . .

Laboratory Evidence

The earliest laboratory studies applied to the repression problem were those of Jung and Riklin both then at the famed Burghölzli Clinic of Eugen Bleuler. Perhaps the best way to grasp the rationale of these studies is first to consider some of Jung's related work on lie detection from which all modern lie-detection systems are derived.

Jung and his colleagues found that a dissimulating criminal—or patient—could unwittingly give himself away through certain anomalous responses, such as changed pulse rates, depth of breathing, elevated galvanic skin responses, or a variety of abnormalities in word associations (unusually long reaction times to critical stimuli; superficial, repetitive, or clang associations, etc.). The emotionally toned topics about which the subject was deliberately (and consciously) trying to lie nevertheless produced emotional reactions that these more subtle "indicators" gave away. For example: Three nurses suspected of stealing some money from their hospital were individually administered word-association tests by Jung. One of the nurses gave unusually slow reactions to stimulus words related to the crime (e.g., *money*), on which basis Jung accused her of the theft. Thereupon she broke down and confessed. The emotional ideation, despite the subject's attempt at dissimulation, had leaked through into the more sensitive indicator system.

The question now arises: What if a subject gives the appearance through these indicators of emotionality of lying, but is not conscious of any attempt of lying or even of what it is about which he is presumably lying? One may infer, as Jung did, that the subject is engaged in a private lie, that he is lying to himself. In this view, then, the patient is treating his own consciousness as an outside agent from which some emotional facts are being hidden but that, as in the case of the public lie, more sensitive indicators register and reveal. It was such evidence of emotional reactivity in the absence of awareness for the ideas behind it (and, often, unawareness for the emotional reaction itself) that led Jung to construe his experiments as demonstrating the existence of "emotionally-toned ideational complexes" existing in dissociation from consciousness.

Though interesting, and certainly heuristic for the field of lie detection, the research program cannot be said to shed much light on the problem of repression. A careful reading of this work reveals a plethora of methodological as well as conceptual flaws that are too numerous to attempt detailing here. We may cite a few of the more major issues. First, anomalous reactions such as delayed reaction times need not indicate emotionality; other factors, such as familiarity or complexity, might yield similar effects, a possibility for which Jung was criticized and for which he had no answer. Then, even if the indicator correctly reveals emotionality as opposed to some other factor (i.e., an emotional hit vs. a false alarm), it still does not follow that the subject is unconscious of the ideation that triggers the emotion. Indeed, a careful reading of Jung's writings on the topic typically shows Jung unveiling a conscious rather than an unconscious secret (i.e., a secret withheld from others rather than from the self). Moreover, in those cases where the subject reports no awareness for the ideation producing emotional reactions, it is never clear what it is he is repressing, if anything. Jung often supplies some inferred complex, but one can never be certain whether the subject's unawareness of it reflects repression or faulty interpretation on the part of the therapist. Thus, it is by no means clear how—if at all—these experimental data extend the insights obtainable in straightforward clinical settings, especially if the demonstration must also hinge eventually on interpretation.
Another early experimental approach to repression was the attempt to demonstrate that memory for unpleasant events is poorer than for pleasant events. Perhaps no other research effort in the area has been as universally criticized by opponents as well as proponents of psychoanalysis. Again, the problems are conceptual as well as methodological. Perhaps the most obvious experimental issue is whether in fact it is true that mem-

ory for the unpleasant is inferior to that for the pleasant. Thus, Cason demonstrated that extremely pleasant and unpleasant experiences tend to be remembered equally but in both cases better than mildly pleasant or unpleasant experiences.

At the theoretical level, it has been claimed that such laboratory work rests on a basic misunderstanding of Freud's concepts in that not all unpleasant, but only anxiety-provoking, materials tend to activate repression. Wolitzky, Klein, and Dworkin have extended the point by insisting that conflict must also be present. This line of criticism, we feel, is probably unjustified. It could be said that in this regard Freud himself had basic misunderstandings about Freud. Certainly not until 1926 (in *Inhibition, Symptoms, and Anxiety*), near the end of his career, did Freud specifically formulate his notion that anxiety instigates repression. Moreover, a broad conception of "anxiety" (including guilt, shame, worry, etc.) is hard to disentangle from the unpleasant, especially in the light of Freud's "Pleasure–Unpleasure Principle," in which unpleasure is defined generally as tension (and pleasure as the reduction of tension). We believe that the more serious theoretical problem with this research approach is the erroneous assumption that unpleasant things in general are repressed. This certainly was never Freud's position. It does not follow that because things that *are* repressed are unpleasant (or lead to unpleasure)—a position that Freud did hold—unpleasant things therefore are necessarily repressed. Such a conclusion is based on a faulty syllogism of the form:

All philosophers are men (or women)
Therefore, all men (or women) are philosophers.

Freud actually addressed this problem directly: "Aren't unhappy memories the hardest to forget, as for example the recollection of grievances or humiliations? This fact is quite correct, but the objection [with respect to the repression notion] is not sound. It is important to begin early to reckon with the fact that the mind is an arena, a sort of tumbling ground, for the struggles of antagonistic impulses." Here Freud is emphasizing that the psychological system is not unitary, based solely on the "Pleasure-Unpleasure Principle." The "Reality Principle" opposes the developmentally primitive "Pleasure-Unpleasure Principle," and it is precisely with respect to the relatively innocuous events experienced or reported in the laboratory that contact with reality is likely to prevail, and perhaps be even amplified. Thus, the innocuous stimuli of the laboratory are precisely the least likely to activate defenses. (Moreover, even if activated, a variety of defensive devices, such as intellectualization, would not necessarily yield a diminution of episodic memory.)

In an effort to come to grips with the problem of ineffective laboratory stimuli, researchers cast about for some experimental manipulation that would be disturbing enough psychologically to activate defensive reactions. A major breakthrough (or so it was thought) was provided by what MacKinnon and Dukes have aptly termed "Zeigarnik's unintentional study of repression." Zeigarnik is best known, of course, for her famous, if often disputed, Zeigarnik Effect, the discovery that uncompleted tasks tend to be better remembered than completed tasks. The relevance of this work for repression is Zeigarnik's discovery of a systematic exception to the Zeigarnik Effect: When the noncompletion of a task was construed by the subject as a personal failure rather than just merely a consequence of insufficient time, that is, when the subject felt stupid, awkward, or inferior because of the failed task, then it was the uncompleted rather than the completed task that tended to be "extremely often forgotten." These tasks—Zeigarnik called them "repressed tasks"—were thought to produce an "ego-threat" of sufficient seriousness as to mobilize repression, accounting for the forgetting of failed tasks.

This approach was systematically explored and extended by subsequent researchers, though the emphasis soon shifted away from the interruption of tasks per se to direct manipulation of anxiety through laboratory induction of feelings of failure or success, guilt, psychopathology, etc.

The performance decrement effects for anxiety-related materials are reasonably robust, particularly if individual differences in defense strategies are taken into account. Nevertheless, the findings—or the conclusions derived from the findings—have been subjected to a variety of criticisms: that diminution in memory is in itself an insufficient demonstration of repression unless the return of the repressed, i.e., hypermnesia for the forgotten, can be effected by the removal of the associated anxiety; that performance decrements in themselves need not arise from repression but might result instead from other mechanisms, such as disturbed attention, response "interference" or "competition", or the general effect of anxiety upon the performance of complex tasks; that since subjects have been found to ruminate about their anxiety-provoking experience before recall trials, that the subsequent memory decrements cannot be a consequence of repression; that the memory decrement effect cannot involve repression, since it appears to be subject to conscious control; that the studies in question do not tap repression, since the ego- or superego-threat manipulations produced in the laboratory are simply not powerful enough to mobilize repression or at least not such gross defensive reactions as outright amnesias; and that—and here we add our own criticism—it has not been demonstrated that the obtained performance decrements reflect true memory rather than merely report bias processes.

Although there is merit in some of these criticisms, many of them may also be shown to be flawed or downright misguided. Aborn's objection, for example, that repression must be a process beyond conscious control is simply wrong. Freud's earliest nonhypnotic technique for recovering repressed materials was nothing other than conscious effort. D'Zurilla's observation that subjects ruminate about their failures is most interesting and certainly in accord with clinical experience, as with the "repetition-compulsion" nightmares of war neurotics, but it simply does not follow logically that the resultant memory failures for parts of the experience are therefore not a result of repression. Zeller's critique has been exceptionally influential but is probably off the point, having more to do with the demonstration of the existence of *the repressed* than the existence of *repression*. At a rote level it is true, of course, that at least some repressed materials should be subject to recovery. This, after all, is the goal of psychoanalytic psychotherapy. However, the return of the repressed is not a necessary condition for the assumption of repression; psychoanalysis in fact maintains that most repressed materials are never recovered. A modern conception of memory, moreover, would specifically suggest that, contrary to Freud, some repressed materials will in fact be lost irretrievably. Thus, although materials rejected from long-term memory are likely to remain available for subsequent retrieval, rejection from other memory buffers, as, for example, iconic memory stores , would result in permanent loss of the material—not because repression erases the memory trace, but because the memory trace in buffers other than long-term memory tend to decay precipitously if not subjected to conscious processing.

The "response interference" or "disturbed attention" arguments per se cannot be viewed as criticisms of repression but only—at best—as theoretical conceptualizations of repression (or at worst, terminological wrangles). Without any doubt, Freud's own concept of repression is an interference one (though he did not, of course, use behavioristic terminology); moreover, Freud specifically viewed the withdrawal of attention ("attention cathexis") as one means by which repression is effected. The really important criticism behind Holmes' response interference position, however, is the question of whether the interference is tendentious, i.e., purposeful, as opposed to being merely a "non-defensive attentional process." This, Holmes is right to assert, has not been proven. His own research has shown, for example, that performance decrements can be obtained not only with ego-threat but with ego-boosting manipulations as well. Unfortunately, it is not obvious how the experimental paradigm under discussion could be adapted to yield the requisite proof of intent. Thus, the fact that the paradigm does not yield such a proof may, as we have already intimated, reflect on the experimental paradigm, not necessarily on repression. . . .

If the frequency with which Freud refers to Bernheim's work on hypnotically directed forgetting (which Freud personally witnesses during a brief visit to Bernheim's clinic in 1889) is any indication, research on intentional forgetting played a significant role in the development of the repression concept. In "astonishing experiments upon his hospital patients," Bernheim would hypnotize a patient, subject him to a variety of experiences and posthypnotic suggestions, direct the patient *not* to recall the hypnotic experiences (but nevertheless to carry out the indicated posthypnotic behaviors), awaken him from the trance, and then question him about the to-be-forgotten, though just experienced, hypnotic events. The patient typically would recall little or nothing (posthypnotic amnesia), though Bernheim also showed that with unrelenting pressure the subject could be made gradually to recover the lost material (hypermnesia), a fact that Freud was later to turn to clinical account.

Bernheim's loose hypnotic demonstrations have since been extensively replicated in the laboratory. Further, as we have already indicated, a major experimental program on *non*hypnotic "directed forgetting" ("intentional forgetting," "voluntary forgetting," "selective amnesia," etc.) has arisen in the modern cognitive literature, though with few exceptions, the relationship of this work to either Bernheim's research or to the issue of repression has been ignored or brushed aside. Nevertheless, this contemporary work on selective amnesia, like the modern research on selective attention and inattention, tends to confirm the basic repression mechanism—if not the defense—posited by Freud, i.e., "the function of rejecting and keeping something out of consciousness." Both literatures, however, have heretofore focused on the rejection of information from unstable memory buffers, iconic stores in the case of selective attention—inattention and short-term stores in the bulk of selective amnesia studies. Only recently have researchers begun to extend the selective amnesia paradigm to long-term memory; it is this latter direction, we predict, that will yield hypermnesia, i.e., "return-of-the-repressed" effects.

Space does not permit a detailed discussion of the methodological or theoretical issues impinging on the selective amnesia literature. In many respects (and for no good apparent reason) the field appears to be recapitulating some of the unfortunate either-or proclivities of perceptual defense theorizing. Thus, a great deal of experimental effort is being invested in attempts to show that a particular locus or a pet mechanism is the critical (or interesting) underpinning of the phenomenon. There is little doubt, however, that the selective amnesia phenomenon, like all complex cognitive phenomena, is multiprocess in nature and that a series of overlapping and sometimes redundant mechanisms operate sometimes singly, other times in unison, in producing the amnesia effects. It is only reasonable that complex phenomena should have complex determinants.

There are, of course, a variety of methodological problems, the major one, once again, being the question of whether the effect is a report bias ("response withholding") or memory bias phenomenon. Especially in early efforts, as in Bernheim's work, where subjects are first instructed to forget, then to remember, one is led to wonder about the crosscurrent of demand characteristics impinging on the subject and the problematical consequence of these conflictual demands upon what the subject is willing to say he does and does not remember.

In order to bypass these obvious problems, many of the recent studies have used indirect measures, e.g., the reduction of interference by (presumably) forgotten items or the memory enhancement of the to-be-remembered items as a function of to-forget instructions for other list items. The disadvantages of these more indirect approaches is that the conclusions that can be drawn are necessarily more indirect as well.

Fortunately, however, despite many unresolved problems, there can be no doubt of the existence of intentional forgetting in at least short-term memory tasks. The very nature of the demonstration of short-term memory—namely that nonrehearsal of new inputs inevitably results in rapid memory loss—necessarily means that the subject can voluntarily effect selective forgetting through selective nonrehearsal. Archer and Margolin have experimentally confirmed this expectation.

Granted, then, that certain types of memories can be intentionally rejected and kept from consciousness, may these experimental demonstrations be construed as proofs of repression? Scholars in the field, to the extent that they have allowed themselves to broach the matter, have tended to dismiss the bearing of selective amnesia on repression (or vice versa) while simultaneously offering up notions that, to us at least, bear remarkable similarities in conception, if not wording, to Freud's own ideas. Thus, Epstein's "selective search" or selective "depth of search" hypothesis may be thought of as recapitulating Freud's attention cathexis notion; similarly, Bjork's "differential grouping" hypothesis appears to be a variant of Freud's early "dissociation" theory; Rakover's "blocking" notion sounds like Freud's "censorship."

Leaving terminological issues behind, the answer to the question ultimately rests on the same considerations that confronted us in the case of selective inattention. The mechanisms clearly exist for the undertaking of the defense; also, aversive stimuli may be shown to disrupt memory; yet, as before, the compound fact, as plausible as it might appear, has not been experimentally demonstrated, i.e., that the available mechanism is in fact deployed for defense against aversive stimuli. It is, moreover, less likely that such a laboratory demonstration will be achieved in the memory realm, since, on account of the immediacy and consequent impact of perception, it is easier to introduce an unbearable visual stimulus than an unbearable memory in the laboratory.

Conclusion on the Evidence for Repression with Some Observations on Methodology

What has been shown? The answer would seem to depend on whether one looks at the clinical or laboratory data, for the two approaches have had palpably different yields. Such differences, we believe, reflect inherent differences in the two approaches, not some peculiar inconstancy of the phenomenon itself.

The genius of the clinical approach is its ability to reveal truly complex cognitive processes. It can uncover compound facts such as the conjoint occurrence of (a) tendentious rejection from awareness of (b) aversive materials (c) for the purpose of avoiding pain (d) often by unconscious means (though the latter fact is not essential for the proof of repression). From the clinical standpoint, the evidence for repression is overwhelming and obvious.

The weakness of the clinical approach, on the other hand, is its looseness of method. The most ubiquitous evidence is the indirect one, based on unregimented interpretation, which up to now has been more of an art form than a scientific instrument—though we should not forget that we use that "art," like syntax, for daily communication. The more direct evidence, namely hypermnesia effects, is methodologically more solid. Quite clearly, people at times forget traumatic events and then subsequently remember both the forgotten material and the defensive intent to forget. Even so, some features of these data cannot be fully verified. Report bias effects have not been formally controlled. Moreover, as far as the paramnesia problem is concerned, one may verify the objective truth of an objective event (e.g., "my mother died") but not the objective truth of a subjective intent (e.g., "I wished not to face the fact that my mother died"). Scientific psychology has yet to develop a methodology of purpose.

The strength of the laboratory-experimental approach, unlike the clinical, is its methodological rigor; its overriding weakness is its inability to deal with truly complex processes.

Thus, none of the four critical facts in themselves are in any doubt within experimental psychology: (a) that there can be selective information rejection from awareness; (b) that aversive stimuli tend to be avoided; (c) that organisms strive to defend themselves against pain; and (d) that many psychological processes occur outside of awareness. All these facts, independently, are not in dispute; what is in dispute, and what has not been demonstrated experimentally, is the conjoint fact, i.e., all the component facts integrated into a higher-order fact. In the absence of a clear-cut demonstration of the compound phenomenon, experimental psychologists have reflexively held the phenomenon accountable. How curious that they should never question the method instead.

Methodology, after all, is only an applied epistemology; as such it is a band of philosophy and, therefore, theory; as such it is subject to verification—and, hopefully, to falsification. If an applied epistemological theory fails, it should be discarded or modified, like any theory. There is nothing sacrosanct or final about theories, whether about the mind (psychological theory) or about how the mind should pursue truth (methodological theories). Like any theory a particular methodology has its "focus of convenience." Rats, pigeons, nonsense syllables, sensory processes, and the like are the focus of convenience of current experimental methodologies. If it now should blur suddenly when applied to new domains—complex cognitive processes like poetry, intention, love, repression—we should hardly be surprised. Nor should we helplessly cling to the hapless methodology, shaping reality to fit the method. Better to search for something in the darkness than to search for nothing in the light (J. B. Watson notwithstanding).

Involuntary Commitment of the Mentally Ill Is Justifiable

JAMES L. LEVENSON

James L. Levenson is a psychiatrist who supports the practice of involuntary commitment for the mentally ill. Levenson argues that it is society's right to protect itself and its mentally ill, through its police power and paternalism, by compelling treatment of those in need. Levenson argues that society's members have as much right to be free from potentially harmful persons as those persons have a right to treatment for their suffering. Here Levenson reviews the history of civil commitment laws and practices in the United States and discusses the ethical justification for their use.

QUESTIONS

1. According to the author, what is beneficence?
2. What are police power and paternalism, according to Levenson?

James Levenson, "Psychiatric Commitment and Involuntary Hospitalization: An Ethical Perspective," *Psychiatric Quarterly* 58 (no. 2, Summer 1986-87):106-12. Copyright 1986 Human Sciences Press. Reprinted with permission.

3. Could an argument be created, from Levenson's viewpoint, that psychiatrists and psychologists have an affirmative ethical duty to commit those who need treatment? How far could this argument be taken (i.e., how relaxed should the criteria for mental commitment be)?

■ ■ ■

Psychiatric commitment is often discussed as presenting a classical conflict between society's needs and individual rights, but we must also consider the needs of the individual. Society's *obligation* to the unfortunate victims of mental illness may seem out of fashion in an era of deinstitutionalization and budget cutbacks, as the mentally ill swell the ranks of the homeless and helpless in our cities. Nevertheless, there has been a tradition in our society since the Enlightenment to provide care and protection for those who are unable to care for themselves. Psychiatrists and other mental health professionals are charged by society with a mission to relieve the suffering of mental illness. When the debate is framed as society's needs versus individual rights, what is left out is the individual's need for, and right to, treatment. We have a collective responsibility to prevent harm and to prevent needless suffering and death. This obligation is what ethicists call the duty of beneficence.

This paper briefly reviews the history of psychiatric commitment, then describes how it typically works in practice, followed by an examination of its ethical justification.

History of Psychiatric Commitment

Before the 19th century, the mentally ill were not hospitalized, let alone treated, but generally regarded as sinful or possessed. With the evolution of the asylum and the development of psychiatric diagnosis and treatment, the pendulum has swung back and forth between the perceived need for treatment on the one hand, and patients' rights to liberty and due process on the other. During the first half of the 19th century, the mentally ill were institutionalized solely on the grounds that they were mentally ill. This was usually decided by physicians, not the courts, but often was initiated by family members. A husband who was unhappy with his wife's behavior could rather easily put her in an asylum. The earliest U.S. statutes (before 1850) formally codified the system already in operation of family and doctor deciding together. In the 1860's and 70's, public protest focused on the disregard for patients' rights, and new procedural safeguards were introduced, including (in some jurisdictions) trial by jury to determine whether to hospitalize. During most of the 19th century, psychiatric hospitalization remained essentially involuntary. In 1881, Massachusetts passed the first law permitting the mentally ill to admit themselves to psychiatric facilities. During the first half of the 20th century, with advances in medicine and psychiatry, the pendulum swung back toward making it easier to get the mentally ill hospitalized, with broader grounds for commitment and loosening of procedural safeguards. By 1949, only ten percent of psychiatric patients were voluntarily admitted in Massachusetts. Not until 1972 were the majority voluntary, reflecting the swing of the pendulum back toward patient autonomy.

Between the 1950's and 1970's, perhaps the most common form of commitment was the two-physician certificate. A necessary and sufficient condition for involuntary hospitalization was the signature of two doctors agreeing to the need. The 1970's brought increased societal concern with the protection of rights (civil rights, rights of the criminally charged, rights of children, prisoners, the mentally retarded, as well as the mentally ill). The relatively informal commitment process was now carefully defined. The justification for commitment was narrowed in most states to dangerousness—danger to others, danger to self, or so gravely unable to care for oneself that one was clearly endangered. Rights to have an attorney, a jury trial, call witnesses, appeal, and other rights were explicitly protected. The focus on proving dangerousness in an adversarial process seemed to many observers a "criminalization" of the commitment process, a view of commitment as a "preventive detention" otherwise abhorred by our system.

Commitment and Involuntary Hospitalization in Vivo

What is the typical course of an actual commitment? There are a number of different routes through which a mentally ill person could be involuntarily hospitalized. A concerned family member or friend may bring him or her to an emergency room, a psychiatrist's office, or a mental health center. The disturbed individual may come himself seeking help, but be unwilling to enter the hospital voluntarily. She might already be in treatment with a therapist who decides hospitalization is required. She may be brought in (to an emergency room or mental health center) by the police after being found acting bizarrely or dangerously in public. Once a mental health professional has evaluated the individual, a decision may be reached to seek an emergency inpatient evaluation. Most states provide for emergency psychiatric observation, typically 48-72 hours. In Virginia, this process is initiated by the professional's contacting a judge who can grant the warrant. Sometimes, concerned family members have been unable to convince the individual to come for evaluation; if so, they themselves can initiate the commitment process by contacting the "crisis" service of their local mental health center. A crisis team may then do the evaluation at the individual's home, or have the police bring him in to a mental health center or hospital emergency room for evaluation.

During this brief period of two or three days, in Virginia, a commitment hearing is held, with a judge presiding. The patient may choose to hire his own attorney, or the court will appoint one for him. A psychiatrist who has not been involved in the case makes an independent assessment and reports during the hearing. The patient has a number of protected rights including the right to call witnesses. The judge decides on the basis of previous clinical history; the emergency evaluation; and testimony by the patient, the independent psychiatrist, and any witnesses, whether to release the patient, or commit her to any willing hospital or to the State hospital, for further evaluation and treatment, for a period of time not to exceed 180 days. At any point in the emergency evaluation and commitment hearing process, a patient can change his mind and become a voluntary patient if judged competent to do so.

On what *basis* do mental health professionals and judges decide whether someone needs involuntary evaluation and treatment? With the tightening of commitment laws in the 1970's, most states limited involuntary hospitalization to those who clearly have a mental illness and who meet one of these conditions: 1. imminent danger of harming oneself, i.e., suicidal; 2. imminent danger of harming someone else, i.e., homicidal; 3. so gravely disabled as to be totally unable to care for oneself. In addition, it is required that less restrictive alternatives, like outpatient evaluation and treatment, be considered and deemed inadequate before hospitalization is allowed. Each of these conditions is a matter of judgment on a continuum. There remains much disagreement over how suicidal or dangerous a person must be to justify overriding their wishes and hospitalizing them. Many psychiatrists, families with a mentally ill member, and others are concerned that these criteria are too narrow. They believe that some people in urgent need who can be helped are left out.

Ethical Issues

On what moral grounds can commitment and involuntary hospitalization be justified? To commit someone is, seemingly, to abridge their liberty rights, to override their autonomy. Our society highly values individual liberty, and it will not interfere unless there are powerfully compelling reasons to do so. Indeed a few in our society, like the psychiatrist Thomas Szasz, believe that involuntary psychiatric treatment is *never* justified. Among other arguments, he bases his position on the belief that there is no such thing as mental illness. Most do not take this extreme position, and consider other moral principles as sometimes outweighing individual liberty. For most of us then, the question of "when is commitment justified?" is a classical ethical dilemma, where the answer to the question must balance the competing moral principles. There are two for us to consider, "police power of the state" and paternalism.

The first of these, "police power" sounds ominous, but it does not refer to storm trooper or gulags. We recognize in our society that we may rightfully restrict an individual's liberties if their exercise will harm others. John Stuart Mill asserted that this was the only justification for interfering with individual liberty. This principle is sometimes called the "harm principle." As our collective representative, the state has the right, and often the obligation, to protect us from individuals who would harm us. This "police power" principle could be invoked mainly to justify committing mentally ill persons who pose a threat of harming other people. Some would also argue that committing suicidal patients is justified under "police powers," because suicide is against the law in many states. In my opinion, society does have a "police power" right to commit a mentally ill person who poses a real danger of assaulting or killing others, but this seems a weak justification for committing suicidal people. There are more compelling grounds for their involuntary treatment.

This brings us to the second moral principle that comes into conflict with individual liberty, referred to in law as the doctrine of *parens patriae*, more commonly as paternalism. Here, the state intervenes on behalf of the welfare of individuals, sometimes without their permission, much as a parent does for a child. Examples outside mental health include FDA restrictions on which drugs one can buy, and mandatory warnings on cigarettes. Via commitment laws, the state paternalistically substitutes the judgment of a mental health professional for that of a mentally ill person, with regard to the need for psychiatric evaluation and treatment. This paternalism is currently limited in scope, for overriding the individual's refusal is allowed only in severe circumstances, when one is very suicidal or totally unable to care for oneself. In other words, involuntary hospitalization is not allowed just because someone is mentally ill.

Paternalistic justification is usually seen as applying to suicidal or gravely disabled individuals, but I believe it also supplements the "police power" justification for committing mentally ill persons who are a danger to others. If a disabled, hallucinating schizophrenic is not treated and he kills someone, his victim suffers the greatest loss, but he is not the only one. The schizophrenic himself may be imprisoned, or confined indefinitely in a forensic ward, and may also suffer, when he is more lucid, the guilt and other consequences of having killed someone.

Is paternalistic intervention via psychiatric commitment morally justified, since it appears to involve overriding individual liberty? It is worth remembering that John Stuart Mill, a philosopher who believed it was rarely justified to interfere with individual liberty, exempted those whose behavior was "incompatible with the full use of the reflecting faculty." Paternalistic intervention is not justified just because someone is doing something we think is crazy. The person must also be crazy. There remains much disagreement, though, over how mentally ill one must be and how dangerous one's behavior to justify beneficent but paternalistic intervention.

Passersby in a campus area observe two young women standing together, staring at each other, for over an hour. Their behavior attracts attention, and eventually the police take the pair to a nearby precinct station for questioning. They refuse to answer questions and sit mutely, staring into space. The police request some type of psychiatric examination but are informed by the city attorney's office that state law (Michigan) allows persons to be held for observation only if they appear obviously dangerous to themselves or others. In this case, since the women do not seem homicidal or suicidal, they do not qualify for observation and are released.

Less than thirty hours later the two women are found on the floor of their campus apartment, screaming and writhing in pain with their clothes ablaze from a self-made pyre. One woman recovers; the other dies. (There is no conclusive evidence that drugs were involved.)

P. Chodoff, a psychiatrist, uses this case to point out the limitations of current commitment laws and the need for broader grounds for intervention. C. M. Culver, a psychiatrist, and B. Gert, a philosopher, discuss the same case, but conclude that the facts do not morally justify detaining the two women because they view the correlation between the women's behavior and subsequent suicide as too low.

The so-called "medical model" of commitment attempts to strike a balance between individual liberties, and paternalism, with a clear bias toward the latter. Seeing this as a classical ethical dilemma of autonomy versus beneficence, the medical model adherents seem to be choosing beneficence over autonomy. However, many who espouse the medical model would reframe this, and argue that the seriously mentally ill are not autonomous. For choices to be truly autonomous, they must be made by an individual who is rational, informed, competent and free of coercion. Does this fit a homeless schizophrenic who is hearing voices commanding him to set himself on fire?

Our training and experience as mental health professionals give us a different view of human motivation, wishes, and actions than that generally held by attorneys and philosophers. Human decisions are ambivalent and conflicted, and this is acutely true for the seriously mentally ill. Someone who is *not* torn over suicidal impulses, who is *sure* he wants to die, rarely gets committed and hospitalized. He kills himself. It is because most suicidal people are deeply ambivalent that they call crisis hot-lines before or just after an overdose, or attempt suicide in circumstances where someone else is likely to discover and intervene in time. Which should we regard as their autonomous wish, the wish to die or the wish to live? They express both. If a hallucinating person comes to an emergency room scared to death and pleading for help, but then is too frightened to voluntarily accept hospitalization, unable to choose between his fear of the hospital and his fear of his internal chaos, which of his impulses should we label as his autonomous preference?

We must be careful, however. When we claim that a mentally ill individual is not autonomous and that we are therefore justified in involuntarily hospitalizing him we are not free of bias. Psychiatrists' medical training conditions them, as practitioners, to reflexively treat illness, and sometimes we have gone too far. Mental health professionals are trained to become very uncomfortable with the prospect of losing a patient to a preventable death. Faced with a person threatening suicide or homicide, or even just someone poorly able to care for himself, we fear being sued if, after the person is not committed, a tragedy occurs. We also fear being shamed or blamed if such a patient is identified in the press as ours. Violent or suicidal individuals create anxiety and aversion even in experienced mental health professionals, and our judgment may sometimes be clouded by our apprehensions. Busy, understaffed mental health services may also err on the "safe side" because the professional feels there is not enough time, information, or capability to consider alternatives consensually with the patient.

Prediction of Dangerousness

One of the arguments directed against the medical model of commitment is that paternalistic intervention to prevent harm to self or others is misguided because it is pointed out that prediction of dangerousness is very imprecise. The often repeated claim that mental health professionals cannot predict danger-ousness at all is an exaggeration based on misunderstanding. For the risk of harm to others, there are a few studies, with methodologic flaws, that show that when a previously violent individual is released after a long hospitalization, it is difficult to reliably predict recurrent violence. Specifically clinicians over-predict the long-term risk. But this finding, even if true, is not relevant to the initiation of commitment. What we need to know is what is the short-term risk when the mentally ill, threatening individual first presents to us if we do *not* hospi-talize him? It would be preferable if our policies here could be firmly based on data, but we are unable to really properly study the question. Not many would advocate a randomized, controlled study in which instead of being hospitalized, half of the psychotic threatening people brought to the emergency room were released to see if our predictions are correct. For prediction of the risk of self-harm and suicide, there is almost no empirical data. Clinicians are better at predicting suicidal and homicidal risk than is generally recognized, but scientific proof one way or the other is not going to solve our ethical dilemma for the foreseeable future.

Summary

As a psychiatrist, I have focused in this paper on the medical model view of commitment. Directed against the medical model is the civil liberties position, mostly put forward by at-torneys, which values autonomy over beneficence and sees psychiatric decision-making as biased, imprecise, and too pa-ternalistic. Like the moral principles they champion, neither of these positions is "wrong." The tension between them is in-evitable and sometimes beneficial. The conflict is inevitable because the proponents differ in their missions and how they think. Attorneys (and philosophers) think in terms of the gen-eral case, of classes of situations, whereas psychiatrists focus on individuals as unique. Chodoff has also pointed out that the medical model is a utilitarian one, i.e., the morality of an act is determined by, on balance, whether it increases the good for the individual or society. The civil liberties position, on the other hand, is a deontological one, i.e. the end does not justify the means; some moral principles must be considered even if they do not lead to maximally good outcomes. This conflict between positions can be ultimately beneficial, if we recognize that each is fighting for a good. As a society, we should expect psychiatrists and other mental health professionals to try their utmost to treat the mentally ill, and attorneys to protect their rights. When we view it as such a moral dilemma, states Chodoff, "we are confronted not with melodrama, a contest of right against wrong, but rather with tragedy, a conflict of one right—to be at physical liberty—against another right—to be free from dehumanizing disease."

VIEWPOINT 4

Involuntary Commitment of the Mentally Ill Is Not Justifiable

STEPHEN MORSE

In this viewpoint Stephen Morse argues against involuntary commitment for the mentally ill. Morse presents four arguments against involuntary civil commitment. First, he contends that the differential treatment of disturbed and non-disturbed individuals cannot be justified. Second, he asserts that involuntary commitment of those with mental illness is misguided by the inaccuracies in the criteria for commitment. Third, he claims that the poor prognosis for treatment of those involuntarily committed does not warrant their deprivation of liberty. Finally, he argues for the use of less intrusive means for the treatment of mentally ill persons. Morse is a professor of law at the University of Southern California Law Center and professor of psychiatric and behavioral sciences at the University of Southern California School of Medicine.

Stephen Morse, "A Preference for Liberty: The Case Against Involuntary Commitment of the Mentally Disordered," Section 1, *California Law Review*, vol. 70, no. 1 (January 1982), pp. 54-106, © 1982 by California Law Review, Inc. Reprinted with permission.

QUESTIONS

1. According to the author, what is the problem with treating mentally ill persons differently than "normals"?
2. According to the author, what is wrong with current mental commitment criteria?
3. What are some of the less restrictive alternatives to mental commitment, according to Morse?

■ ■ ■

The Argument Against Involuntary Commitment

Involuntary commitment is an extraordinary exercise of the police power and paternalism of the state. Although liberty is constantly infringed in various ways by state action—preventive detention through certain bail practices is but one example—the deprivation of liberty authorized by involuntary commitment laws is among the most serious restrictions on individual freedom the state may impose. Moreover, it may be imposed on the basis of predictions, without the prior occurrence of dangerous acts or other legally relevant behavior. Typically, the state must have exceptionally weighty interests in order to justify such an exceptional deprivation of individual freedom. It must therefore be asked whether, in light of our national preference for liberty, a system of involuntary commitment that is based on wide substantive standards and relatively lax procedures can be justified. It is argued in this Part that it cannot.

The objections to involuntary civil commitment are both theoretical and practical. First, it is difficult or impossible to support, with theory or data, the differential treatment of mentally disordered persons that allows them, but not normal persons, to be involuntarily committed. Second, the system is unlikely to identify accurately those persons who should arguably be committed; consequently, large numbers of persons who are not properly committable will be unjustly and needlessly deprived of their liberty. . . .

Mentally Disordered Persons Should Not Be Legally Distinguishable from Normal Persons

The primary theoretical reason for allowing involuntary commitment of only the mentally disordered is the belief that their legally relevant behavior is the inexorable product of uncontrollable disorder, whereas the legally relevant behavior of normal persons is the product of free choice. It is believed, for example, that a normal person who experiences an impulse to commit a crime is capable of repenting or being deterred by the sanctions of the criminal law, and hence, may choose not to commit the crime. Thus, to preserve the person's autonomy and dignity, a normal person cannot be incarcerated until he or she actually offends the criminal law, even if the person's future dangerousness is highly predictable. On the other hand, the disordered person is thought to lack understanding or behavioral control, and therefore cannot change his or her mind or be deterred. Because the individual will ultimately have little or no choice in deciding whether to act violently, it does not violate the disordered person's dignity or autonomy to hospitalize him or her preventively, even in the absence of strong predictive evidence of future dangerousness.

The belief that disordered persons particularly lack competence or behavioral control is a strongly ingrained social dogma that underlies the special legal treatment accorded mentally disordered persons. But what is the basis for this belief? A major distinguishing aspect of most behavior labeled serious mental disorder is that it is inexplicably irrational—it is crazy behavior that makes little or no sense to others. When a person behaves in such a way, there is a tendency to believe that the person is out of control. After all, who, in his right mind, would choose to act crazily? Thus, when we cannot make sense of the behavior of another, we believe that there is something wrong with the person, something beyond the actor's control in most cases. For example, if a patient tells us that he will not take his medicine because the doctor is a hostile agent trying to poison him, we are likely to believe the patient is mentally disordered—the reason for drug refusal is delusional, after all—and that this refusal of treatment is incompetent because it is the product of the delusion and not of the patient's free, rational choice.

But the assertion that the crazy behavior of mentally disordered persons is compelled, in contrast to the freely chosen behavior of normal persons, is a belief that rests on commonsense intuitions and not on scientific evidence. Indeed, the degree of lack of behavioral control necessary to justify involuntary commitment is fundamentally a moral, social, and legal question—not a scientific one. Social and behavioral scientists can only provide information about the pressures affecting an actor's freedom of choice. The law must determine for itself when the actor is no longer to be treated as autonomous.

In fact, empirical evidence bearing on the question of the control capacity of mentally disordered persons would seem to indicate that mentally disordered persons have a great deal of control over their crazy behavior and legally relevant behavior related to it; indeed, often they may have as much control over their behavior as normal persons do. Even in apparently easy cases where it seems clear that the legally relevant behavior is the product of mental disorder—for example, the delusional person who refuses needed medication or attacks the doctor because he believes the doctor is a hostile agent—we cannot be sure that the person is incapable, as opposed to unwilling, to behave rationally or to control him- or herself. All that is certain is that the person did not behave rationally compared to dominant social standards.

For comparison, imagine the case of a habitually hot-tempered person who takes offense at something his doctor says and threatens to harm the doctor. Is this person more in control or rational than the delusional person? Or, consider the case of a severely ill cardiac patient who refuses to modify dietary, exercise, or smoking habits because the person prefers his or her habitually unhealthy lifestyle. The person's behavior can disrupt the well-being of the family, help drive up health care and insurance costs, and, if the result is an untimely death, impoverish the family. Is this person more in control or rational than the delusional person, and if so, in what sense? Of course, we all "understand" the behavior of the hot-tempered person and the cardiac patient, while the behavior of the delusional person makes no sense whatsoever. Still, there is no conclusive means to prove that any of these persons has greater or lesser control than any of the others. Despite this, civil commitment is possible only for the delusional person; the hot-tempered person may be detained only *after* striking or attempting to strike the doctor and the cardiac patient cannot be forced to enter a hospital or to change his or her lifestyle.

There is thus little support for the proposition that the mentally disordered, in contrast with normal persons, lack the ability to control their behavior. The mere intuition that the mentally disordered lack control should not be sufficient to deprive such persons of their freedom. A system of involuntary commitment for only disordered persons therefore cannot be justified on the basis of the mentally disordered's alleged lack of free choice or capability for rationality.

A second possible reason that only crazy persons may be committed is the belief that they are especially dangerous. If so, society might be justified in instituting special measures that would make it particularly easy to intervene in the lives of crazy persons for either their own good or the good of society. This argument, however, may be disposed of with relative ease. Mental disorder is both an over- and underinclusive predictor of dangerousness; most crazy persons are not dangerous and many normal persons are.

Indeed, although it is hard to obtain firm data on this question, mentally disordered persons are probably no more dangerous than normal persons. At one point it was believed that mentally disordered persons were especially prone to violence, but later empirical studies tended to support the opposite conclusion, which in turn became the accepted wisdom for many years. In the last few years, however, a series of studies has tended to show that ex-mental-hospital patients have higher arrest (not conviction) rates than nonpatients. Such findings have led some to conclude that mentally disordered persons may be especially dangerous. But close analysis of the data reveals that prior arrest rather than mental status is the variable that accounts for the recently increased arrest rates among mental patients—patients are now more likely to have been previously arrested than formerly. Moreover, ninety percent of ex-patients are not arrested. In sum, mental patients are not especially dangerous, and, if they are slightly more dangerous than nonpatients, it is not a consequence of their mental disorders. Finally, the mentally disordered account for much less violence in absolute terms than normal persons. Therefore, if social safety is a primary goal of involuntary hospitalization, it will not be served by singling out the mentally disordered.

A third reason given for allowing commitment of only the mentally disordered is that such persons are especially incompetent, that is, incapable of rationally deciding what is in their own best interests. The concept of incompetence is difficult to analyze, but it is clear that it refers to an *inability* to decide rationally or to manage one's life, rather than to the fact that the individual in question makes decisions that might be considered irrational or based upon seemingly irrational reasons. In order to protect liberty and autonomy, the legal system focuses on the decisionmaking process rather than decisional outcomes: so long as a person is capable of rational decision making and managing, the person will be left free to make irrational decisions or to mismanage his or her life and to suffer the consequences; only if the person is not so capable does overriding the actor's judgment and substituting the judgment of the state appear justified. Of course, a person who consistently demonstrates bad judgment or gives apparently irrational reasons for his or her decisions is often assessed as being *incapable* of exercising sound judgment, at least in particular areas of his or her life. Nevertheless, it is generally believed that unless the person is crazy, he or she is probably capable of deciding rationally, even if most of the evidence is to the contrary.

Are the mentally disordered particularly incompetent? The question is crucial because involuntary commitment substitutes the state's judgment about the necessity for hospitalization (and often for treatment as well) for the judgment of the individual. Although commitment rarely includes a formal finding of legal incompetence at present, it at least implies the judgment that in some cases the person cannot cope or make decisions in his or her own best interest. Indeed, the commitment schemes proposed by Alan Stone and Loren Roth place crucial weight on a person's decisionmaking competence.

There is, however, little empirical or theoretical justification for the belief that the mentally disordered as a class are especially incapable of managing their lives or deciding for themselves what is in their own best interests. Available empirical evidence demonstrates that the mentally disordered as a class are probably not more incompetent than normal persons as a class. Indeed, there is no necessary relationship between mental disorder and legal incompetence. As it was with dangerousness, mental disorder is an over- and underinclusive indicator: many normal persons are incompetent and many, if not most, mentally disordered persons are not. Consequently, the premise of the commitment system that crazy people are particularly incompetent is unsupported. While some disordered persons are clearly incompetent according to any reasonable criteria, the social goal of reducing the consequences of incompetence is not well-served by allowing involuntary hospitalization, guardianship, or treatment of only the mentally disordered.

A final reason for allowing commitment of only mentally disordered persons is the belief that they are especially treatable. The mental disorders themselves and the dangerous and incompetent behaviors that allegedly ensue from mental disorder supposedly are particularly ameliorable by mental health treatment methods. Although this assertion seems reasonable, once again there is little evidence to support it. There is every reason to believe that normal persons who are dangerous or incompetent are equally treatable. Indeed, there is good reason to believe that normality is positively correlated with likelihood of treatment success. Moreover, the consequent social disabilities, which are in many cases more worrisome than mental health symptoms, are far harder to treat than the symptoms themselves. Differential treatability is thus not a supportable rationale for allowing involuntary commitment of the mentally disordered.

These comments on the lack of self-control, dangerousness, incompetence, and treatability of the mentally disordered do not imply that no seriously mentally disordered person lacks self-control or is dangerous or incompetent as a result of his mental disorder; nor do they mean that the disordered are per se untreatable. A person who is assaultive because of delusions is of course dangerous. And although lack of self-control and incompetence are hard to assess, in some cases a common-sense determination that a crazy person lacks control or is incompetent can be made. Finally, many mentally disordered persons are of course treatable with some likelihood of success. Both data and theory indicate, however, that the mentally disordered as a class are not particularly lacking in the capability for self-control and rationality, nor are they particularly dangerous, incompetent, or treatable. There would thus seem to be little support for an involuntary commitment system that is imposed only on the mentally disordered. Such a system will neither protect society nor protect large numbers of persons from themselves with special efficacy. What such a system will do is cause large numbers of citizens to lose their liberty based on faulty premises that rob them of dignity.

At the very least the analysis offered in this section should suggest that if involuntary commitment of only the mentally disordered can be justified at all, it should be limited to cases of persons who, first, are so clearly crazy that all reasonable persons would agree that their capability for self-control or rationality fails to pass even the lowest of legal thresholds; second, are so dangerous or incompetent, as demonstrated by objective acts, that preventive confinement is clearly and absolutely necessary to prevent grave harm; and, third, are clearly and only treatable on an inpatient basis. Only in such cases can singling out the mentally disordered for involuntary hospitalization be reasonably justified on theoretical and utilitarian grounds.

The Involuntary Commitment System Will Produce Unacceptable Numbers of Improper Commitments

Proponents of commitment often concede that in the past the commitment net ensnared many persons who did not need to be committed. But, they argue, there are persons for whom involuntary commitment is truly appropriate. Involuntary commitment, therefore, should be properly limited rather than abolished. In that way, the excesses of the past will be avoided, the system will operate fairly, and the small amount of liberty sacrificed will be justified by the benefits flowing to society and those committed. This argument has plausibility and appeal if one accepts, as many do, that the mentally disordered are different enough to warrant a commitment system applicable only to them and that proper limitation of involuntary commitment is possible. This section challenges the latter assumption and argues that it is highly unlikely that the involuntary commitment system will operate so as to commit only properly committable persons and that, to the contrary, unjustifiably high overcommitment will necessarily result from the existence of any commitment system that applies only to the mentally disordered.

One factor that is likely to lead to the overuse of civil commitment is the use of commitment as a mechanism for the control of "overflow" deviance. As a social control system, involuntary commitment provides a solution to the problems caused by troublesome, annoying, scary, and weird persons. Even if such people are not particularly harmful to themselves or others, they often disrupt—frequently severely—their families, friends, colleagues, and the public. In short, they tend to cause interpersonal problems and to make those around them feel profoundly uncomfortable. The criminal justice system may be unable to control this type of deviance because in many instances the deviant behavior may not constitute a crime. Still, the severity of social disruption and nuisance is undeniable. Involuntary commitment thus satisfies a perceived need to have an alternative system to deal with this type of conduct.

Family and interpersonal problems and the discomfort of others, however, are not sufficient reasons in a free and pluralistic society to deprive people involuntarily of their liberty: the right of people not to be bothered is important, but it is far less weighty than the right of the bothersome person to be free. Nor will it do to say that we must have commitment for such cases because society will insist on it. To date, few of the "horribles" predicted by opponents of enhanced rights for the disordered have occurred as a result of greater freedom for the disordered. Society has tolerated and can manage to tolerate crazy behavior without resort to incarceration.

Although limited involuntary commitment laws seek to avoid undue incarceration, the social pressure to incarcerate troublesome, crazy deviants is so powerful that such laws are likely to be misapplied. People who do not fit the commitment criteria will be held to do so, and the system will continue to sweep into hospitals persons who are capable of living freely without significant danger to themselves or others. Civil commitment is such a simple, although unfair, answer to interpersonal, family, and comparatively mild social problems that it is certain to be overused.

Another factor that increases the likelihood of improper overcommitment is the difficulty attending proper conceptualization and diagnosis of mental disorder. There is much disagreement among mental health professionals about how to define and categorize disorders. Further, there are those who go so far as to claim that mental disorder does not exist, that a medical model of deviant behavior is misguided and perhaps dangerous. A common theme in many of the criticisms of the medical model is that it is far too easy to declare any deviant behavior to be the symptom of a disorder, thus bringing that behavior within the ambit of the commitment system.

The debate about the medical model and the proper conceptualization of crazy behavior has been intense for at least two decades and shows little sign of abating. At present, a more medical view seems to have regained its ascendency within the psychiatric profession. Nevertheless, the problems associated with the medical model cannot be gainsaid by discoveries of biological causes for some disordered behaviors or by the apparently clear success of some somatic treatments, most notably chemotherapies, in reducing crazy behaviors in significant numbers of patients. The controversy concerning the medical model will not disappear, and indeed, it will probably reappear with renewed intensity with the almost inevitable failure of the new biological psychiatry to fulfill the lofty hopes it has engendered. And so long as the debate is unresolved, the group with the power to define disorders will retain the ability to overinclude deviant behaviors as mental disorders. . . .

A third basis for the belief that commitment criteria will be overapplied is that the relevant behavioral component standards are too vague and require predictions that are beyond the present capability of mental health professionals or anyone else. Standards such as "dangerousness" or "need for hospitalization" have no generally agreed upon meaning among lay persons or professionals. Of course, there is likely to be a great deal of agreement about extreme cases, but such cases are unusual. Thus, it may be claimed, each witness, lay or professional, along with each factfinder, injects his or her own private meaning into the criteria, rendering the system essentially lawless.

It would be possible to ameliorate such vagueness by rewriting the criteria to allow commitment only if rather specific behavioral criteria were met. For instance, the dangerousness criterion might be written and interpreted to mean only substantial physical danger—for example, death or serious bodily harm to oneself or others as evidenced by a recent (*e.g.*, within the past seven days) act or attempt. While such a standard is no more vague than many substantive criminal law criteria, a few observations are in order. In a free society, preventive detention should be authorized, if at all, only for serious harms. Additionally, persons whose dangerousness is evidenced by acts or attempts can be removed from society by the criminal justice system. However, if dangerousness is evidenced only by a threat (or less), the question of the predictability of real harm, discussed in detail below, is raised. Finally, there is the fundamental question of whether it is the proper role of the state to intervene massively in the life of an individual to prevent the person from doing harm to him- or herself. Thus, philosophical and political objections to paternalistic commitment are not resolved by developing more precisely defined criteria that refer to relatively specific behaviors. Although less vague criteria ensure that the system will operate more fairly, the system's foundation remains unsound.

When commitment laws authorize preventive detention, predictions of future behavior are almost always required. For example, commitment criteria often require that the person is "likely" to be a danger to self or others. On occasion no qualifying phrase referring to probability will be found, and a person may be committed if he or she is simply "dangerous to others." There are two related problems with these criteria: first, it is rarely if ever clear what specific probability of the requisite harms is required; and, second, only poor predictive ability exists.

The former difficulty could be remedied by more precise statutory specification of the probability required. What probability of harm is required (and which harms are required) is a political, legal, and constitutional question. It is clear, however, that in a free society there should be a high probability of the occurrence of the harm prior to any preventive detention. But how high is sufficient? If "likely" or similar standards are interpreted to mean 51% probability, this will mean that persons may be incarcerated when there is just slightly more than a 50-50 chance that they will actually cause the specified harms. Assuming that the probability data are accurate, it is therefore possible that just under half the people committed will not pose the requisite danger in fact. This number of wrongly committed "false positives" is completely unjustified in a society that values liberty. Most informed persons would probably agree that the "correct" probability required for preventive detention is much higher, say, in excess of 80%. But even then, it should be noted, one person in five will be unnecessarily committed. It might be argued that the probability of harm required and the degree of harm required should be inversely related: the greater the harm predicted, the lower the probability of its occurrence that is required. But if such an inverse sliding scale were permissible, the probability of harm required for even great harms should still be quite high.

Even if the predictive criteria are defined more clearly and at a sufficiently high probability level, there is little evidence that future legally relevant behavior, especially in the long term, can be accurately predicted by anyone except in a few clear cases. Most cases will not be clear and many false predictions will result. Indeed, studies of the prediction of violence to others demonstrate that an accuracy rate of 30-40% is unusually high. For predictions of suicide, an accuracy rate of about 20% appears to be the upper limit of present predictive skill. Of course, if the probability of harm required for commitment is lowered enough, fewer improper commitments will ensue. But, since most persons would probably agree that preventive detention should not be authorized on the basis of a low probability of harm, the prediction problem cannot be solved in this fashion.

The problem is particularly acute in the involuntary commitment context where the increased use of dangerousness criteria has amplified the necessity for relying on predictions to make commitment decisions. Many false predictions appear inevitable, and it is virtually certain that there will be many more false positives than false negatives since mental health professionals tend to err in the direction of overpredicting rather than underpredicting legally relevant behavior. For many reasons, professionals are more likely incorrectly to believe that harm will occur or that involuntary treatment in a closed institution is necessary than incorrectly to believe the opposite. As a result, lack of predictive accuracy leads far more often to incorrect commitment than to incorrect release. The improper incarceration of a vast number of hapless citizens who safely could and properly should remain at liberty is the unfortunate result.

Inaccurate predictions create a powerful objection to involuntary commitment because a society with a strong preference for liberty should seek to minimize incorrect involuntary commitments, even at the risk of increasing the number of "incorrect" rejections of commitment. The analogue to the criminal justice system, of course, is that our society does "not view the social disutility of convicting an innocent man as equivalent to the disutility of acquitting someone who is guilty." Until predictive accuracy becomes immeasurably greater, the involuntary civil commitment system will result in unacceptable numbers of unjust commitments.

A final reason that overcommitment is inevitable is the procedural laxness that apparently characterizes commitment proceedings nearly everywhere, including those jurisdictions where the law requires rather stringent protections. Hearings tend to be perfunctory, rarely applying fully the procedural protections required; there is not a reasonably complete exploration of either the factual basis for commitment or the possibility of less restrictive placements. Furthermore, since appeals are infrequent, judges are left relatively free to apply substantive criteria too loosely and to fail to insist on the requisite procedural safeguards. Most importantly, the lawyers who represent the allegedly mentally disordered often fail to act in a fully adversary manner, even when trained to do so. Finally, although the standard of proof required for involuntary commitment under the Constitution is stricter than the civil preponderance standard, it creates a much higher risk of wrongful commitment than the criminal standard of "reasonable doubt."

It is sometimes argued, by those who are aware of the overcommitment danger, that the problem is not serious. Even if some persons are wrongly committed because they are not significantly dangerous to themselves or others, it is contended, these persons probably are mentally disordered and will therefore benefit from a regime of hospital care and treatment. This argument must fail for at least two reasons. First, society has decided that provision of treatment does not outweigh liberty interests in those cases that do not meet the statutory criteria for commitment; wrongful commitment is unjustified, abusive, and stigmatizing even if treatment is provided. Second, state mental hospitals (and many private hospitals) are unlikely to provide quality care and treatment, even to those who arguably need it the most. . . .

In sum, for a variety of reasons—the desire to control deviance, difficulties in the proper definition and diagnosis of mental disorder, vagueness of commitment standards, difficulties in accurately predicting future behavior, and procedural laxity—the involuntary civil commitment system will produce unacceptably high numbers of improper commitments and thus will continue to function as an unjust system. This will be true even in those jurisdictions that have reformed their commitment statutes in an attempt to limit their application only to those persons who allegedly truly require involuntary hospitalization.

The claim that a high likelihood of overcommitment is inevitable is supported by empirical studies of the application of reformed commitment statutes. Careful studies demonstrate that as many as half the persons committed in a jurisdiction do not meet the jurisdiction's statutory criteria for commitment. Thus, both theory and data indicate that there is little reason to believe that civil commitment can be reasonably limited. As the studies show, statutory reform does not seem to make much difference. At best, as suggested above, one can try to develop precisely defined standards that would be satisfied by rare, clear cases. If such standards were accompanied by rigorous, adversary procedures, reasonable limitations on wrongful commitment might result. Such standards and procedural behavior appear unlikely to be instituted, however; and, as we have seen, statutory reform does not appear to make much difference.

Is a system that improperly incarcerates a substantial percentage of its inmates—perhaps as many as half or more—supportable in our society? It is clear that if the standards and procedures of the criminal justice system led to a fifty percent erroneous conviction rate, the system would be blatantly unconstitutional. Until recently, the justifiability of the involuntary commitment system has been accepted without much question and the burden of demonstrating its inequities has been firmly on the opponents of involuntary hospitalization. The burden of persuasion in the commitment debate should now shift to the proponents of the system to demonstrate that commitment can be appropriately limited. If they cannot, our duty to protect the liberty of all persons must lead us to forego commitment in those few cases where many persons might agree that it is warranted. Unless the system can be demonstrably reformed, too little benefit will be provided at the expense of far too much deprivation of liberty.

Rational Suicide Is a Valuable Practice

DEREK HUMPHRY

In 1986 Derek Humphry, as spokesperson for the Hemlock
Society, presented the following article at a bioethics confer-
ence on the question of rational suicide. The following year
the article was published in the *Journal of Suicide and Life-
Threatening Behavior*. The Hemlock Society is an organization
dedicated to the furtherance of an individual's right to die in
a dignified and respectable manner. It is generally characterized as a more liberal proponent of the right to die and a supporter of planned, reasoned autoeuthanasia. Here Humphry
asserts the Hemlock Society's position on rational suicide.

QUESTIONS

1. What are the criteria for a rational suicide, according to
   Humphry and the Hemlock Society?
2. What types of cases are inappropriate candidates for rational suicide, according to Humphry?

Derek Humphry, "The Case for Rational Suicide," *Suicide and Life-Threatening Behavior*, vol. 17, no. 4, Winter 1987. Reprinted by permission of The Guilford Press.

The Hemlock Society is dedicated to the view that there are at least two forms of suicide. One is "emotional suicide," or irrational self-murder in all its complexities. Let me emphasize that the Hemlock Society's view on this form of suicide is approximately the same as that of the American Association of Suicidology and the rest of society, which is to prevent it whenever possible. We do not encourage any form of suicide for mental health or emotional reasons.

We say that there is a second form of suicide, "justifiable suicide"—that is, rational and planned self-deliverance. Put another way, this is autoeuthanasia, using suicide as the means. I don't think the word "suicide" really sits well in this context, but we are stuck with it.

What the Hemlock Society and its supporters are talking about is autoeuthanasia. But we also have to face up to the fact that it is called "suicide" by the law. (Suicide is not a crime in the English-speaking world, and neither is attempted suicide, but giving *assistance* in suicide for any reason remains a crime. Even if the person is requesting it on the grounds of compassion and the helper is acting from the best of motives, it remains a crime in the Anglo-American world.)

The word "euthanasia" comes from the Greek—*eu*, "good," and *thanatos*, "death." But it has acquired a more complex meaning in recent times. The word "euthanasia" has now come to mean doing something, either positive or negative, about achieving a good death.

Suicide can be justified ethically by the average Hemlock Society supporter for the following reasons:

1. Advanced terminal illness that is causing unbearable suffering to the individual. This is the most common reason for self-deliverance.
2. *Grave physical handicap, which is so restricting that the individual cannot, even after due consideration and training, tolerate such a limited existence.* This is fairly rare as a reason for suicide, despite the publicity surrounding Elizabeth Bouvia's court cases.

What are the ethical parameters for autoeuthanasia?
1. *The person is a mature adult.* This is essential. The exact age will depend on the individual.
2. *The person has clearly made a considered decision.* The individ-

ual has to indicate this by such indirect ways as belonging to a right-to-die society, signing a Living Will, or signing a Durable Power of Attorney for Health Care. These documents do not give anybody freedom from criminality in assistance in suicide, but they do indicate clearly and in an authoritative way what the intention was, and especially the fact that this was not a hasty act.

3. *The self-deliverance has not been made at the first knowledge of the life-threatening illness, and reasonable medical help has been sought.* We certainly do not believe in giving up the minute a person is informed that he or she has a terminal illness, which is a common misconception of our critics.

4. *The treating physician has been informed, and his or her response has been taken into account.* What the physician's response will be depends on the circumstances, of course, but we advise our members that as autoeuthanasia (or rational suicide) is not a crime, there is nothing a doctor can do about it. But it is best to inform the doctor and hear his or her response. The patient may well be mistaken—perhaps the diagnosis has been misheard or misunderstood. Usually the patient will meet a discreet silence.

5. *The person has made a will disposing of his or her worldly effects.* This shows evidence of a tidy mind and an orderly life— again, something that is paramount in rational suicide.

6. *The person has made plans to exit this life that do not involve others in criminal liability.* As I have mentioned earlier, assistance in suicide is a crime. (However, it is a rarely punished crime, and certainly the most compassionate of all crimes. Very few cases ever come before the courts—perhaps one apiece every 4 or 5 years in Britain, Canada, and the United States.)

7. *The person leaves a note saying exactly why he or she is committing suicide.* Also, as an act of politeness, if the deed of self-destruction is done in a hotel, one should leave a note of apology to the staff for inconvenience and embarrassment caused. Some people, because of the criminality of assistance in suicide, do not want to put their loved ones at any risk; such people will leave home, go down the road, check into a hotel, and take their lives.

Many cases of autoeuthanasia through the use of drugs go absolutely undetected by the doctors, especially now that autopsies in this country have become the exception rather than the rule. Autopsies are performed on only 12% of patients today, compared to 50% in 1965, because of the high cost and the pointlessness of most autopsies. Also, of course, autopsies often catch doctors' misdiagnoses. One study showed that 29% of death certificates did not correlate to the autopsy finding. Many doctors these days prefer not to have an autopsy unless there is good scientific reason or foul play is suspected.

We in the Hemlock Society find that police, paramedics, and coroners put a very low priority on investigation of suicide when evidence comes before them that the person was dying anyway. Detectives and coroners' officers will walk away from the scene, once they are satisfied that the person who has committed suicide was terminally ill.

But, having considered the logic in favor of autoeuthanasia, the person should also address the countervailing arguments.

First, should the person instead go into a hospice? Put bluntly, hospices make the best of a bad job, and they do so with great skill and love. The euthanasia movement supports their work. But not everyone wants a beneficent lingering; not everyone wants that form of treatment and care. Hospices cannot make dying into a beautiful experience, although they do try hard. At best, hospices provide appropriate medicine and care, which everybody deserves. A major study has recently shown that most hospitals have adopted hospice standards, so the hospice movement has done a marvelous educative job. We do not feel there is any conflict of interests between euthanasia and hospices; both are appropriate to different people, with different values.

The other consideration is this question: Does suffering ennoble? Is suffering a part of life and a preparation for death? Our response here is that if that is a person's firm belief, then that person is not a candidate for voluntary euthanasia; it is not an ethical option. But it should be remembered that in America there are millions of agnostics, atheists, and people of varying religions and denominations, and they have rights, too. We know that a good 50% of the Hemlock Society's members are strong Christians and churchgoers, and that the God they worship is a God of love and understanding. As long as their autoeuthanasia is justifiable and meets the conditions of not hurting other people, then they feel that their God will accept them into heaven.

Another consideration is whether, by checking out before the Grim Reaper calls, one is depriving oneself of a valuable period of good life, and also depriving family and friends of love and companionship. Here again, there is a great deal of misunderstanding about our point of view and what actually happens. Practitioners of active voluntary euthanasia almost always wait to a late stage in the dying process; some even wait too long, go into a coma, and are thus frustrated in self-deliverance.

For example, one man who was probably this country's greatest enthusiast for autoeuthanasia, Morgan Sibbett, had lung cancer. He not only intended at some point to take his life, but he was going to have an "educational" movie made about his technique. I thought the plan was in poor taste myself, and would have nothing to do with it, but it shows the level of his enthusiasm. As it happened, Morgan Sibbett died naturally. He had a strong feeling for life, and he hung on, not realizing how sick he was; then he suddenly passed out and died within a couple of hours. Obviously, he didn't need autoeuthanasia.

My first wife told me her intention to end her life deliberately 9 months before she actually did so. When she died by her own hand, with drugs that I had secured from a physician and brought to her, she was in a pitiful physical state; I estimate that she was between 1 and 3 weeks from certain death. Her doctor, by the way, when he came to see her body, assumed that she had died naturally—it was that late.

From my years since then in the Hemlock Society, hearing the feedback of hundreds, maybe thousands, of cases, I can assure you that most euthanasists do enjoy life and love living, and their feeling of the sanctity of life is as strong as anybody's. Yet they are willing, if their dying is distressing to them, to forego a few weeks of the end and leave under their own control.

What is also not generally realized in the field of euthanasia is that, for many people, just knowing how to kill themselves is in itself of great comfort and often extends their lives. Once such people know how to make an exit and have the means to do so, they will often renegotiate with themselves the conditions of their dying.

An example quite recently was a Hemlock member in his 90s who called up and told me his health was so bad he was ready to terminate his life. He ordered and purchased the latest edition of *Let Me Die Before I Wake*, Hemlock's book on how to kill oneself, and called back a week or so later to say that he had gotten a friend in Europe to provide him with the lethal overdose. So everything was in position. "Where do you stand now?" I asked cautiously. "Oh, I'm not ready to go yet," he replied. Now that he had the means to make his exit, he was convinced that he could hold on longer. Thus, with control and choice in his grasp, he had negotiated new terms concerning his fate. Surely, for those who want it this way, this is commendable and is in fact an extension rather than a curtailment of life.

VIEWPOINT

6

"Rational" Suicide Is a Misnomer

JOSEPH RICHMAN

Joseph Richman is a therapist who has published extensively on suicide and clinical psychology. The next piece, Richman, was written in response to Derek Humphry's viewpoint. Richman argues that even for the terminally ill, "rational suicide" is a misnomer. He contends that by its very nature the choice to commit suicide shows an inability to see alternative pathways, which by definition obviates a rational choice toward suicide. Richman argues that society's misperception of suicidal persons clouds the distinction between rational and irrational suicide. This tendency to misperceive the needs of suicidal persons threatens the utility and efficacy of psychotherapy for such individuals.

QUESTIONS

1. How does Richman's definition of rational suicide differ from that of Humphry's? How does this difference affect their arguments?
2. Does Richman's definition of rational suicide allow for any cases of legitimate rational suicide?

Joseph Richman, "The Case Against Rational Suicide," *Suicide and Life-Threatening Behavior*, vol. 18, no. 3, Fall 1988. Reprinted by permission of The Guilford Press.

I write as a clinical suicidologist and therapist who has interviewed or treated over 800 suicidal persons and their families since 1965. I have been impressed by the similarities in stresses and strains among these people—similarities that cut through cultural, socioeconomic, psychosexual, and ethnic barriers. Those from diverse backgrounds who are suicidal are more like each other than different, including, I submit, those who choose "rational suicide."

A major difference between Derek Humphry and myself lies in the idea of suicide as a unified versus a pluralistic concept. Mr. Humphry postulates that there are at least two types of suicide, one emotional and irrational and the other justifiable and rational. For reasons that I elaborate upon later, I do not see this as a justifiable position.

As Humphry put it during our debate, I, Dr. Richman, am a healer of sick people, whereas, "A person like myself goes amongst healthy people. . . . The cases of rational suicide I know of directly and indirectly are of intelligent, thoughtful, caring people, who do not need a therapist, who would not go near a therapist or psychiatrist. There are some of us in this world who can handle and work through our own problems . . ." and so forth. Thus, "at least two types of suicide" are dichotomized into "them," the weak and the sick, and "us," the strong, the intelligent and the healthy.

Not coincidentally, that is precisely the attitude expressed by those most vulnerable to suicide, because of what it means to them to accept help. As these people and Mr. Humphry both see it, those who are strong and healthy would not go near a therapist or psychiatrist; *ergo*, to go for help means that one is not strong or healthy. Such a division is itself neither rational nor healthy. It has been my experience that many of my patients are strong, intelligent, and basically healthy people who have been faced with a major life crisis, and possess the good sense to seek help. Those who perceive the acceptance of such help as a sign of weakness are not necessarily strong.

My position, therefore, is that the concept of rational suicide and its accompanying attitudes are at best irrelevant and misleading, and at worst the basis for unnecessary deaths. As a therapist, my attitude is inseparable from my effectiveness.

When someone is suicidal and fate dictates that our paths cross, it is my goal to practice my profession, not to determine whether the person should live or die.

Originally, I had thought that Mr. Humphry's work would help reduce the stigma of being suicidal by bringing the topic of suicide out of the closet. Help would then become more acceptable for those who might want it but believe that being suicidal is too much of a shame or stigma. What Humphry has said has disabused me of that belief. His attitude is simplistic, because *all* suicides, including the "rational," can be an avoidance of or substitute for dealing with basic life-and-death issues.

Six other reasons why I disagree with the concept of rational suicide include the following:

1. The suicidal person and significant others usually do not know the reasons for the decision to commit suicide, but they give themselves reasons. That is why rational suicide is more often rationalized, based upon reasons that are unknown, unconscious, and a part of social and family system dynamics. I began my work as a proponent of rational suicide, but direct experiences with those who chose "rational suicide" led me to a major questioning of that concept. "Rational suicide" prevents rather than facilitates genuine understanding and decision making.

2. The proponents of rational suicide are often guilty of tunnel vision, defined as the absence of perceived alternatives to suicide. Their attitude can become a generalized narrowing of vision, in which the alternatives are automatically disregarded.

At a gathering, some supporters of the Hemlock Society asked me what, in my opinion, was the cause of suicide. I outlined my fourfold theory: the exhaustion of both individual energies and family or social network resources; the presence of a crisis felt to be insoluble by everyone; and the idea of suicide as a solution. They said, "Of course, people should commit suicide in that case." In that response lies the crux of the difference between the Hemlock Society and myself. What I see as the basis for treatment, they see as the basis for rational suicide.

3. Ageism and bias against the ill, the severely disabled, and the poor, especially those dependent upon society, is frequent. Life has become a question of dollars and cents. Rational? Age is not an illness, but ageism is a social disease, which is also not rational. The April 1987 issue of the *Hemlock Society Newsletter*, for example, reported indignantly that a 103-year-old man with pneumonia was placed on a respirator for 6 days. Some members of the hospital staff thought life support systems inappropriate "at such a great age." The *Newsletter* report did not give any other reason for not using life support systems. However, it did see the family as interfering: "One problem was that the centenarian's children were divided about the heroic measures, illustrating in our view the necessity in such cases for a durable power of attorney for health care, designating one person to make health care decisions."

Evidently, the mere fact that some of the man's children wanted him to live and be placed on a respirator was seen by the Hemlock Society as justification for eliminating the family from the treatment and decision process. That is not a rational view. It is rooted in the refusal to recognize the crisis nature of suicide and the role of others. It would be more rational to work with the divided family members, to help them resolve disagreements and deal with their anticipatory grief and other problems. It is not a reason for leaving them with their splits and differences.

4. The dying process is a complex event that includes biological, psychological, family, and social factors—both past history and current stresses. It is a systems phenomenon, in which the family is central. The proponents of rational suicide do not recognize the degree to which reactions to death are related to family pressures and conflicts. An example is the enormous stress placed upon families with cancer in one of their members. In one study, 60% of the spouses of such patients described the presence of suicidal ideation. Lyons and I also found that 65% of the figure drawings of the spouses of cancer patients contained suicidal features. Many of these well spouses assist their sick spouses in what they consider rational suicide. The stresses placed on the family members and other loved ones, and the wish to alleviate *their* suffering, are related to the decision of the terminally ill person to end his or her life.

However, the Hemlock Society's wish to exclude family members when they are not in agreement with the decision to die could place formidable obstacles to the possibility of the best resolution for all. I suggest two alternatives to suicide. First, the family members are people in pain who should be offered help and counseling. Second, family members should be included, not excluded from the dying process of a family member or from the basic life-and-death decisions.

5. Other people's turning away is often more painful than dying itself. Friends and family turn away when they find the state of a dying person and the pain of losing him or her unbearable. This inability to deal with the mourning process facilitates rational suicide. The dying person may be seen unconsciously as abandoning the family. The result of such turning away and pain in the others is a dreadful loneliness in the dying person, because the need for others continues to the very end. Such a need can be the basis for a truly good death as well as a good life. Feelings of abandonment call for a restoration of cohesion, an affirmation of belonging, and a renewal of love.

6. I wish to emphasize, finally, that effective psychotherapeutic treatment is possible with the terminally ill, and only irrational prejudices prevent the greater resort to such measures. These prejudices are perpetuated by the rational suicide movement. It is true that the treatment of the seriously ill and suicidal person places an enormous strain upon everyone's resources. Major transference and countertransference issues emerge. The major one, perhaps, is the inculcation of hopelessness in the therapist or physician by suicidal and despairing patients and families. However, the proponents of rational suicide compound the problem, in that the hopelessness of those involved is not understood for what it is—a problem—and worked through. Instead, it is seen as a rational response to the real, not perceived, hopelessness of the patient. Thus, at the end, we return to the beginning, the primacy of tunnel vision.

Let me emphasize, in conclusion, that although I am opposed to suicide, I respect a person's genuine choice. Although I believe that suicide is intimately based upon family relationships and the social system, even in our individualistic society, I also believe that it is the individual's responsibility. My goal is to make a genuine choice possible. Self-sacrifice to relieve others of being burdened, for example, is not my idea of a genuine choice. Instead, I would want people who are contemplating suicide—rational, emotional, or whatever—to feel free to go for help without being stigmatized as sick or weak, in full confidence that they will be heard and listened to and that their wishes will be respected. Needed are the following: a greater voice by the patients in determining their treatment program; respect for the needs of family members and other loved ones; the elimination of bias and other barriers against the realization of our common humanity; and respect for a patient's wish to live or die, with a full realization that if there is a right to die, there must be a right to live.

FOR FURTHER DISCUSSION

The following questions have been provided in order to better understand the debates surrounding each chapter. As you answer them, consider each of the viewpoints presented in each chapter. You may want to make a chart to record your answers.

Chapter 1

1. What does the theorist hypothesize is the motivating force of human beings?
2. What does the theorist hypothesize is the source of psychological disturbances?
3. What are the key elements of therapeutic change in each of the theories?
4. What characteristics must the therapist hold in each of the different theories in order to be an effective practitioner of the particular form of therapy?
5. What is a successful outcome under each of the theories?

With a better idea of the basic components of each of the theories of psychotherapy, the reader should now be able to apply these theories in the following cases. How would each of the several theories discussed in this chapter deal with clients in the following situations? It will become obvious as you attempt this task that the tenacity of the debate over which psychotherapy is best is rooted in the fact that different problems may warrant different treatments.

Case History One

A client comes to you despondent about her career. It seems that she was passed over again for a promotion that was long past due. She reveals to you that because it is her second time to be overlooked for the supervisory job, she is sure that it means the management is considering letting her go or keeping her in her current position eternally. The client reports the desire to terminate her position with the company because the eleven years that she has invested in the company "just don't seem to be paying off." However, because of her limited education and job skills, she worries that she will not be able to find another position in today's declining job market.

Case History Two

A man shows up at your office late for his scheduled appointment. He reports that he is having difficulty making an important decision in his life and wants your help. He explains that he has been offered "his dream job" at a much higher rate of pay but that if he accepts the job he will be forced to leave his fiancé, Cheryl. "I don't want you to think that I am callous," he says, "but this is the chance of a lifetime, and if I give up the job, I'm afraid that I will grow to resent Cheryl. But . . .

if I give up Cheryl, I don't think that I'll ever be able to enjoy the benefits that come with this job. And then what happens if I don't do well in this new job?"

Case History Three

A woman arrives in your office with obvious signs of physical abuse. She says that she has been beaten routinely by her husband for the last three years but now wishes to seek help. She is unsure whether the remedy for this situation lies in her escape from the situation or whether she is wiser to stay and wait for him to change. She tells you that he was supposed to show up for today's session, but, like so many times before, he apparently "forgot." She reveals, almost lightheartedly, that "when I was growing up, I swore that I would never turn into my mother. But you know, next week is my 35th birthday, and you know what? . . . I think I am married to my father."

Case History Four

A man arrives for his first therapy session in your office and tells you that he is there for you to help him quit smoking. He tells you that he has tried several times before but "fallen off the wagon when the stress got real bad." He says that he can generally quit for several months, but when he goes out with old friends that knew him in his smoking days, he always reverts to his old behaviors. "I don't know," he says, "there's something about Super Bowl Sundays and dingy bars that makes me crave nicotine."

Chapter 2

1. How does each of the authors propose that personality develops?
2. What are the similarities and differences between each of the several theories of personality?
3. How do the personal lives of the authors influence their theories of personality development?
4. Do the authors provide an explanation for poor personality development? A solution? What are they?
5. What does each of the theories say about human nature? Are humans basically good or basically evil? What do you think?

Chapter 3

1. Is the theory one of continuity or discontinuity? Explain your answer.
2. Does the theory support a nature or a nurture argument of human development?
3. How does the theory hold up today?
4. What implications does each of the theories have on child rearing today?
5. Do the theories provide any information relative to appropriate discipline for children?
6. How does the social context of the time influence the author's theory?

Problem One

You are an engineer working for a children's toy manufacturing company. A current media surge touting the inadequacy of the American educational system has invoked a renewed interest in educational toys. Your task is to create the most marketable toy possible. Remember that a toy that can be used for the longest duration (i.e., can be interesting and educational at each of a child's developmental stages) will most likely sell better than a more limited toy. How would your toy differ depending on which theory you use? Can you create a toy that would satisfy more than one theory? In this exercise give yourself two marketability points for each stage/age group your toy stimulates; five points for each toy created to meet all or most of the needs of a particular theory throughout its course, and thirty extra points if you can create a toy that meets all theories. The toy with the most points wins.

Chapter 4

Problem One

The nature/nurture debate in abnormal psychology has endured for centuries because its ethical implications are enormous. Why is the debate surrounding the origin of alcoholism such an important topic? If it could be definitively determined that alcoholism was a product of either nurture or nature, what implications would it have on the following:

1. The structure of treatment programs for alcoholism?
2. Private insurance coverage for alcoholism treatment?
3. Federally subsidized medical programs for alcoholism treatment?
4. The penalties and sentencing provisions for alcohol-related crimes (i.e., drunk driving or drunk-and-disorderly conduct)?
5. Alcohol prevention measures?

Problem Two

If it could be definitively determined that criminal behaviors were a product of either nature or nurture, how would it affect your answer to the following questions:

1. Should individuals with antisocial personalities be subject to the death penalty like the rest of the criminal population?
2. Should individuals with antisocial personalities be allowed access to the insanity defense?
3. Could an argument be made for and against genetic engineering or selective childlessness to reduce crime?
4. Should familial criminal records be included in the criminal files on prospective sociopaths?

Problem Three

1. What are the implications for finding that depression is a product of genetics?
2. Of environment?

Chapter 5

Problem One

1. What role do psychotherapists play in unearthing repressed memories?
2. How has this role changed since Freud's original conceptualization of repression?
3. Suppose that we assume that repressed memories are as frequent and accurate as their advocates assert; does it necessarily follow that all of these memories should be proved and brought to a client's consciousness? Could an argument be made for letting memories that were once so traumatic that they were buried for self-preservation continue to stay dormant? Explain.
4. How can a legal solution be reached to protect both the survivor and the suspected perpetrator of child sexual abuse?
5. Should the statute of limitations be extended for sexual abuse survivors who have repressed their memories?

Problem Two

1. How do definitions of "rational" and "irrational" differ for each of the authors on rational suicide?
2. Providing that we could come up with an accurate assessment of rationality, what role should psychologists play in determining who are acceptable candidates for suicide and who are better candidates for therapy?
3. After reading the articles on rational suicide, where do you stand on the issue?

Problem Three

1. What interests are balanced in a debate on involuntary commitment of the mentally ill?
2. What are the concerns with involuntary commitment?
3. What role does data on mental illness play in a discussion of involuntary commitment?

Problem Four

What is the appropriate role for psychologists in each of these three debates? At what point have psychologists gone too far in the application of their theories?

Suggestions for Further Reading

Chapter 1

Arron Beck, "Cognitive Therapy: A 30 Year Retrospect," *American Psychologist*, vol. 46, 1991.

Albert Ellis, "The Revised ABC's of Rational Emotive Therapy (RET)," *Journal of Rational Emotive and Cognitive Behavior Therapy*, September 3, 1991.

Sigmund Freud, *The Standard Edition of the Complete Psychological Works of Sigmund Freud* (23 vols.). Ed. & trans. by J. Strachey et al. London: Hogarth Press, 1953-1966.

Wolfgang Kohler, *Gestalt Psychology*. New York: Liveright Publishing Company, 1947.

Albert Lazarus, *Behavior Therapy and Beyond*. New York: McGraw-Hill, 1971.

Robert Nye, *Three Views of Man: Perspectives from Sigmund Freud, B.F. Skinner, and Carl Rogers*. Monterey, CA: Brooks/Cole Publishing, 1975.

Carl Rogers, *On Becoming a Person*. Boston: Houghton Mifflin, 1961.

B.F. Skinner, "The Machine That Is Man," *Scientific American*, November 1961.

Thomas Szasz, *The Myth of Mental Illness*. New York: Harper Colophon Books, 1974.

Chapter 2

Alfred Adler, "Individual Psychology," *Journal of Abnormal Social Psychology*, vol. 22, 1927.

Alfred Adler, *Superiority and Social Interest*. New York: W.W. Norton & Company Inc., 1979.

Gordon W. Allport, *Becoming: Basic Considerations for a Psychology of Personality*. New Haven: Yale University Press, 1955.

Gordon W. Allport, *The Nature of Personality: Selected Papers*. Cambridge, MA: Addison-Wesley Press, 1950.

Raymond Cattel, *The Description and Measurement of Personality*. Yonkers, NY: World Book, 1946.

Hans Eysenck, *The Biological Basis of Personality*. Springfield, IL: Charles C. Thomas, (year T.K.)

Abraham H. Maslow, *Motivation and Personality*. New York: Harper & Row, 1970.

Abraham H. Maslow, *Toward a Psychology of Being*. Princeton, NJ: Van Nostrand, 1968.

CHAPTER 3

Albert Bandura, *Agression: A Social Learning Analysis*. Englewood Cliffs, NJ: Prentice-Hall, 1973.

Albert Bandura, *Social Foundations of Thought and Action: A Social Cognitive Theory*. Englewood Cliffs, NJ: Prentice-Hall, 1973.

Erik Erikson, *Childhood and Society*. New York: Norton, 1963.

Lawrence Kohlberg, *The Cognitive Developmental Approach to Socialization*. In *Handbook of Social Theory and Research*, edited by D.A. Goslin. Chicago: Rand McNally, 1969.

Lawrence Kohlberg, *The Psychology of Moral Development: The Nature and Validity of Moral Stages*. San Francisco: Harper & Row, 1984.

Jean Piaget, *The Origins of Intelligence in Children*. New York: International Universities Press, 1952.

Jean Piaget, *The Psychology of the Child*. With Barbel Inhelder. New York: Basic Books, 1969.

Robert Sternberg, *Beyond IQ: A Triarchic Theory of Human Intelligence*. New York: Cambridge University Press, 1985.

Robert Sternberg, *Intellectural Development*. Edited by Robert Sternberg and Cynthia Berg. New York: Cambridge University Press, 1992.

CHAPTER 4

Richard Block, "Community, Environment and Violent Crime," *Criminology*, May 1979.

Ray Bixler, "Nature Versus Nurture: The Timeless Anachronism," *Merrill-Palmer Quarterly*, April 1980.

John Brim and Michael Nelson, "Moral Idiocy: A New Look at an Old Concept," *The American Journal of Psychiatry*, March 1980.

Philippe Cappeliez and Robert Flynn, *Depression and the Social Environment*. Montreal and Kingston: McGill-Queen's University Press, 1993.

James Coyne, *Essential Papers on Depression*. New York: New York University Press, 1985.

William George and Alan Marlatt, "Alcoholism, the Evolution of a Behavioral Perspective," *Recent Developments in Alcoholism*, vol. 1, 1986.

Donald Goodwin, "The Genetics of Alcoholism: A State of the Art Review," *Alcohol World*, Spring 1978.

Sarnoff Mednick, *Genetics, Environment and Psychopathology*. Amsterdam: North-Holland Publishing Co., 1974.

Sarnoff Mednick, Patricia Brennan, and Elizabeth Kandel, "Predisposition to Violence," *Aggressive Behavior*, vol. 14, 1988.

Robert Plomin and Gerald McClearn, *Nature, Nurture, and Psychology*. Washington, DC: American Psychological Association, 1993.

Stanton Peele, "The Dominance of the Disease Theory in American Ideas About the Treatment of Alcoholism," *American Psychologist*, March 1986.

Stanton Peele, "The Implications and Limitations of Genetic Models of Alcoholism and Other Addictions," *Journal of Studies on Alcoholism*, January 1986.

P. Clayton Rivers, *Alcohol and Addictive Behaviors: Nebraska Symposium on Motivation, 1986*. Lincoln: University of Nebraska Press, 1987.

Robert Sampson and W. Byron Groves, "Community Structure and Crime: Testing Social Disorganization Theory," *American Journal of Sociology*, January 1989.

Joseph Schneider, "Deviant Drinking as Disease: Alcoholism as a Social Accomplishment," *Social Problems*, April 1978.

John Searles, "The Role of Genetics in the Pathogenesis of Alcoholism," *Journal of Abnormal Psychology*, May 1988.

CHAPTER 5

William Amis, "Perspectives on Involuntary Hospitalization: An Evaluation," *Sociological Symposium*, Summer 1977.

Paul Chodoff, "The Case for Involuntary Hospitalization of the Mentally Ill," *American Journal of Psychiatry*, May 1976.

James Finnerty, "Ethics in Rational Suicide," *Critical Care and Nursing Quarterly*, September 1987.

L.R. Grossman and M. Pressley, "Introduction to the Special Issue of Recovery of Memories of Childhood Sexual Abuse" (and accompanying articles), *Applied Cognitive Psychology*, August 1994.

James Humber, "The Involuntary Commitment and Treatment of Mentally Ill Persons," *Social Science and Medicine*, December 1981.

Elizabeth Loftus, "The Reality of Repressed Memories," *American Psychologist*, May 1993.

Elizabeth Loftus and Hunter Hoffman, "Misinformation and Memory: The Creation of New Memories," *American Psychologist*, March 1989.

David Mayo, "The Concept of Rational Suicide," *The Journal of Medicine and Philosophy*, May 1986.

Richard Ofshe and Ethan Watters, "Making Monsters," *Society*, March/April 1993.

Stephen Rachlin and Janet Milton, "Civil Liberties Versus Involuntary Hospitalization," *American Journal of Psychiatry*, February 1975.

Georgia Sargeant, "Victims, Courts and Academics Debate the Truth of Recovered Memories," *Trial*, May 1994.

Karolynn Siegel and Peter Tuckel, "Rational Suicide and the Terminally Ill Cancer Patient," Omega vol. 15, 1984-1985.

Robert Simon, "True or False Memories of Abuse? A Forensic Psychiatric View," *Psychiatric Annals*, September 1993.

Jerome Singer, *Repression and Dissociation: Implications for Personality Theory*. Chicago: University of Chicago Press, 1990.

INDEX